BILLY JOEL

THE LIFE & TIMES OF AN ANGRY YOUNG MAN

HANK BORDOWITZ

BILLBOARD BOOKS

An imprint of Watson-Guptill Publications/New York

DEDICATION

To my wife, Caren, who put up with my bitching and moaning as this book took on a monstrous, Frankensteinish life of its own, and who shrugged off the tight times when the advance ran out. "I'm shameless when it comes to loving you."

To Bruce, Rachel, Justin, and Charlotte Gentile, who are the finest demonstration I know that "just surviving is a noble fight."

To J-Mo and J-9. We "love you just the way you are."

To Tom and Melissa. "We never knew what friends we had."

To Larry. "Sing us a song, you're the piano man."

To Mike and Billy. "This is the time to remember."

Executive Editor: Bob Nirkind
Production Manager: Katherine Happ
Cover Design: Bob O'Brien / Elizabeth Mandel
Interior Design by Leah Lococo Ltd.

Copyright © 2006 by Hank Bordowitz

First published in 2006 by Billboard Books,
An imprint of Watson-Guptill Publications,
A division of VNU Business Media, Inc.,
770 Broadway, New York, NY 10003
www.wgpub.com

Library of Congress Cataloging-in-Publication Data
The CIP data for this title is on file with the Library of Congress

ISBN-13: 978-0-8230-8248-3
ISBN: 0-8230-8248-2

Printed in the United States

First printing, 2006

1 2 3 4 5 6 7 8 9 / 10 09 08 07 06

CONTENTS

ACKNOWLEDGMENTS

All thanks to:

* Jim Fitzgerald, who casually brought this up over beer and sandwiches at the Pig and Whistle one afternoon, knowing it would snowball.
* Bob Nirkind, who bought this hair-brained scheme and got a few more gray hairs in the bargain. Bob is a very proactive editor, a tough taskmaster who gives his writers no slack! Beware this monster, fellow writers. He will make your book better than you thought it could be.
* Sandy Gibson, my first interview subject for this project, who helped shape various aspects of my perceptions, if not the book; and Todd Everett, for hooking us up.
* Kenny Wallace and Jonathan Moorehead. J-Mo did so much legwork toward the end, he made me look lazy.
* Bruce Gentile, the Plain White Rapper, who is responsible for vast amounts of great stuff in this book, not to mention helping to vet it, keep the timeline honest, and catching a bunch of my dumb mistakes!
* Irwin Mazur and Artie Ripp, who I thought would be hostile witnesses but had very few negative things to say about Billy.
* Howard Bloom and Elaine Schock, two people in Billy's camp who consented to be interviewed on the record for this project. Several other folks who had off-the-record conversations with me shall remain nameless, though as any lawyer will tell you, the testimony that shapes a trial is the testimony the jury is ordered to ignore.
* Jerry Schilling and Bill Thomas, who were extremely forthcoming about their Billy Joel experiences.
* The cast and crew at the Lincoln Center Library, the Suffern Free Library, and the New York Public Library for the Humanities.
* Barney Hoskins of Rock's Back Pages.
* Burt Goldstein at Big Daddy for crucial information in record time.
* Turnstiles.org, former home of a most excellent Billy Joel archive.
* Jeff Jacobson, my longtime legal guardian.
* The people at All Music Guide, one of the greatest online resources ever, and at Lexis-Nexis, Ebsco, Gale, and all the other online resources.

PREFACE: STRANDED IN THE COMBAT ZONE

To really know Billy Joel is to know that he's been living in his own personal combat zone, fighting, his whole life—fighting for love, fighting for fame, fortune, and acceptance. Billy the Kid, the piano man, the stranger, the entertainer, the innocent man, the angry young man, our own home boy, and probably one of the world's best songwriters. Has Billy really written the last words he's got to say? Has he turned his back on rock and roll forever? Did classical music and Broadway steal him away from rock for good?

I've known Billy since around 1968. At the time, a local band called the Hassles had given him and his sidekick, drummer, and best friend Jon Small their first pro taste of the music biz. Billy sang his heart out. He reminded people of Steve Winwood, who played keyboards and sang tunes like "Gimme Some Lovin'" for the Spencer Davis Group.

The mid to late '60s were a magical time on Long Island. Local bands were becoming stars so fast it was like we had a galaxy of our very own. Groups like the Vagrants, with a guitar player named Leslie West, the Young Rascals (who were actually from New Jersey, but keep that quiet), and Soft White Underbelly, Vanilla Fudge, Mynd's Eye, the Rich Kids, and the Good Rats started to infest the Island with their brands of distinctive rock.

Long Island clubs like the Golden Pheasant, My House, and the In Crowd were sort of a hippie scene. The Pheasant was probably the club where Billy and a guy like me had our first groupie. The club had a lot of places to hide—Billy and I were both underage, and the owner, Tony, would tell me and a few other cats to hide under the stage when cops would show up. Those were good old days, when Billy was differently "polished from his head down to his toes," a veritable fashion plate in English clothes from Granny Takes a Trip in downtown Manhattan.

Billy was a rocker with a kind of magical control over his B3 organ and Leslie cabinet. You could hear Jimmy Smith, Ray Charles, and Felix Cavaliere in his style. It was always rumored that Billy could duplicate a lick with either his right hand or his left hand, in total control. They'd say, "That short cat with the bug eyes is really hot. Sings good too; boy's got soul."

The years 1967, 1968, 1969 were great and a very special time to grow up on the Island. But getting back to the combat zone . . .

Back then, Billy was rooming with Jon and Elizabeth Small and their very young son, Sean, in a large stone home in Dix Hills that we called the Rock House. Billy and Elizabeth started to become smitten with each other after the breakup of the Hassles and the making of an album he would rather forget called *Attila*, which he recorded with drummer, heavy metal lover, and good pal Jon Small. Trouble was in the air.

I remember hanging out with Billy and Jon at clubs like Dean's College Inn, around the corner from the Rock House, and the Action House and Leone's in Long Beach. Lots of hot chicks, mostly fans of the Illusion, one of the first hair bands.

Billy was always a blackout drinker in those days. Now he's well known for his taste in good, expensive bottles of wine. These days, most of my friends on the comedy circuit refer to him as America's new crash-test dummy.

It was during the late '60s and very early '70s when Billy wrote "Everybody Loves You Now," "She's Got a Way," and a couple of other songs that he recorded later for the *Cold Spring Harbor* record. I started to jam with Billy at the Rock House as he was getting ready for that project. This was Billy's first solo album deal, the one contract every young musician signs without reading, and it was a joke. When Billy told us the producer's last name was Ripp, we thought that should have been an omen. Billy has been ripped off for millions since then by managers, lawyers, and a lot of other sharks in his inner circle of people.

Finally there came that real bad day when Billy, Elizabeth, and Sean left for LA. Elizabeth was "Always a Woman" to Billy, his best buddy's old lady. He went through a lot of feelings about that. He also wrote some great songs about her. After all the feelings he must have put himself through—falling hard for Elizabeth, the *Cold Spring Harbor* album's failure, splitting for LA—I would have lost it, too. But Billy is a survivor, always has been.

He's also always been pretty open about his past. A ninety-day stay at a local flight deck is well known to his fans. He did run with a dangerous crowd, but it was the one inside his head! He talked about it on VH1's *Storytellers* and *Behind the Music*. "You're Only Human" is a tribute to that experience. All monies from that record were donated to suicide prevention. Let's never forget this about Billy Joel: He's helped raise millions of dollars for Long Island, from Charity Begins at Home to the plight of the East End baymen. He truly loves this Isle of Long we live on.

As time went by, Billy was offered another shot at the big time. He got signed to Columbia and did the *Piano Man* album. He always had more talent than business sense. With the help of Elizabeth, at that point his wife, on the biz side—everyone knows that old saying about there being a woman behind every successful man—and his time spent underground as William Martin, lounge piano player, he produced a hit song. "Piano Man" made the long-struggling musician a musical force to be reckoned with.

With the 1970s ending and the new decade approaching, Billy found himself in the lap of luxury. He became a musical monster, winning Grammys and seeing his music finally get the respect it truly deserved. While he became the toast of the country, it seemed that everyone who worked for him became a millionaire except him.

He survived, though, and continued to produce hit after hit. It was around this time that Billy was once again single, and he embarked on a relationship with one of the world's top models, Christie Brinkley, a dream come true for a dude like Billy. One night, at the party for his longtime sound engineer Brian Ruggles's fortieth birthday at a place called Rocky's Sports Arena—Rocky was one of those Vietnam War vets who helped Billy Joel write his powerful social message called "Goodnight Saigon": "We would all go down together"—there was Christie, towering over Billy, yelling at him like the mother superior at some Catholic school. She said she was tired of hanging around his friends. "All they do is smoke dope, and don't think I don't know what they are passing around in that cigarette case," meaning all the coke they were snorting. There goes that dangerous crowd crap. Christie was good for Billy and, if he had let her, could have been better. She kept the man in check.

Doug Stegmeyer (to whom I dedicate this preface) helped Billy out a lot for seventeen years, from Pintos to limos, as he would say.

Not long afterward, I was playing in Cold Spring Harbor. Tom Davis—another refugee from the Rock House—and I used some glaucoma medication in the park across the street from the club. I said to Davis, "This would be an excellent place to name a park after Long Island's favorite son, to let Billy know he has some friends who really want to turn the *Cold Spring Harbor* experience into a special tribute to what he has done for many Long Island causes." Thank God for people like Helen Lutz and then councilman—now a Suffolk County judge—Bill Rebolini. We had a plaque and sign put in the park, right on the harbor, and a big dedication ceremony.

Being the victim of desire he has always been, Billy had the best years of his life to that point in time with Christie. I had the feeling something was going on when Billy's wife and daughter didn't show up at the park dedication. After his second marriage split, Billy went out with several women. He just married his third wife, a very young lady—so young, she's four or five years older than Billy's daughter. Billy is nine years older than his new wife's dad.

Most people working with Billy have to sign non-disclosure agreements, as well as being bound by gag orders resulting from lawsuits and other litigation, so we may never find out everything there is to tell about Billy's life and times. What we do know is that he's emerged from the combat zone to face a storm front of trouble and controversy, peers, and paparazzi. He may never be an innocent man again, but on Long Island, he'll always be ours.

—BRUCE GENTILE

INTRODUCTION

Over the course of the late '70s and through the '80s, Billy Joel was second only to Elvis as the most successful male solo artist in the music business. Ironically, Garth Brooks overtook him sometime during the '90s, not too long after Brooks had a #1 hit with Billy's song "Shameless."

A look at just some of Billy's accomplishments (a more comprehensive one appears in the appendices at the back of the book) offers testimony to just how popular he became and, to an extent, remains:

He's sold more than 100 million albums worldwide, including:

* Two diamond® albums, each award signifying sales in excess of 10 million copies in the United States
* The *Greatest Hits, Volume I & Volume II* collection, which has sold more than 23 million copies worldwide
* Nine multi-platinum® albums, each having sold over 2 million copies in the United States
* Two albums that each earned single-platinum® status for sales of at least 1 million copies in the United States
* One gold® album signifying U.S. sales of 500,000 copies
* Four albums that topped the *Billboard* 200 Albums chart

He's had thirty-three Top 40 pop hits:

* Three #1 singles on the *Billboard* Pop Singles/Hot 100 chart
* Ten Top 10 singles on the *Billboard* Pop Singles/Hot 100 chart
* Two platinum singles, each with sales of more than 1 million copies in the United States
* Five gold singles, signifying sales of more than 500,000 copies in the United States

He's won five Grammy® Awards, including the prestigious Grammy Legend Award, and received twenty-four Grammy nominations.

Billy was the first artist to perform, in 1990, to back-to-back, standing-room-only audiences at 54,000-seat Yankee Stadium. In 1992, he was inducted into the Songwriters Hall of Fame, and in 1999 into the Rock and Roll Hall of Fame. In 1994, he received the *Billboard* Century Award, and he's been awarded doctorates in humane letters.

Billy's popularity helped power the series of "Face to Face" tours with Elton John into some of the most successful live events of all time, setting attendance records around the world. Despite not having written a song in more than a decade and having turned his compositional talents to the composed classical music arena, he remains one of the few acts that can practically guarantee a sellout on the touring circuit.

If this weren't enough, a Broadway show, *Movin' Out*, featuring Billy's songs and Twyla Tharp's choreography to tell a story in the best tradition of ballet, has been running for nearly three years as of this writing, and has spawned a touring company, allowing Billy to have his music tour while he stays home in the Hamptons.

That said, anyone who has followed his career and his very public (much to his chagrin) private life doesn't need to be Freud to figure out that Billy Joel has, as modern parlance would have it, issues.

He has spent most of his career at war with the media in general and music critics in particular. Early in his career, he was not entirely wrong to rail. Critics didn't "get" the musically mercurial Billy. "Critics have accused Joel of trying to have it all ways," *Time Magazine* writer Tony Schwartz noted as Billy started flirting with stardom in the late '70s, "but it's precisely his capacity to blend old-fashioned melodies, literate lyrics and a rock 'n' roll spirit that makes him special."

Many critics didn't agree. While reviews ran both ways for the first four albums of his career, when he finally broke pop in a big way with *The Stranger*, and especially the hit ballad "Just the Way You Are," Billy became the rock and roll sellout, the borderline rocker who went over the line into crooner-ville. In one of the most scathing of these reviews, *New York Times* critic Robert Palmer wrote: "He has mastered the art of making lyrics that are banal—and, when they are about women, frequently condescending—sound vaguely important. He has mastered the art of making the simplest drum accent sound as portentous as a peal of thunder and of introducing his side-men's solos with such dramatic flourishes that they almost sound like gifted, sensitive musicians rather than like the hacks they are. He has won a huge following by making emptiness seem substantial and Holiday Inn lounge schlock sound special."

Billy takes criticism *very* personally. He often equates the songwriting process with giving birth. Like a parent shielding his child, early on Billy could be very defensive of his music. It took many years for him to compartmentalize how he felt about his songs from what others felt. "When he got criticized it really hurt him . . . ," said Elaine Schock, his publicist for close to two decades. "He would call me all ticked off because of things he read."

"I think of myself," Billy himself conceded, "as a real sensitive and vulnerable person, like a bad review could destroy me."

Fans love his songs, though. He remains especially popular in the New York City area, and particularly on his home turf on Long Island. He could play the 14,000-seat Nassau Coliseum five nights a week and probably sell it out for years.

Billy Joel's personal life has never quite worked out as well as his professional life. This, of course, has caused the press—especially the mainstream, celebrity-obsessed press—to swarm around him like bees around honey. Billy's answer to this is to withdraw.

"I don't feel that I have to be very accessible," he says. "I don't feel I need to keep myself exposed, because the private life being sacrosanct is the fodder for the artistic cannon."

Because of this generally adversarial relationship with the media, the picture it paints of him is often not flattering. And since he paints the media with a wide roller, all the same shade, Billy remains wary of even those who would have nice things to say about him. When the "Face to Face" tour with Elton John kicked off, a colleague from TV-1 in Finland called me and asked me to help him set up some Billy Joel footage and interviews. I scouted locations in Hicksville, set up interviews with people who had worked with Billy, and thought, since I had nearly two decades worth of connections in the music business, getting a few minutes with Billy before or after a show he was playing at Nassau Coliseum would be a no-brainer. The obstacles the people from both his office and his record company threw in our way were astounding.

"Everybody who knows Billy cares a great deal about him," Schock admits. "I think he's been through plenty, and we just want to be sure that he'll be as okay as possible . . . Billy has always been good to work with, always been fair and a lot of fun. Everyone wants his back."

Schock's comment about him wanting him to be "as okay as possible" is telling. For a guy who frequently claims to have everything he ever dreamed of, Billy rarely looks particularly happy. This brings to mind a couple of legends. The first has to do with a sultan, one of the wealthiest men of his era. As he's dying, he tells his vizier, "I have counted up all the days I can recall being totally happy. They numbered eleven." The second is the legend of the monkey's paw—"Be careful what you wish for, you might get it."

The most public evidence of Billy's struggle to be "as okay as possible" has to be his bouts with alcohol, which might or might not have led to a spate of car wrecks through the early years of the third millennium. Stories abound, both in print and on the grapevine. One person tells of watching Billy spend time in a Chelsea sidewalk café while allegedly walking his ex-girlfriend's dog. As the dog hunkered under the table, this person claims to have seen Billy, over the course of about an hour, polish off the contents of a bottle of Rémy Martin.

Celebrities often get a break when they become entangled in automotive mishaps, especially when the only damage done is to property. While some of Billy's accidents may have resulted from driving an older car on a wet and winding road, many of his friends and his ex-wife have urged him to get a driver.

Billy has been married three times. As I write this he has just tied the knot with a woman about a third his age. His first wife, Elizabeth, was the sister of the man he replaced in the first band he put out a record with, the Hassles, and the ex-wife of that band's drummer. His second wife was Christie Brinkley. One of the first women the fashion industry dubbed a supermodel, she continues to be successful and beautiful into her fifties. Both of these unions ended in traumatic, if not acrimonious divorces. The divorce with Elizabeth proved disastrous in many, many ways that will become evident as Billy's story unfolds.

Relationships were never Billy's strong suit. He once claimed he had only two friends at Hicksville High, one of them his cousin. That might have had to do with his appearance. He was from one of the area's less well-to-do families, and there was not a lot of cash for cool clothes. He admits to feelings of economic inadequacy early in his life. He also claims that, on occasion, the family went hungry.

Like so many of Billy's musical idols, from James Brown to Ray Charles to John Lennon, the relative deprivation of his youth found an outlet in music. There always seemed to be enough money for piano lessons. This might have had to do with his parents' European backgrounds. His father grew up in Germany, and he left the country with his family while in his late teens, just ahead of the Holocaust. His mother's parents were cultured English Jews. The arts played an important part in the Joel household.

However, Billy's father apparently found America not to his liking. Nearly twenty years after leaving Europe, he returned to Vienna, leaving his family to muddle through as best they could in the working-class Long Island suburb of Hicksville, a part of the larger Levittown development that provided an alternative to city life for returning World War II veterans (Billy's father is one). While Billy's father sent support checks regularly, that was about all the contact he had with the family from the time Billy was seven until he was an adult. It was a, perhaps *the*, watershed event in Billy's life.

"I don't know what happened with his father," says longtime confidant and former publicist Howard Bloom. "I don't know why his father and his mother split, but I have the impression that when his father was cut off from him, his right to intellect was cut off from him. It's just a feeling."

"Billy has his own distrust of people," concurs his first manager, Irwin Mazur, "and his own tendencies that stem from his father leaving the family. I don't think Billy ever really got over that. I think Billy has an uneasy feeling about that."

This, then, is where the story begins.

CHAPTER 1

AND NEVER SAW HIS FATHER ANYMORE

By the time he became a parent, Howard Joel was employed as an engineer for General Electric, helping the company put together huge infrastructure projects in Central America and Europe, though he officially worked out of the company's New York City headquarters. Even when his marriage worked, he was rarely home. When he did get home, he would fill his children's ears with such uplifting thoughts as, "Ahh, life is a cesspool."

Howard Joel left home when his daughter, Judy, was nine years old and his son, William, was seven. He and his wife, Rosalind, officially divorced a few years later. Abandoning his family may have proved the pivotal point in the life of his son, William Martin Joel. Gone were the Schumann and Bartok that would emanate from the cheap upright piano with fifty coats of paint that sat in a place of honor in the Joel living room in Hicksville. Gone too was the bitterness and contention that filled the house.

Howard Joel had never really felt that he fit into the role of an American, despite having served in the U.S. Army. He missed the European gestalt of his youth—without, of course, the bitterness of exile and the horrors of the Holocaust. When Howard Joel thought about going home, it wasn't to the four rooms on a slab in a rehabilitated potato field on Long Island; it was to the cultured splendor of prewar Germany.

But it hadn't always been like that for Howard Joel.

At the turn of the nineteenth century, the Joels were one of the wealthier families in Nuremberg, Germany. They had started small, with Billy's great-grandfather's tailor shop, but by 1923, when Helmut (Billy's father, who later changed his name to Howard) was born, the Joel family was well on its way to building the country's second-largest mail-order fabric company. They owned a manufacturing plant and had a very nice home in town.

The nature of the Joels' fortune, however, offers a glimpse of what was going on in Germany at the time. It was the height of the industrial revolution, and even in Europe most people dressed in ready-to-wear clothing as opposed to making their own. After World War I, however, the economic sanctions levied against Germany were weighing heavily on the nation and the people. The economic depression of the late '20s and '30s was a global phenomenon, but it hit hardest in a defeated and downcast Germany, where it took a wheelbarrow full of marks to buy a loaf of bread.

By the 1930s, Nazi party leader Adolph Hitler was in power, and things were changing rapidly for Jews all over Germany. The center of that change was Nuremberg. In 1935, the Nuremberg laws were passed, stripping the Jews of Germany of all their rights as German citizens. The Joel home was a block away from one of the focal points for the Nazi rallies that endorsed these laws. The upshot was hard for them to miss, even for Helmut Joel, who was just in his early teens.

"What is a child supposed to do about that?" Howard Joel wondered. "What is a grown-up to do about such things? Withdrawing was the only option."

"My father, Carl . . . had to leave and couldn't take [his business] with him, so he sold it. He was detained in Berlin for a week or so and then he joined my mother and me in Switzerland."

When war consumed Europe, the Joel family left for Cuba, then a friendly place for Europeans and Americans alike, if not necessarily for the native Cubans. Pre-Castro Cuba, the Cuba of Ernest Hemingway and U.S.-friendly dictator Fulgencio Batista, was a Caribbean playground for the rich, a place to drink rum and sit in the sun by day, gamble and enjoy a variety of entertainments by night. The Joel family spent some three years there, during which Helmut studied engineering at the University of Havana.

The Joel family finally immigrated to the United States, settling in the Riverdale section of the Bronx in 1942. While Carl managed to salvage some of the capital from his business, he was forced to leave most of it behind when the family became refugees. By the time he arrived in the Bronx, he needed to get back into business, and he started a hair-ribbon company.

Helmut changed his name to Howard as the family settled into their new life. At one time, during happier days, he had thought of becoming a concert pianist. He expressed his musical interests by getting involved in life at the City College of New York, joining the school's Gilbert and Sullivan Players as a non-matriculating member. There he met Rosalind Hyman.

Howard and Rosalind performed together in the college's productions of *The Pirates of Penzance* and *The Mikado*, the latter conducted by Julius Rudel, who would later become the conductor of the New York City Opera.

Gilbert and Sullivan played an important role in the life of Rosalind Hyman. Her parents had met at a Gilbert and Sullivan production at the Royal Albert Hall in London. Rebecca Hyman had trained in the traditional British art of nannying. Phillip wrote books and plays. As their daughter described their circumstances, "My family didn't have a pot to pee in, but we were cultured English Jews with a lot of pride."

Phillip and Rebecca had brought their pride over from England and gave it, themselves, and their daughter a home in a tenement apartment in Flatbush, Brooklyn.

Howard and Rosalind played and sang together for about a year before Howard was drafted into the army in 1943. He was assigned to an Engineer Combat Battalion. Initially he served in Italy, fighting in the battles of Anzio and Monte Casino. Then his unit was redeployed to Germany. Traveling through Nuremberg, he drove a Jeep past the ruins of his father's old factory, with one smokestack still enduring, the name "Joel" painted on the side, standing tall among the ruins. In April 1945, he was among the troops that liberated the Nazi concentration camp at Dachau, outside Munich.

"We . . . took pictures of the heaps of . . . dead people," he recalled. "And then we moved on, because we were a combat troop and never stayed anywhere . . . It was terrible. We were too late to help."

The war experience must have torn at Howard as he drove through the city of his youth, now in ruins, with the military force that had rendered it such. He saw the factory that had created his family fortune, now as ruined as that fortune. He saw the remains of hundreds of his people, the Jews of Germany, stacked like loaves of bread, with no time for incineration or burial, so hasty was the German retreat. And yet, in a strange way, it was home, it was what he knew better than Switzerland or Havana or the Bronx.

"He was never the same when he came back," says Rosalind Joel. "All his cynicism and sourness came from his experiences in the war."

❧ ❧ ❧

In 1946, shortly after Howard returned from his tour of duty in Europe and was demobilized, he and Rosalind Hyman married. Howard took an apartment on Strong Street in the Bronx, not far from his parents. Their first child, a daughter they named Judith, was born in 1947. Their second child, William, came along on May 9, 1949.

There was not a great deal of love between the Joel parents and the Hyman parents. Carl Joel was a businessman. Phillip Hyman was a bohemian. The Joel family lived in a large apartment in a still-fashionable area of the Bronx. The home had a sunken living room with expensive furnishings and oriental rugs. It wasn't the grandeur of Nuremberg, but it wasn't bad.

Howard's job at General Electric allowed him to move his young family out of the city and into a private house in a better environment. He became one of the hundreds of thousands of returning GIs commuting from Long Island to New York City.

Long Island earns its name. It is the largest island adjoining the continental United States, extending approximately 118 miles east-northeast from the mouth of the Hudson River, adjacent to Manhattan. Twenty miles at its widest point, the 1,723-square-mile island is separated from the mainland on the north by Long Island Sound and bounded by the Atlantic Ocean on the south and east. The New York City boroughs of Brooklyn and Queens make up the western end of the Island. The city is bordered by Nassau County, and the eastern end of the island is Suffolk County. The closer to the city, the more valuable the property, save for the far-eastern area, the summer resort towns and countryside known collectively as the Hamptons.

The Levitt communities took over the former farming area of Long Island, about three-quarters of the way into Nassau County. Levitt paved the potato fields with grids and streets of virtually identical two-bedroom homes with a living room, kitchen, and dining room on a slab of cement. These houses were created as inexpensive dwellings for the servicemen returning to post-war prosperity. Sixty years later, modified Levitt homes still constitute a huge number of the dwellings in Long Island communities like Levittown, Jericho, and Hicksville. They gave a lot of former apartment dwellers a bedroom and a lawn for the kids, a little land they could call their own. Among the other musicians who came out of the Levitt developments were producer George "Shadow" Morton, who built a recording studio in the basement of a non-Levitt home, and Hall of Fame songwriter Ellie Greenwich.

Howard took his family to their new Levitt home on Meeting Lane in Hicksville. There was one thing that set the house, overlooked by the Hicksville water tank, apart—it was the only house on the block that had no driveway.

They did, however, have a piano. This was Howard Joel's refuge, his escape into the cultural. While he'd given up on a career as a classical pianist, at his father's urging, he still loved to play and would work his way through folios of Chopin and Bartok, laboring with each composition until he had mastered it. This was Howard's idea of a good time, and it impressed his very young son mightily.

"My father was my idol as a pianist as a kid, because he was classically trained and could read music," Billy says. "But he thought he was never good enough; he never gave himself any slack. He said, 'I'm a hack, I can't play, I'm just doing it for me.'"

The piano fascinated Billy from the time he could reach it. He recalls writing early compositions, in which he would very impressionistically create storms on the piano, playing the very low notes and the very high notes. Howard and Rosalind discovered that their son had inherited their ears and love for music. By the age of four, young Billy was picking out Mozart by ear on the piano. So they trundled him off to a local piano teacher, and thus began a dozen years of classical pedagogy.

"After four years of little Billy's storm song," he says, "my mom said 'enough!' and dragged me to Ms. Francis's to take lessons."

"I hated every minute of it until I quit," Billy recalled.

Howard didn't hear much of his young son's early (or even later) musical travails, however. After the war, things that Americans took for granted, like electricity in their homes, became the standard around the planet. Howard Joel became one of the engines of that development in developing nations. As part of the technology team that went traipsing around the globe on projects for General Electric, he spent large chunks of time developing the power grid all over Latin America. This left Rosalind alone a great deal of the time with her children—Billy, who was a year old when they moved to suburbia, and Judy.

Life at the Joels became acrimonious. When Howard was there, he and Rosalind would fight. When he wasn't, she had to cope with parenting two growing children. The split was inevitable and came when Billy was seven, in 1956. Howard left and took a position with GE in Europe, finding himself comfortably back in the civilized, German-speaking world of Vienna. Eventually, in Vienna, Howard remarried.

CHAPTER 2

CHILDREN LIVED IN LEVITTOWN

The mid-1950s were the days of Ike and *Donna Reed*, where home-baked cookies awaited well-dressed, well-groomed kids when they came home from school with books strapped neatly. If aliens land and do their anthropological research in the Museum of Broadcasting, they'll think that every family was a nuclear one (except for poor Steve Douglas, the father on *My Three Sons*, who was a widower), that moms vacuumed their deep-pile carpets in designer dresses, high heels, and pearls, that every dad went to work in an office, and woe to the children who misbehaved when their father came home.

Howard, however, was not coming home. By all accounts the Joels were the neighborhood's only single-parent home. Rosalind was still a relatively young and attractive woman, and a single woman so close to home made all the local wives very wary (a decade would pass before the Women's Movement took hold). At that time, though, the only jobs for a working mom were generally those reserved for single girls—stenography, filing, bookkeeping, and the like. Howard sent a monthly check, but between that and the living Rosalind could eke out doing jobs that, at the time, would barely support a single girl, the Joels barely got by. It toughened up Rosalind Joel pretty quickly.

"We weren't like everybody else on the block," Billy says. "We were kind of wackos, the weirdos. If you weren't—at least, imagewise—the nuclear family, if you didn't keep your lawn trimmed, you know, there was tension with the neighbors . . . My mom didn't have many friends in the neighborhood. I didn't have many friends in the neighborhood."

"We were blue-collar poor people, which is different from *poor* poor people," Billy explains. "You don't go to welfare when you're blue-collar poor. You somehow work. You never ask for a handout—you would die first. Your kids would starve to death first. It was very hard for my mother. We were the gypsy family, the only family where there had been a divorce, the only one that wasn't Catholic, the only one without a driveway."

"We went hungry a lot. Sometimes it was scary not eating . . . Do you know what it's like to be the poor people on the poor people's block? . . . There was a lot of insecurity as a kid. It was a drag and I guess that it gave me the drive not to let it happen again. I'm not gonna be hungry again—ever!"

"Roz did the best she could by Billy," says Bruce Gentile, Billy's longtime associate, former housemate, and a civil servant in the somewhat more upscale Huntington area, not too far from Hicksville, where Roz moved when Billy had the money to move her, "with lessons, etc. Just ask any Huntington resident who has come across Roz when she's going on about it after having a few drinks."

For young Billy, things were even more complicated. For better or worse, living in a house of women with his mother and older sister, he had no strong male role model at home. On the other hand, this gave him what he describes as a very loving, nurturing home. Unlike most of his contemporaries, he did not have to fear "waiting for his father to come home." While he didn't have a present father to pattern after, he also didn't have a father who might beat him just "to make a man" of him. His home life also didn't make pursuits like playing the piano and reading seem "wimpy." The one sturdy, steady male in his life, his grandfather Phillip, was especially helpful in this regard.

"My grandfather . . . was the most inspiring presence in my life," he says. "He was a very proper, well-mannered and well-read Englishman, although none of his breeding had brought him wealth or position . . . he didn't have a dime because all of his energies were funneled into the pursuit of knowledge . . . He didn't respect anything but knowledge, and you'd better know what you were talking about or he would devastate you. He could be a pain in the neck, but he was a happy man, the only self-fulfilled soul I've ever known."

"He would sneak us into operas, ballets, and Gilbert and Sullivan by slipping the usher a pack of Luckies, and we'd be sitting in almost the front row."

While Billy may have inherited his father's ear and talent, he didn't have his patience. It used to astound him when his father would stagger through a Chopin piece until he came out at the other end able to play it. Billy didn't have that inclination, certainly not as a pre-teen. With pre-teens there's the inherent problem of their attention span.

What Billy did have, even then, was a phonographic memory. If he heard something, he could generally play it back, and if he couldn't, he could fake it well enough that most people wouldn't know.

"I guess I started writing when I was about seven years old," he recalls. "I was too lazy to read my Bach or Schubert, so I'd make up some of the parts to fake out my mother."

Early in his lessons, Billy decided that he never wanted to be a classical pianist. His peers with such ambitions were always nervous, practicing constantly, devoting their entire being to this pursuit. They were in competition with everyone else with such intentions, and this was not the kind of life young Billy Joel was about to choose for himself. He enjoyed playing baseball and having fun, and practicing the piano was not his idea of fun.

Billy's first years of school were fomentive years in America. As he would later encapsulate in his hit "We Didn't Start the Fire," it was the era of communist plots and cold wars. Billy sucked it all in.

He was, by his own admission, a model grade schooler, albeit he didn't feel the need to actually *study*. He read voraciously, however, reading history books for entertainment before the Joel home had a television.

"By the time he was seven," his mother confirms, "Billy was a bookworm, and if I went to the library, I had to bring home twenty books: picture books, storybooks, history books."

It was a habit that has continued throughout his life. His longtime publicist and confidant Howard Bloom observed (and approved of) this habit: "Billy reads books the way other people eat M&Ms."

The '50s in America were like the fire Billy didn't start, a peat fire that burns quietly underground, occasionally sending a flare through to the surface, generally looking for places to ignite for real. One of those points of ignition was rock and roll. The focus of that flash point was a young truck driver from Tupelo named Elvis. He certainly caught the pre-adolescent attention of Judy Joel and her friends, exposing her classically trained, piano-playing brother to the joys of rock and roll.

"I . . . remember doing an Elvis Presley impression when I was in the fourth grade. It was the first thing I ever did in front of people. I sang 'Hound Dog' and I was jiggling my hips like Elvis. I remember because the fifth-grade girls started screaming. I really dug the fifth-grade girls. I thought, 'Hey, this is pretty neat.' When the girls started screaming, the teacher pulled me off the stage. . .

"When I got pulled off the stage for singing Elvis . . . it was kind of like I beat the system. I got away with something before they could stop me."

This story points to one of the continuing tensions in Billy's life. On the one hand, he enjoys getting away with something. On the other hand, he admits that he has had a lifelong fear of being caught, of being sent to the principal's office, of getting pulled over by the cops, of dealing with lawyers, of anyone chiding him about not following the rules. To paraphrase one of his contemporaries (and another Howard Bloom client), John Mellencamp, he fought authority. Authority has a nasty habit of coming out on top, though.

"I think it was because of his father leaving the family like that," postulates Irwin Mazur, who managed Billy in the early years of his career. "Billy has had, in my eyes, a distrust of male figures. Not male figures that are cronies of his, but any kind of more adult, authority figures."

Ironically, despite the classical influences of his parents and his teenage sister's interest in the pop idols of the day, Billy recalls that the first record he actually went out and bought was a copy of Dave Brubeck's cool-jazz recording of his sax player Paul Desmond's tune "Take Five," a song that shattered any number of stereotypes. It was on the first jazz LP certified gold, the lyrical yet experimental album *Time Out*. The sales of the album become even more surprising when you consider that the songs on the album were in rhythms rarely heard even in classical music, let alone jazz or pop. "Take Five" bounced around in a 5/4 time signature. Other songs on the album used 9/8. This was the album's artistic statement—hence its title. It testifies to the artistic gifts of Brubeck and Desmond as players and composers that tunes like "Blue Rondo a la Turk" and "Take Five" have become jazz standards.

"The way Brubeck messed around with time signatures appealed to the musician in me," Billy recalls. "It was, 'This is impossible, this should not be allowed to happen,' but he made it work in a melodic, musical way."

Brubeck and Billy also had common ground that they would discover later—both were students of classical music who, when they were allegedly reading their lessons, used to fool their mothers with the music they had memorized or improvised with their massively musical ears and pianistic prowess.

In addition to being something of a bohemian, Phillip Hyman, while born a Jew, became what the Jews call an *apikoros*, an educated agnostic. He raised his daughter Rosalind in that manner.

Perhaps it was the fact that they were the only non-Christians on their street. Perhaps it was that, historically in America, religion, and particularly the Christian churches, have served as the refuge of the poor—spiritually and financially. For whatever reason, Rosalind Joel had her children baptized in an evangelical church when Billy was twelve, the years that most of his compatriots were getting *bar* and *bat mitzvahed* and many of Judy's were preparing for Sweet Sixteen parties and other rites of passage.

However, you can take the Jew, even an *apikoros*, out of the faith, but it's much harder to separate the faith from the Jew. It was a lesson Howard's family might have taught them, but Rosalind, Billy, and Judy had to learn it the hard way. That happened the day the evangelical preacher got up to sermonize. He held up a dollar note and proclaimed, "This is the flag of the Jews."

This didn't sit well with the Joels, who left and never went back.

CHAPTER 3

YOU MIGHT HAVE HEARD I RUN WITH A DANGEROUS CROWD

Adolescence is a bitch. Ask anyone who's been through it. Lots of peer pressure affects the way you look, the way you act, who you hang out with. And that doesn't even take into account the raging hormones. Junior high school is not merely a battlefield, it's an entire war complete with daily skirmishes, potential land mines, a hierarchy of ranks, sorties of all sorts, negotiations, attacks, and retreats. And that's just the hallways. It's a time when you start making decisions about yourself.

"You got into junior high, you could go one of three ways," says Billy. "You could be a collegiate, a hitter, or a brownie—the kid who wears brown shoes with white socks, carries a school bag and always gets the monitor jobs." Initially, Billy hung with "the hitters," a group of guys called the Parkway Green Gang.

The Parkway Green was the Hicksville version of the town square. A Gilbert and Sullivan fan would have been amused by the gang's name, as it was reminiscent of Gilbert placing his Pirates in a popular English beach resort like Penzance. The Parkway Green Gang were local kids who banded together for mischief and security. At the Hicksville Middle School, it meant they had each other's backs. It was an all-white, playtime version of *West Side Story*, without the deadly violence.

"We'd just play handball all day, kick over garbage cans, sniff glue, and use phony draft cards to buy beer," Billy says. "Every evening I'd say goodnight to my mom, go up to my room, crawl out on the roof, and sneak away. I'd run over to the green to . . . drink Tango wine and screw around with the gang."

"We were hitters. I mean I had a gang and that's what we did.

They called us punks—we didn't call ourselves punks—we thought we were hoods."

"We used to sneak off to find Italian-style clothes, tight black shirts, and stuff. Some guys had the really pointy shoes, casino pants . . . Me? I was one of those crewcut guys with white sneakers. That was before punks, before greasers. 'Punk' was an insult. 'Whaddya mean, I'm a punk? I'm a hitter.' We didn't really know what to call ourselves. We thought we were just cool."

The gang reflected the times. Not as dangerous certainly as gangs can get today, those of the early '60s on Long Island represented yet another teenage rite of passage, juvenile adventures in delinquency. As the Los Angeles Police Department points out, one of the attributes of belonging to a gang fit Billy to a tee: "adopting a defiant attitude toward authority figures (may be expressed by violent behavior at school or home)." The violence was not really a problem at home or school. Billy hung with the gang for a feeling of belonging more than as an outlet or even protection.

"I never said I was tough," he says. "I suppose some of the guys I used to hang out with were kind of wild, but I was a cream puff."

Still, Billy had several needs that the gang didn't or couldn't serve. The male bonding he found on the Parkway Green didn't fulfill that need, his need for a place to channel his aggression, or, ultimately, his need for protection, to seem less of "a cream puff." The gang might have offered safety in numbers at school, but on the street it was a different matter, especially on the way to piano lessons. For one thing, Ms. Francis taught both piano and *ballet*.

Now, piano lessons were bad enough, but a boy that his peers even *thought* was studying ballet might as well have had a big bull's-eye painted on his back. Despite being a heavily Catholic area, the "turn-the-other-cheek" ethic was not one of the dictates that Hicksville lived by. Rather, the rule was that if you got hit, you had to hit back, harder if possible.

For Billy, it was a big problem during junior high and into high school. According to people who attended school with him, he was slight, studious (despite his wilder tendencies), and he was the kid that got picked on and beat up for shits and giggles.

The need to smack, and to defend himself, led Billy to the gym. There he demonstrated some impressive prowess and developed a reputation as a pretty good amateur boxer, learning how defend himself and keep the bullies at bay. Between the ages of sixteen and nineteen, he earned a 22–4 record in the ring and acquired a wiseguy's broken nose.

"I've got two different sized nostrils," he points out. "I used to be cute, believe it or not. I think about it now and I must have been out of my mind . . . But I really enjoyed it while I was doing it."

Beyond enjoying it, he performed well as a boxer. He won twenty-two of his twenty-six fights, losing two by decision and two by knockout. He decided it was time to quit, though, when his final opponent had arms that seemed as big as Billy. However, Billy would maintain that the boxing helped him work through the male-identity issues brought on by his life in the house of women.

§ § §

While the boxing might have helped Billy deal with his male-identity crisis, it didn't wipe out his rebellious streak. He would run away from home, escaping, if just for a moment, from the flip side of the nurturing "house of women," the hassles and arguments inherent in all parent-child and sibling relationships, especially when the tensions are high because the money's tight. One night, he got more trouble than he bargained for.

"I just wanted to break out in general," he recalls. "I was sitting on the stoop of this anonymous house in Hicksville in the darkness, pondering my fate, when a patrol car pulled up.

"Now, unbeknownst to me, this particular house had been robbed earlier that night. The cops came up to me, grabbed me, and threw me in the clink.

"I knew, of course, that my own father had spent time at Dachau. All I could think about . . . was they were going to shave my Jewish head, beat me, slap the soles of my feet bloody and force me to live on gruel."

While the charges were dropped the next day, many of his fellow gang members wound up in jail for real. Within a few years, many others would find themselves half a world away in Asia, fighting on a remote peninsula they had never heard of before, a divided country called Vietnam.

Billy would find another outlet, however. In fact, by the time he was seventeen, he was already knee deep in it, though it had started two years earlier.

The year 1964 was amazing, especially for pop music. America was recovering from the ramifications of potential nuclear Armageddon supplied by the Cuban Missile Crisis, followed by the devastating assassination of President John F. Kennedy. The country needed a good scream, both physically and metaphorically. America needed distraction.

Over the previous year, across the pond, all of England seemed to be in thrall to the point of distraction over a quartet of young men who called themselves the Beatles. These four actually had quite a bit in common with Billy Joel. One of the Beatles' main songwriters, John Lennon, was raised in a "house of women." They all were working-class blokes living close to the ocean. Their personal taste in music ran toward the soulful sounds of African Americans like Little Richard, the Isley Brothers, and Chuck Berry, whose songs they honored by recording them. They also harbored a sneaking fondness for show tunes, as illustrated by their version of "Then There Was You" from *The Music Man.*

From the release of their second single on EMI, "Please Please Me," in 1963, the Beatles, under the shrewd, savvy, and watchful eye of their manager, Brian Epstein, did something few acts before had—they delivered the full monty. Beyond the musical goods, the Beatles had the look, the offstage demeanor, and the onstage attitude.

While opening a show for one of their heroes, Roy Orbison—who recalled being lucky to even get on stage that night after the Beatles' fourteenth or fifteenth encore—they asked him how to make it in the States. To that point, English bands had not been accepted in America, the chauvinistic Americans begrudging the English, who the Yanks felt were bringing their own back to them. Orbison offered them this bit of advice: "Dress like you're doing, keep the hair, say you're British and get on a show like *The Ed Sullivan Show.*"

On February 9, 1964, Americans discovered what all the fuss was about. They actually kind of knew, as by the time Sullivan booked them, the Beatles had already topped the U.S. pop charts twice: "I Want to Hold Your Hand," had spent seven weeks at #1 during that winter, at which point "She Loves You" replaced "I Want to Hold Your Hand" at #1 and stayed there for another two weeks.

As it was for Elvis, the key moment came with that evening's hyped-up appearance on the CBS Sunday-evening television staple, *The Ed Sullivan Show*. More than 73 million Americans tuned in and saw everything musical change forever, once again. The Beatles performed their two #1 songs and "Till There Was You" (a clever choice for the parents in the living room). Suddenly, every song in the Top 10 featured the vocal stylings of John Lennon and Paul McCartney.

Nearly as suddenly, it seemed that every young man who wasn't a football hero (and even some who were) had picked up an electric guitar and was making noise with his friends in the garage or the basement.

The Beatles presented a crossroads for Billy Joel. At fifteen years old, he'd studied classical piano for eleven years. However, he knew he would never be a concert pianist. He didn't have the temperament.

"If you're going to be a concert pianist then you've got to practice six hours a day and devote your whole life to it. You become a high-strung maniac," Billy observed. "It doesn't seem to be a lot of fun. And I wanted to have fun."

"I had no intention of becoming a concert pianist. And rock and roll, the entry level is a lot lower criteria. And it's a lot more forgiving. If you learn to play a couple of chords on a guitar or crash-bang-boom on the drums, you can come in. It's very welcoming."

Billy was, of course, familiar with rock and roll—he didn't live in a cave (there are none in Hicksville). After *The Blackboard Jungle*, the 1957 film that opened with early rock and roll star Bill Haley and the Comets singing "Rock Around the Clock"—bringing the music to Hollywood and thus the mainstream—rock and roll became the sound of young America rebelling mildly. It was, to Billy's generation, what big-band swing had been to their parents' generation: that horrible noise that kids dance to these days.

While the Beatles impressed Billy on a visceral and musical level, there was more to the attraction. Up to that point, his perception of rock—colored, no doubt, by his sister and her friends—were the Philly teen idols of that afternoon teen soap opera called *American Bandstand* (most kids, especially young women, watched it not as much for the musicians performing as for the drama on the dance floor—who was dancing with whom that week). The Beatles were an antidote to the middle-of-the-road pretty boys pretending to rock.

"I thought, 'these guys don't look like Fabian. They don't look like they were manufactured in Hollywood,'" says Billy. "I would see this look in John Lennon's eyes that told me something. They were irreverent, a bunch of wise guys like me and my friends!"

Beyond his total adoration (and absorption) of everything the Beatles ever recorded, he also honed in on their influences, especially latter-day R&B, both blue-eyed and brown. He also fell in love with Phil Spector's mini-operas for kids, the Righteous Brothers' overwrought ballads, and the puissance, passion, and power in the gutbucket soul of Sam and Dave, Wilson Pickett, and Otis Redding.

"When I was a teenager," he adds, "music progressed because people were exposed to a lot of everything. On the radio, one pop station would play new music, blues, soul."

Another thing any red-blooded, heterosexual male couldn't miss about the Beatles on *Sullivan* (and subsequently) was the reaction of the heterosexual females in the audience. They yelled, they screamed. It was clearly evident there wasn't a dry panty in the house. This naturally appealed to the non-football heroes. Now they could attract sex, too. An intelligent young man, Billy realized this.

"I became a musician partially because of my physical limitations," he admits. "I wasn't tall, I don't have Cary Grant looks. I had to transcend somehow . . ."

So when his neighbor Howie Blauvelt, who played bass in a band called the Echoes, asked Billy if he would be interested in employing his classical knowledge of the keyboard in the service of rock and roll, at first Billy was suspicious, but he decided to give it a go. The band wore velvet-collared blue jackets, and eventually they got good enough to play covers of British invasion bands like the Kinks, the Zombies, the Rolling Stones, and, of course, the Beatles at the local teen canteens, and dances at the high schools and forward-thinking churches.

"When these guys first asked me to join them, I couldn't figure out why," he says, "but we'd play at parties and when somebody wasn't singing, they'd drop the microphone in the back of the piano, which sounded terrible, so I got an organ. It was a Vox Continental with the orange top, same as the Dave Clark Five's: looked great, sounded dinky as hell—just like theirs did . . . If you were a musician, you got to meet more girls than most." This became especially clear at one of the Echoes' early gigs. From the stage, Billy noticed a girl he had a huge crush on.

"Her name was Virginia Callaghan, and she didn't know I was alive," he recalls. "Then my band did its gig, playing songs like 'I Want to Hold Your Hand' or whatever was popular then and she *looked* at me.

"Then, at the end of the night, the priest gave each of us fifteen dollars. I thought, 'You mean you get paid for this?' That was it."

Not only would the young women look at the short kid with the wiseguy's nose, many would do more than look. And a better class of young woman, too.

"If you were from the more industrial, blue-collar part of Long Island, you wanted to go out with girls from the North Shore," he recalls. "Those girls weren't supposed to go out with us . . . and that made the girls want to, of course."

۞ ۞ ۞

Billy got the rock and roll bug in a big way. He could have fun with his friends, make music, attract girls, and get paid while he did it. What could be wrong with that?

It's a connection that Howard Bloom sees, and one that he feels explains a lot about Billy's subsequent career. "Rock is a religion," Bloom says, a position with which Billy definitely agreed, "that says you have the right to rebel and you have the right to an identity of your own."

The Echoes' increasing visibility also opened up doors that Billy hadn't previously dreamed of. Shortly after the band debuted, he got drafted to work with soon-to-be-legendary producer George "Shadow" Morton. The story goes that Morton had contacted an old friend of his, Ellie Greenwich, who had become a very successful songwriter with her partner, Jeff Barry. At the meeting, Morton told Barry that he, too, wrote songs.

Barry challenged Morton to bring one in, so Morton arranged a session with some girls he knew who had already had some flop singles, the Shangri-Las. On his way to the session, he wrote two songs, "Remember (Walkin' in the Sand)" and "Leader of the Pack" for the group. It may very well be these sessions on which the fourteen-year-old Billy played.

"The first time I remember actually being in a professional recording situation was in a basement studio in Levittown called Dynamic Studios," he says. "It was 1964 and I was fourteen years old, and the guy producing the sessions for Red Bird Records was named Shadow Morton. I was asked to play piano on these two songs, 'Remember (Walkin' in the Sand)' and 'Leader of the Pack' . . . There were no singers at the time, and whether I cut a demo or the final master, I don't know, but I played on the recordings of those two songs, never got paid, and I was thrilled to even be in a professional recording situation."

Audiences also heard Billy's unbilled keyboard work on an ad for Bachman Pretzels, a campaign that capitalized on Chubby Checker, "the Twist" dance craze, and the fact that pretzels—classic pretzels—have that twist in the middle: "There's a new 'twist' in Bachman."

Even this limited success gave him the license to think bigger. When he got into New York City, he would find himself on 57th Street, in front of Steinway Hall, ogling the concert grand pianos in the window. He went to concerts at places like the Apollo Theater in Harlem, renowned for performances by African-American artists ranging from Duke Ellington and Ella Fitzgerald in the '30s to the ground-breaking stagecraft of James Brown—one of the artists Billy went to see—in the '60s.

Around this same time, he also began to learn about the dynamic nature of rock and roll. Not just about the dynamic nature of the music, but about actually playing the music. Being in a rock band is an intense experience, with everyone having their own point of view as to what to play and how to play it. This dynamic is what causes bands to be great if they can work through the differences and come out with something that doesn't sound compromised at the other end. It is also the thing that causes so many bands, successful or otherwise, to implode, explode, break up, or jettison musicians.

Billy's band, the Echoes, had been around since Blauvelt had been in fifth grade. Now they were freshmen in high school, and the name began to seem anachronistic in the wake of the Beatles, the Rolling Stones, the Zombies, and even the Rascals. Briefly, they became known as the Emeralds. A few months later, the Emeralds became the Lost Souls.

The change in name to the Lost Souls coincided with the band adding original material to their show and weaning themselves away from doing covers of popular hits. Cover bands could gig regularly at high school dances and events like that, but to play the clubs, you needed original material. While they didn't know whether Billy could write music, his bandmates couldn't help but notice his reading habits. They asked him to be the word man.

"What are you looking at me for?" he asked.

"Well, you read a lot, you read a lot of books," they replied.

"So what?" he countered. "That doesn't make me Robert Browning. It doesn't make me Bob Dylan."

"Well," they said, "give it a shot."

And with that auspicious beginning, Billy Joel became a songwriter.

۞ ۞ ۞

Because of Long Island's proximity to New York City, and because a lot of record company people commuted from Long Island, the mid-'60s became a banner time for Long Island musicians. By 1966, the Young Rascals had already introduced the archetypal Long Island rocking version of blue-eyed soul, topping the charts with their tune "Good Lovin'." They were used to the limelight, as the band's members—Felix Cavaliere on keys, Gene Cornish on guitar, and Eddie Brigati on percussion, guitar, and vocals—had all been part of Joey Dee and the Starliters, a group that continued to ride high long into the '60s on their 1962 addition to the twist craze, "The Peppermint Twist." (The Starliters that featured the future Rascals also had a very young Jimi Hendrix as a member.) All of this added to the allure of Long Island musicians. Long Island became a hotbed of blue-eyed soul bands of all stripes.

"Long Island was the soul counter to the West Coast psychedelic counterculture," says Bruce Gentile, who played drums with a number of bands on the scene, most notably Mynd's Eye. "Long Island was a floodgate for music."

Lost Souls signed with Mercury Records. Mercury was in something of a slump at the time. The last hit record they had had was the novelty instrumental "A Walk in the Black Forest," by middle-of-the-road keyboard player Horst Jankowski in July 1965. Earlier that year, they had landed a hit with Julie Andrews's "The Wedding." Their biggest pop/rock artist, by far, was Leslie Gore. The rawer garage sound of the Lost Souls must have befuddled the people at the label who had to deliver the music to radio.

It should have been an instructional time for Billy, but he was probably too caught up in the excitement of recording for a major record label to notice the group's innocence being chipped away. The first aspect of that innocence to fall by the wayside was their name. They recorded under the moniker of the Commandos, as another act was already using the name the Lost Souls. During the sessions, the Commandos set down the earliest recordings of songs by William Martin Joel.

"The first song Billy ever recorded—and a great song, too—was entitled 'Journey's End,'" said Howie Blauvelt, who was playing bass with the group. "Billy and I also wrote a song together called 'Time and Time Again.'"

The Commandos' recording career was short and undistinguished. They cut demos, but their music was never released.

❡ ❡ ❡

Another casualty of Billy's fealty to the religion of rock and roll was school. Billy would gig until early in the morning or practice until very late at night. When he wasn't doing either of those things, he was boxing. Needless to say, it became tougher and tougher for him to answer the bell at seven in the morning and go another ten rounds at Hicksville High. He would arrive three classes late. His eyes would be bloodshot from lack of sleep. He drooped. His teachers thought he had come to school stoned. In a way he had, but not from drugs, just the natural disorientation of the sleep-deprived.

"I started playing with my friends at night," Billy quips. "School never got in the way."

Ironically, he managed to keep up his grades despite his only occasional appearance in class. Being as well read as he was, he already seemed to have a grasp of much of the material, and he also admits to being good at taking tests. (He would have done well in college.) He might have dropped out entirely, except that, despite all the internal bickering *chez* Joel, he didn't want to disappoint his mother. So he continued showing up when he had the strength. Unfortunately, that was not enough. Despite having a passing average, his truancy prevented him from graduating with his class.

"I told them, 'The hell with it,'" he says. "'If I'm not going to Columbia University, I'm going to Columbia Records and you don't need a high school diploma over there.'"

CHAPTER 4

THERE'S A NEW BAND IN TOWN

One of the gigs the Lost Souls played was the 1965 World's Fair in Flushing Meadows, Queens, 15 miles from Hicksville. The event was billed as "New York State Battle of the Bands Day." It took place in the New York State Tent of Tomorrow and included a demonstration of "the latest dances: frug, monkey, jerk, etc." The program described the Lost Souls as "five members, ranging in age from twelve to nineteen."

Another band that also played the fair was the Hassles, who were fellow Long Islanders and favorite sons on the flourishing local scene. The Hassles were managed by Irwin Mazur, a piano player a few years older than Billy who grew up in North Massapequa, about 7 miles from the Joels' Hicksville home. He, too, played in bands. Despite the fact that his family was heavy-duty into the music business and the local music scene, he realized that, while playing music was a fine way to make a few bucks in high school, he had other, better opportunities when it came to making a living. Paired with that piece of self-knowledge was his understanding that he really didn't have the talent to take his musical career to the limit, at least as a player.

His family, however, owned one of the hottest rock clubs on Long Island in the '60s. My House was located in the Plainview Shopping Center, off Old Country Road in Plainview—actually a bit closer to where Billy lived than to the proprietors' home. Every night of the week, along with clubs like the Golden Pheasant, the Daisy, and the Action House, My House would present two, three, or four bands, many of them national headliners like the Four Tops or local heroes like the Young Rascals.

By 1966, Mazur was already attending the University of Pennsylvania with the goal of becoming a dentist. Weekends, he would come home to Long Island and work at the club. One of his jobs was auditioning bands for the opening slot. That's how he met John Dizek, Jon Small, and the rest of the Hassles.

A band very much in the mold of such fellow Long Islanders as the Young Rascals and Vanilla Fudge, the Hassles were a soulful rock quintet, soulful enough to win a battle of the bands that preceded a James Brown show at the Forest Hills Tennis Stadium (now Arthur Ashe Stadium, home of the US Open). They were popular enough to be asked to play a Hamptons birthday party for New York State Senator Robert Kennedy.

Like any successful band, the Hassles had a following, a large group of fans who would turn up at local shows. A major part of the draw, especially for the young women in the crowd, was the outright charisma and unbridled sex appeal of both lead singer John Dizek and drummer Jon Small.

"Jon Small always used his penis as a brain," recalls Bruce Gentile, a drummer who had his own band, Mynd's Eye, and also worked bills with the Hassles. Gentile wound up rooming with Jon and Elizabeth Small and Billy at a place they called the Rock House, a large home in Dix Hills with a stone exterior and lots of rooms. "There was no going after anyone if Jon had his eyes on her.

"Jon was one of the best bullshit artists on the scene. We usually went home alone, but Jon got laid. He looked like Rod Stewart. Jon had the lines, Jon had the moves, Jon had the make, Jon owned the car. Jon was banging everyone's girlfriend. He could do that because he was Jon Small.

"The very first time I met Jon Small, I was in eleventh grade, playing at the Golden Pheasant on one of those big bills with like four bands. I was sitting at his drum set, banging it. But no one really wanted to play on Jon's drum set, because Jon needed a gimmick. He wasn't really a good drummer. So, what was Jon's gimmick? He used his bass drum set up like a floor tom tom, and the pedal hit it like a cocktail drum.

"At the time, the Hassles had a van that was like the Magical Mystery Tour. It was professionally painted with flowers. These two little Italian guys were their roadies. This was all very impressive for someone who was in the eleventh grade, getting to play with this band with almost a hit record.

"Jon was like, 'Who the fuck told him he could get on my drum set?' I said, 'Well, Tonio,' who was the promoter or the owner. 'He doesn't want the setups up and down, so it was suggested that everyone use your drum set. So I was just wondering what it was like to play on something where the tom tom is over here, the other one is way over there, and you have a floor tom tom, and you have a bass drum that you're using like a cocktail drum. What am I, Desi Arnaz?'"

The Hassles were a working band, playing very regularly. Mazur convinced the group to let him manage them. "The Hassles had really become one of the hot bands on Long Island," Mazur says. "Those days, on Long Island, were great music days. We had the Rascals, a band called the Vagrants who were a very popular band. You had a band called the Pigeons, which became Vanilla Fudge, who were monumental. Each band had its own gang, had its own people. The Hassles would appear somewhere and a thousand kids would show up. In those days, that was big time."

Like so many bands, the Hassles had their problems. In 1966 the biggest was their keyboard player, Harry Weber. The brother-in-law of the group's drummer, Jon Small, Harry had developed into a major huffer.

"Harry Weber suffered from debilitating depression before the advent of Prozac and the incredibly effective psychotropic medicines of the last quarter of the twentieth century," laments Sandy Gibson, who worked with Billy later on with Family Productions and became very friendly with Billy and Elizabeth. "He was handsome and talented, and so ahead of the curve he was practically the first person in America to have a subscription to the British *New Musical Express*."

"He was sniffing a lot," recalls the group's vocalist, John Dizek. "One time, on stage, I was singing my part and waiting for Harry to come in. I looked back to see where his harmony was . . . Harry was playing the organ with one hand and had his head in a bag sniffing! Harry was crazy . . . as he became more into the glue, the scenes got uglier and uglier."

A working band couldn't function with an unreliable player, so the group started to look to replace him. My House was very close to Hicksville, and a natural target gig for an up-and-coming young band. It was only a matter of time before the Lost Souls/Commandos showed up for an audition. As it turned out, for half the band their timing was kismet.

"Billy had come in," says Mazur. "He must have been fifteen or sixteen at the time. He had a little Farfisa organ, and he played with a band that would do Top 40 stuff. I heard his playing and thought he was phenomenal. I convinced him to leave his band and join the Hassles as the keyboard player. The Hassles were always working. I told Billy I'd buy him a Hammond organ and he'd be working constantly. He said, 'Cool! I'm in.'"

"I'm a better organist than I am a piano player," Billy says. "I can scream when I'm playing an organ! When I got my first Hammond organ—I think I was seventeen—I bought every Jimmy Smith album there was . . . I'd play that stuff with my eyes closed. Actually, I have more fun playing organ than playing piano."

Billy took along Howie Blauvelt. The Commandos disbanded.

Not too long after he was dismissed from the Hassles, Harry Weber died. "I was told," says Mazur, "—and by no means do I know this for an absolute fact—that Harry was a heroin addict. I was told he was killed when he fell in front of a train."

"Harry laid himself on the tracks one night," confirms Gentile. "He couldn't handle the rejection. After he got the boot from the band, Harry the party animal started getting worse. He was drugging and drinking to the max, and being very depressed. Harry was a user of mood- and mind-altering somethings, so the people who turned their backs on him had something to blame it on. Harry ended up sitting on the railroad tracks near Jericho between Syosset and Hicksville while he faced the train. The engineer didn't see him and ran right through. Harry died instantly.

"Everything was kept hushed up until time passed and the real story came out—that it was not an overdose of drugs. Harry took his life over the band. The band was Harry's life. No one really cared and just blew it off."

"I saw the Hassles' first gig with Billy on the keyboards at My House," said one of Harry Weber's old schoolmates, Mark Perry. "I knew that magic had just been added to the band, even while I was wondering what had happened to Harry. You could tell right away that Billy was the new voice and new stand-out member."

Soon the revised Hassles were working all over the East Coast, with a heavy concentration on Long Island. In addition to regular gigs at the Mazur family club, during the summer they would play five shows a night at The Eye in the Hamptons. Back in the '60s, the Hamptons was not the see-and-be-seen place it has become. Rather, it was a placid scene where old money folks and young bohemians could find a separate peace, a pleasant ocean breeze, and nice surf among the cottages and candle-lit cafés. And, of course, there were rock clubs like The Eye where the bohemians (and the old-money kids) could get their ya-yas out of a night.

"Billy sang," Mazur says, "and there was a front man named John Dizek who all the girls loved. They were the two main singers. Billy, at that time with the Hassles, always sat behind the keyboard. He never got on the stage, on mike up front. He just stayed behind the organ."

"Dizek was really the glamour part of the Hassles," Gentile confirms.

The rest of the band consisted of Billy's old Commando pal Howie Blauvelt on bass, guitarist Richie McKenner, and drummer Jon Small. By 1967, the Long Island scene had established itself in the national popular music marketplace. Bands like Leslie West's Vagrants and Vanilla Fudge had major-label deals. As the Hassles solidified as a live unit, it was time for them to make the next move.

"I arranged for somebody from United Artists records to come down and hear the band," says Mazur, "and we got a record deal with United Artists. That was pretty exciting."

At that time, United Artists was experiencing enormous middle-of-the-road success with artists like Bobby Goldsboro, whose tune "Honey" spent a good portion of 1968 in the Top 20, and the Hassles' New York neighbors Jay and the Americans, who enjoyed a string of hits from 1962 through 1970—their biggest, the gold version of "This Magic Moment," coming while the Hassles were also on the label.

"We recorded our first single and album. The first single we recorded was 'You've Got Me Hummin',' the old Sam and Dave song. It charted in the Top 100 in *Billboard*. The album didn't do that much, but we were excited."

In addition to that tune, they did the first version of Traffic's "Coloured Rain," even before Traffic got to release it. Traffic's young keyboard player, Stevie Winwood, was something of a hero to Billy, and to most of the kids playing keyboards in bands at the time. In 1967, when he was fifteen, Winwood had led the Spencer Davis Group to two massive Top 10 hits, "I'm a Man" and "Gimme Some Loving." Traffic was Winwood's new venture, and with the heavy organ and soul influences, it bore no small resemblance to the Hassles, who heard the song through a publisher's test pressing.

The Hassles' first (eponymous) album was a local hit. It didn't get beyond that, though, as the band couldn't secure a national tour.

"Our management was bad," John Dizek maintains. "They used us to support themselves. They kept the Hassles at My House during the most crucial time. We should have been touring to support our album."

"I didn't really know the inner workings of the record business," Mazur concedes. "So I decided the only way I was really going to learn about the record business was to work for a record company. I took a leave of absence from dental school and got a job working for Morris Levy."

If the music business had a godfather in the '50s through the '70s, that figure was Morris Levy. Known by his intimates as Moishe (the Hebrew/Yiddish for Moses—more than likely Levy's Hebrew name), Levy ran Roulette Records. The company had made stars of Frankie Lyman and the Teenagers with hits like "Why Do Fools Fall in Love," and of Tommy James and the Shondells, who had more than a dozen hits, including the #1 song "Hanky Panky," without making anyone but Moishe wealthy.

Levy was the point where the music business and crime blurred. Moishe was a kingmaker, though Roulette Records, his most visible company, wouldn't have seemed to warrant that. Levy also had interests in nightclubs like Birdland—one of the legendary venues of the bebop era of jazz—as well as record distribution, publishing, and every other conceivable area of the music business. During the '50s he had partnered with legendary disc jockey Alan Freed in a variety of business enterprises that made both a lot of money.

Moishe's publishing, recording, live venue, and even retail music ventures had made him fabulously wealthy in both the bebop era and the golden age of rock and roll. He also was reputed to have ties to organized crime, ties that were never legally verified (that is, he was never convicted) but were generally understood—ergo, you didn't cross Moishe.

"If you wanted to learn the record business," Mazur asserts, "and you were privileged enough to work for Morris Levy, you learned the record business."

❁ ❁ ❁

In the meantime, by 1966 President Lyndon Johnson had escalated the conflict in Vietnam. Thousands of young Americans were going there, and many didn't come home. It was a nightmare for any eighteen-year-old who couldn't afford college and had to register for the draft. In 1967, Billy Joel turned eighteen.

Privately, he decided, "To hell with this, I'm not going." When he appeared before the draft board, however, his story was slightly different.

"I'm my mother's sole support," he told the induction officer. "My X amount of dollars a year as a musician is supporting the family."

The officer looked at him, and said, "Oh, OK."

Billy had mixed feelings about not going to war. Like so many of his generation, he didn't understand what it was all about. It was a conflict much older than most of the kids fighting it, though the rhetoric surrounding it was couched in terms of communism versus "our way of life."

Many of these young men found the "salami theory"—you take a slice here, a slice there, and pretty soon the whole thing has gone commie—to be so much baloney. However, Billy eschewed the general anti-war movement. In a blue-collar suburb like Hicksville, in the heart of conservative Long Island, you went and you did your bit. This was, after all, the suburb built specifically to accommodate returning World War II vets.

✿ ✿ ✿

With their keyboard player safely deferred, the Hassles could concentrate on making their second album. Unlike the mix of covers and originals on *The Hassles*, the group's sophomore effort, 1968's *Hour of the Wolf*, featured all William Joel originals, many co-written with other members of the band. Rather than going with their strength—rock heavily informed by soul—the album leaned more toward the tenor of the times, and the times were going psychedelic. Around this time, Jimi Hendrix's turned-on guitar, Pink Floyd's mix of blues and electronics, even the extended jams of the Grateful Dead were all part of the psychedelic movement, as were harder-rock bands like the Iron Butterfly, who's side-long epic "Inna-Gadda-Da-Vida" became the surprise hit of 1969. Similarly, the title track of *Hour of the Wolf* ran 12 minutes long and featured the band actually howling.

The problem with the Hassles as a psychedelic band was . . . they weren't. After the experience with Harry Weber, drugs were likely a sore subject. They might have tried to look and act the part of hippies; however, they had the words but not the music. Billy's background went against any notion of him as a successful hippie. Indeed, try as he might, he failed at it utterly.

As big a failure as Billy was at being a hippie, that was how badly the album failed. The high point of that time with the Hassles was an opening slot for José Feliciano at a Schaefer Music Festival concert in Central Park.

Irwin Mazur, who was still toiling for Morris Levy while trying to shepherd his band through the record release process, defends the album: "It was a pretty good album for its time, but it didn't see the light of day."

The lack of success on a wider-than-local level started to wear on the band, and the musicians lost their spark. When the album had run its course, so had the Hassles.

"After three confusing years of screaming teenies and bad music (and two albums)," Billy says, "I quit to look for something heavy."

"Billy was always alright with me," said Dizek. "We had a ton of fun, he's a pretty funny guy. He was always so focused—he knew that he wanted to be a star from the beginning. That always impressed me."

After leaving the Hassles, John Dizek was born again, and the closest he got to the music business was directing his church choir. McKenner was one of the people Billy knew from his youth who wound up in jail for real, after being involved in a gas station holdup. He later became a postal worker.

While Jon Small and Billy had begun to really loathe the Hassles, they enjoyed playing together and had become fast friends. Billy even lived with Jon and his wife, Elizabeth, in Dix Hills, along with drummer Bruce Gentile and a rotating bunch of other roommates. "After gigs, very early in the morning," Gentile recalls, "by the time we'd get back to the Rock House, even if we were playing locally, it was about 4:30 in the morning.

"Every week, whatever new cop got assigned to this sector would follow us up the driveway, thinking we were the Manson Family or something. A bunch of long-haired freaks in this house? Something's off. So we'd get to the end of the driveway and the cop would be behind us flashing his lights. Jon and Elizabeth's room was upstairs. Jon would have to open his window and say, 'It's okay. They live here.'

"The rent on the Rock House was $350 a month. The reason the house and rent came so cheaply? Me, Jon and some friends were doing LSD one night. Jon says, 'I gotta tell you something, but don't let it freak you out. You know the room Bruce lives in? There was a murder in this house, and there were three bodies found in that room.' The only reason Elizabeth got such a great deal on that house was the last people who owned it, there was a big murder committed there. Someone slaughtered his family."

Billy and Jon wanted to continue playing together and started looking for a context. It came when Billy discovered that by modifying his Hammond he could sound like three-quarters of Led Zeppelin, all by himself. That was the "something heavy" he and Small wound up creating.

Jon Small says, "Billy and I . . . wanted to continue to play together so we formed a two-man army called Attila the Hun. We spent most of our time practicing in the basement of my parents' wallpaper store in Jericho."

"Jon and Billy no doubt thought they were going to have a break-through heavy-metal album with the recording of *Attila*," recalls Bruce Gentile. "When Billy kicked his B3 organ on, at high volume, rats scurried across the floor of the Rock House! Billy and Jon were, at this point, consumed with the idea of looking like English rock stars, from fringe jackets to boots imported from London to Granny Takes a Trip in Manhattan."

"It was some ridiculous concept that they had," says Mazur, who continued on as their manager, "but I supported it. It would be a group with just drums and organ, with Billy doing vocals. I hocked everything I had to get a big stack of Marshall amplifiers, I took a demo of *Attila* to Larry Cohen, who was the head of Epic Records at the time; I had met him through various things. It was just based on that. They even, in those days, cut a video of Billy and Jon, of Attila. There was no MTV in those days, but they played that video at the big Columbia Records convention for the major new releases. If you ever saw that album cover, that's a hoot. We shot that in a meat locker on the West Side."

While the way Attila executed the concept might have been ridicu-lous, the concept itself was nothing new and had worked before. Oklahoma-bred, Detroit-based artists Teegarden and Van Winkle had a 1970 hit with "God, Love and Rock and Roll" using the organ and drum duo. Lee "Do You Know What I Mean" Michaels worked often in a similar setting, with a 300-plus-pound drummer named Frosty. So while Billy's experiments in volume and distortion might have been different, the format itself was essentially sound.

"The *Attila* record came out," Mazur said. "Nothing happened."

"*Attila* received rave reviews from two people," Billy quips, "both of them our road managers." Indeed, critic Stephen Thomas Erelwine, an admitted and unabashed Billy Joel fan and collector, has described the album leaving the listener feeling "as if a drill has punctured the center of your skull."

The duo played perhaps a dozen gigs together, and even those were disasters. "Billy and Jon were getting gigs opening for Grand Funk Railroad," says Gentile. "They bombed, to say the least. I'll bet Billy wishes he could buy every Attila album ever pressed."

Unlike its namesake, Attila did not conquer, and Epic dropped the band. As 1970 went into summer, once again Billy and Jon were at loose ends.

After the fall of Attila, Billy hooked up again briefly with Howie Blauvelt in a band called El Primo. "I went to see Billy play with El Primo at the Daisy in Amityville on Route 110," Gentile recalls. "Two keyboard players, Gerard Kenny and Billy, and Howie on bass. It was the first time Billy sang lead with only a mike stand in front of him, no keys. By Billy's account, Howie talked him into the front man thing. Anyway, after Howie died, Billy used to come out front in concert and dedicate 'Innocent Man' to Howie and tell his story about Howie. Fact is, when alive, Howie couldn't cop an after-the-show pass to see the star who credits Howie with making him a front man."

El Primo didn't last long. Over the next decade, Blauvelt went through a succession of local bands before landing in Ram Jam, a group that also featured Lemon Pipers' (who had a chart-topping hit with "Green Tambourine" in 1968) guitarist Bill Bartlett. Blauvelt finally got a taste of the limelight that had eluded him for so long when the band had a fair-size hit in 1977 with a hard-rock version of Ledbelly's "Black Betty," a song that, despite its pedigree, earned the ire of CORE and the NAACP as being "insulting to black women," while becoming a Top 20 hit at the time and an international hit in a remixed version a decade later. Blauvelt died not too long after that, a victim of a heart attack at the age of forty-four.

CHAPTER 5

WE ALL FALL IN LOVE, BUT WE DISREGARD THE DANGER

As Attila broke up, so did Jon and Elizabeth Small's marriage. As it happened, Billy was living with them at the time, and had become involved with his best friend's wife. "Liz was wise to Jon from jump street," says Gentile. "She needed a place to live and she needed a cash flow. The Webers were not rich people. There were a lot of people in that family.

"We were all living together. Elizabeth is coming and going as she pleases. Billy is hanging around in the house because Jon has a white baby grand. The house was big enough for that. He would lie in wait for me to play with him back then.

"Jon and Elizabeth started to part. It became common knowledge that the marriage was going to go. No one really knew that Billy was the cause of it. Jon had no idea.

"It wasn't common knowledge that Billy was doing Elizabeth every day, and Jon didn't even suspect. It was like, 'My best friend would never do anything like that, man. Billy Joel and me are like Mutt and Jeff.' The only reason Billy hung out with Jon was that Jon was a chick magnet.

"It wasn't until Billy had kind of left for an extended period that I realized how the whole affair went down so easy. There was a closet that ran the whole back wall of the house, so if you went into the closet in my room, you could walk right into Elizabeth's bedroom if you wanted to. That's exactly what Billy was doing every day. Jon would leave for his folks' home decorating store, Billy would go into the closet, take a little walk and hop into Liz's bed there."

Attila was no more, so there were no more imminent gigs for either of them, at least not at the level they had enjoyed with the Hassles and even Attila. In the meantime, Elizabeth had a job working for a doctor, as Mazur recalls. Billy was largely at loose ends, to the point where sometimes he couldn't pay the rent. When that happened, he would go out and live rough, sometimes breaking into homes of people who were away, sometimes sleeping in all-night laundromats. In retrospect, he tends to allude to this period with a certain amount of almost pride, but at the time it couldn't have been a great deal of fun.

"I got a call from Billy one night," Irwin Mazur recalls. "He has to talk to me. It's midnight, one in the morning. He wants to meet at this diner on Long Island. He looks like hell. He's all depressed. I find out that Billy and Elizabeth are having an affair behind Jon's back, and Billy doesn't have any money.

"Billy doesn't have any income. It's his famous 'living in a laundromat' scenario. I convinced Billy to stay with us. He moved in with us and he slept on the couch. I said, 'Listen, you've got to be a solo artist. This Attila bullshit is not going to happen. You've got to write me some great hit songs and we're going to make you a star.'"

Throughout his time as a member of the Commandos, the Hassles, and even Attila, Billy Joel was developing as a songwriter. He began to find his voice and his niche. It reflected both his musical interests, from classical to the Beatles to James Brown, and his background. Billy Joel was a suburban kid, and he recognized that the bulk of his audience could relate to that.

"There's a lot of frustration living in the suburbs—you don't have an identity as you would if you came from the city or the country, there's city music and there's country music, but there's no suburban music, you kinda copy the city," he said.

"As it turns out, well, most of us are from suburbia. That's a lot of what America is."

With this in mind, he set out to develop a body of work that he and Mazur could sell. In the meantime, though, he had to make a living. It became one of the major frustrations of living in the suburbs for Billy. At this point, Gentile recalls Billy moving up from the Tango wine of his gang days to becoming "a blackout drinker."

Yet starting to make some kind of money became especially important to Billy, because if he wanted to continue his relationship with Elizabeth, he had to make enough money that she could leave Jon. He alternated between staying with the Mazurs, sleeping in a cedar closet in the Rock House, and crashing in places like the all-night laundromat. He would go to the Rock House to work out material on the baby grand and work out with Elizabeth.

"Billy was very excited that he was turning into a balladeer," Gentile laughs at the memory, "writing songs about different aspects of the human condition. Love was the force behind songs like 'She's Got a Way' and 'She's Always a Woman.' Billy was writing these intense love songs about Elizabeth."

He also tried a variety of things to turn a buck. He put his knowledge of music and literary aspirations to work for him and tried his hand at music criticism, writing some reviews for *Changes*, a New York–based, bi-monthly music magazine, but he didn't like having to criticize fellow musicians.

"I did like two-dozen reviews at twenty-five dollars a pop, but when I saw, in print, a bad review I'd given the album *Super Session*," he says, referring to the ground-breaking 1968 album by Stephen Stills, Mike Bloomfield, and Al Kooper, "I realized, I don't have the stomach for this."

Among the other odd jobs he had were painting houses, factory work, and landscaping. "Landscaping sucked," he says. "They call it landscaping—it's mowing."

Billy spent some time on an oyster dredge in Oyster Bay as well. "It was hard work," he recalls. "It gave me such an appreciation for how hard those guys work. In the middle of winter, and your hands are cracked and bleeding, and it's freezing. And these old guys kept making fun of me, 'Oh, there comes the piano player. He's going to be moaning and groaning about his hands.'"

One of the last jobs he held was inking typewriter ribbons. "When the guys started telling me, 'You'll get a raise when you're forty and a pension when you're sixty-five,' I thought, 'I gotta go, goodbye.'"

He also worked at his chosen craft, playing piano whenever he got—or could make—the opportunity. He would play from the always-damp stage to people gathered in the subterranean, pew-like seats of The Gaslight, a Greenwich Village institution on MacDougal Street from the days of the Beat poets. There, people would pay a buck to hear him. He also occasionally got the opportunity to play on television as an accompanist on a TV show hosted by Woodstock stage manager and announcer Chip "Don't Take the Brown Acid" Monck.

"I tuned in once and the guests were Jackson Browne, Bonnie Raitt, and Steve Miller, along with a then-unknown accompanist, Billy Joel, who didn't even rate a name check," *Ice Magazine* editor Bill Wasserzieher recalls. "The three name performers each did a couple of songs and gabbed a bit. Things got interesting when Raitt fired off a crack about masturbation in Miller's direction. Steve was at his career peak then but already turning into the sort of guy who wears polo shirts and plays golf—in fact, he had on the former and had been boring everybody with the latter, which is what caused Bonnie to more-or-less call him a jerk-off (this was, after all, the '70s).

"Anyway, Miller starts yelling and acting like he is about to smack her, while Browne gets very interested in looking the other way off-camera and Monck weakly tries to mediate. Billy Joel, still seated behind them at the piano, simply starts playing what must have been one of his own tunes, ignoring the whole fracas. It was one of those 1 A.M. TV moments that you tell friends about the next day.

"About six months later, Billy Joel's first album came out. I remember looking at the cover and recognizing him as the guy who kept his cool when Monck's show turned ugly."

§ § §

It was easy to see why Billy was willing to work so hard to keep his relationship with Elizabeth on a more or less even keel. For one thing, she was (and many say she remains) a beauty. "Billy is two years younger than Elizabeth," Sandy Gibson says. "Elizabeth stayed in great shape. Elizabeth is healthy, she's the same size she was, she hikes, she goes to a trainer. Billy looks like her father now."

In addition to being the most consistently employed person in Billy's circle at the time, Elizabeth was probably the best educated as well. She studied business at Adelphi University. With the exception of a penchant for getting involved with musicians, Elizabeth Weber Small was and is, according to people who know her, a smart, savvy, and tenacious woman.

Billy continued to see Elizabeth. By all accounts it was a stormy relationship, and when you think about it, an unlikely one. For one thing, she'd been married to the drummer Billy worked with for several years, and even had a child with him. Now she was involved with the keyboard guy, two years her junior, who had replaced her brother in a band and had even less money and formal education than the drummer.

The tempestuous nature of the relationship didn't help Billy's state of mind any. At twenty-one, life, to Billy Joel, looked like it was over. After investing seven years as a professional musician, giving up his high school diploma because of it, suddenly he wasn't making even the tentative living he had made with music anymore. As 1970 wore on, he no longer had a steady band. His attempts at becoming a recording artist had all come to naught. He was writing songs that no one but he and his manager, his friends at the Rock House, and small gatherings of people down in Greenwich Village ever heard. His lack of that high school diploma prevented him from making much more than minimum wage at anything but music.

The thought of going back to his mother's house, even just to regroup, felt too much like defeat, made him feel like a bum. Which wasn't too far from the case. For all intents and purposes, he was homeless.

At the same time, he was wracked with guilt about his personal relationships. He was cheating on his best friend with his wife. True, Jon would fuck anything in a skirt, but technically he was still married to Elizabeth. Billy wanted to tell Jon about the affair. Elizabeth told Billy that if he did, she was through with him and Jon. Beyond that, he had nothing to bring to the relationship but himself and his limited economic expectations. This was Billy's breaking point. "I was absolutely devastated," he said. "I couldn't bring anything to the relationship. That was the driving force behind my suicide attempt."

Billy made that attempt in a most unlikely and half-assed way, more a cry for help than a real attempt to end it all. He drank a bottle of furniture polish.

"We found Billy in the cedar closet," Gentile recalls, "with some goof balls and a solvent of some kind."

"I was into a real self-pity trip," Billy says. "Isn't it easier to just cut your throat or slit your wrist?"

Jon hauled him off to Long Island's Meadowbrook Hospital, where Billy was admitted in a coma. Irwin Mazur remembers: "One day, I get up and I go into the living room. There's a note on the table. It's a poem, or obviously the lyrics of a song. It's called 'Tomorrow Is Today.' I don't know if you're familiar with that song. That was Billy's suicide note, because I got a call about two hours later that Billy is in a coma. He had overdosed on something. Needless to say, it was fairly crazy and emotional."

Billy landed in the psych ward at Meadowbrook. When he came to, the doctors put him on a suicide watch and committed him for three weeks of observation. His cry for help was getting attention, at least.

Mazur went up to visit him. "It's like a snakepit in here," a doped-up Billy told him. "Irwin, you gotta get me outta here. These people are really fucking crazy."

"Billy, what did you do to yourself?"

"I drank furniture polish. All I've been doing is shitting lemon juice."

"Furniture polish!?"

"Well, yeah. It looked tastier than bleach."

Billy was in there for a couple of weeks, hating it more and more. Finally, they figured out a way to spring him. Until about a year and a half before, Mazur had been a dental student and had learned his way around medical and hospital bureaucracy. He put on a suit and his white lab coat, took an attaché case, and went to Meadowbrook.

"I somewhat represented myself as a doctor," Mazur admits. "They wanted a shrink to release him, so I did a little impression of somebody who was an authority figure."

The one positive thing that came out of the experience was that Billy had a good look at both where self-pity could get you and what it was like to be really crazy. After that experience, he vowed that he would never get that low again. Mazur sees it a little differently.

"Billy had a tendency in those days—and I think he still does—to take steps beyond where they need to go. He tried heroin in his youth once or twice. It's a good thing he didn't like it, or maybe it's a good thing he liked it so much he said, 'I'd better not do it anymore.' I think probably that was the case.

"Billy had a great philosophy about stuff like that, which stays with me to this day. 'You can't treat your body like a temple. You've gotta show it some bad stuff so it will understand the good stuff. Otherwise it has no reference.'"

CHAPTER 6

SO MUCH TO DO AND ONLY SO MANY HOURS IN A DAY

As Billy left Meadowbrook Hospital, he turned to Irwin Mazur and told him, "That's it, I'm quitting. Elizabeth is going to leave me. She's pretty much left Jon. She doesn't want any part of anybody."

"Billy," Mazur replied, "you can't do this. You've written some great songs."

Indeed, in his post-Hassles/post-Attila phase, Billy had been turning out some very good, if often elegiac, music. The irony was that the conventional wisdom was a catch-22—to sell the songs, he had to record them and get them out there. Once again, he needed to wade into the waters of the record business that had so far left him unsullied with fame and fortune.

"You've got to give me thirty days to find you a record deal," Mazur told him.

"Okay," Billy relented. "I'll give you thirty days to get a record deal. Otherwise, I'm going to the Midwest. I'll be a bartender, I'll be happy. I don't need this shit anymore."

Mazur's brother worked as an art director for the fledgling Gulf & Western edition of Paramount Records. The company's head of A&R, the Artist and Repertoire department, responsible for signing artists and vetting their material, had given Mazur a first-look deal to cut demos with Billy. They made a five-song, voice-and-piano songwriter demo that included such new songs as "She's Got a Way," "Everybody Loves You Now," and "Tomorrow Is Today." Initially, Paramount turned him down. They already had a singer/songwriter/piano player from England named Elton John who had just written songs for a

Paramount movie, a teensploitation flick called *Friends*. Paramount Records was preparing to release the soundtrack and hopefully break this new artist with it. It would be John's first stateside release—a coup, since he had not yet released his own solo debut.

With Paramount not exercising their first-look option, Mazur started taking the demo to all his contacts in the record business. And he heard such responses as, "Oh, he sounds like Elton John" and "He sounds like Paul McCartney." Mazur took to walking along the industry grotto that was Sixth Avenue between 42nd and 57th Streets, muttering, "Man, you fucking guys don't get it! You just don't get it."

During this time, Mazur continued his music-business apprenticeship, marketing records for Morris Levy. Mazur, not desperate enough to place his artist at Moishe's tender mercies, was still interested in what the godfather of popular music had to say about his artist. He played his boss the demo.

"Moishe," Mazur said, "I want you to hear something."

Moishe replied, "What is it?"

"Just listen. It's a kid I'm working with. "

Mazur played him the piano-and-vocal demo. Levy listened, staring down at his desk. Several songs played. Finally Levy stopped the tape. He looked at Mazur and said, "You're fired."

Mazur was dumbfounded. His wife is in her ninth month of pregnancy, and suddenly he's unemployed; his steady, albeit not princely, $150 a week has evaporated. "What?!"

"You're fired," Moishe repeats. "Get out of here."

"Why are you firing me?"

"'Because you don't want to be a sales and promotion man," Levy says. "You want to be an A&R man."

A shocked Mazur got up slowly from Levy's desk and walked toward the office door. As he reached for the knob, Levy asked, "How much do you want for the kid?"

Even with just a month to find Billy a place to record, Mazur was not going to hitch that wagon to the godfather's star. After all, what good was there in owning a piece of an artist who recorded for a label notorious for not paying royalties? With nowhere else to go, he went up to Paramount Records to hunker down in his brother's office.

Mazur was hanging out there, playing the tape for his brother when a mop of curls poked through the door. They were attached to the formidable head of Woodstock promoter Michael Lang. Before hooking up with his partners in the Woodstock venture, Lang had already run one of Florida's most successful head shops, managed bands, and produced a smaller festival. In the wake of the Woodstock Festival, he had formed a label called Just Sunshine, one of the dozens of small sublabels that made up the Paramount empire.

"What's that?" Lang asked.

Mazur said, "It's a kid I manage."

"Really? What's his name?"

"'Billy Joel."

"Could I borrow the tape?" Lang asked.

Mazur was running out of time and was not about to turn down someone who actually *asked* for a copy, especially someone who had a record company with major distribution. "Sure," he said.

While Lang wasn't interested in the demo for himself, he told the Mazur brothers, he knew by the sound of it that it might be of interest to a friend of his, a friend it happened he was going off to California to see.

That friend was Artie Ripp. When Billy Joel was seven years old, just dealing with his father leaving, Artie Ripp was a teenager singing in a group called the Four Temptations who recorded for ABC/Paramount. Even then, Ripp realized that he had no future as a performer. "I sucked," he concedes. "I was no Elvis Presley and I wasn't a writer."

What Ripp *was* was a tough kid from Queens, the New York City outpost of Long Island. He had decided that he didn't need school around the same time school decided it was better off without Ripp. The Four Temptations experience had, if nothing else, solidified one thing in Ripp's mind: He knew his future was in the music business. Now all he had to determine was how.

In many ways, the 1957 edition Artie Ripp and the 1970 model Billy Joel had a lot in common. They were both obsessed with music. They both wanted to make it in the business but weren't sure how to go about it. They'd both had a taste of fame. Neither had a high school diploma.

In 1958, Ripp hooked up with George Goldner, an independent record guy who owned his own companies (Gee and Rama Records), produced records, and owned copyrights—an entrepreneurial, creative hustler. Ripp spent weeks hanging around Goldner's office until Goldner finally grabbed him by the ears and asked him what he wanted. Satisfied with the answer Ripp gave him, that he wanted to be the next George Goldner, he hired Ripp to be his gofer.

Goldner taught Ripp how to work a studio and how to structure a record contract. Goldner also instructed Ripp on such fine points as getting a record on the radio, how to get the girls to the hotels for the deejays, and directing that particular kind of traffic. Ripp learned how to, as he put it, "sell a hundred records over the table and a thousand under the table." He was one of the last of the Moishe-inspired, old-line music-business gonifs.

By 1965, Ripp discovered the Shangri-las, probably encountering Billy Joel for the first time without knowing it, as Billy had done the demo sessions with Shadow Morton for the group a year earlier. Ripp produced Doris Troy's Top 10 hit "Just One Look," started his own record company—Kama Sutra—and signed the Lovin' Spoonful.

The Spoonful was a band of Greenwich Village folk-rock stalwarts, led by John Sebastian and Zal Yanovsky. Yanovsky had worked in a group called the Mugwumps that would also spawn members of the Mamas and the Papas. Sebastian had already cut his studio teeth with a variety of artists, playing the harmonica, an instrument that his father also played, often in a classical context. With such huge hits as "Summer in the City" and "Do You Believe in Magic," they helped to turn Kama Sutra into a pop-music powerhouse and earned Artie Ripp a considerable reputation in the music business and a lot of money.

"Artie produced some great, great records and was hip enough to know about the Lovin' Spoonful," recalled Gibson. "He had a great contract with the Lovin' Spoonful."

MGM had a contract for three years to distribute Kama Sutra. The label, in turn, had a five-year deal with the band. However, when the deal with MGM ran out, the larger company thought they could squeeze Ripp out and keep Kama Sutra for themselves by not renewing his contract. Instead, Ripp formed a new record company, Buddha (a lesson learned from Goldner, who must have formed more than a dozen labels at various times). Transferring the Lovin' Spoonful's contract to the new company, he had bona fide hitmakers from the git-go. He was able to get his distributors to actually fund the label, a move that was quite ahead of its time.

Unfortunately, soon after he did this, the Lovin' Spoonful got busted for drug possession after a show at the legendary San Francisco night spot the Hungry I. Zal Yanovsky was a Canadian national and faced deportation if he didn't turn in his dealer. However, when he did that, although he was allowed to stay in the country, his cooperation with the authorities destroyed the group's counterculture credibility, a very important element in record sales during the mid-'60s. This effectively put an end to both Yanovsky's music career and the Lovin' Spoonful. After one more halfhearted effort with producer, musician, and scenester Jerry Yester filling Zal's zany shoes, the group called it a day in 1968. Yanovsky went into filmmaking, and Sebastian went on to a successful solo career that peaked with his theme for the 1975 TV show *Welcome Back, Kotter.*

After the Spoonful fell by the pop music wayside (as big a curb as there ever was), Ripp segued into the next phase of his career. Buddha Records became the home of bubblegum music.

Bubblegum music has been described as pop music's dirty little secret, the kind you find stuck under a chair in the movies or a desk at school. On the face of it, bubblegum expanded what Phil Spector set out to do in terms of creating three-minute Wagnerian operas for kids, though in a leaner, more modern way. Like its namesake, it was sweet and disposable. It also featured some of the best-respected musicians and pop song writers, under heavy guises. Howard "Flo" Kaylan and Mark "Eddie" Volman of the Turtles did scads of bubblegum sessions after their tenure in the band of progressive rock iconoclast Frank Zappa ended.

Before he got involved with rockers like Joan Jett, producer Ritchie Cordell was the brains and brawn behind the 1910 Fruitgum Company, with hits like "Simon Says," "1,2,3, Red Light," and "Indian Giver," gold records all. Other bands on Buddha included the Ohio Express, which minted gold with such timeless tunes as "Chewy Chewy" and "Yummy, Yummy, Yummy." Another was the "made for TV" version of the mother-and-children family group the Cowsills and one of the ultimate prefab bands of all time, the Partridge Family.

Ripp saw these records as musical escapism in a time of unsettling political and societal unrest and change, comfort food for teenage ears. Just as he was, with the good-time, jug-band music of the Lovin' Spoonful, capitalizing on folk rock in a pop context, so was Ripp correct in assessing the musical needs of the late '60s. He made a fortune.

In 1968, at the height of the company's pop power, Ripp sold Buddha and Kama Sutra to Viewlex, a public company that made educational equipment like filmstrip projectors and mini-planetariums for schools, in addition to owning a plant in which they pressed the records that often went along with those filmstrips. The capital he got by selling out to Viewlex allowed Ripp to buy out his partner while staying on as president and continuing to release records. Initially, he enjoyed a laissez-faire relationship with the company— he continued to bring in hit records and the company let him. Soon after the deal was consumated, though, the company founder—with whom he made the deal—passed on. The business fell into the hands of the founder's son.

Ripp and the new CEO didn't see eye to eye on much. Whereas the father treated Ripp and his business with benign neglect as long as it didn't hurt the overall bottom line, the son was, if anything, more conservative than the father. This disagreement spelled the beginning of the end for Ripp and Kama Sutra/Buddha. As the '60s slipped into the '70s, Artie Ripp was looking for new worlds to conquer and capitalize on.

He found them with an auld acquaintance. In 1970, Paramount Records, his label way back in his days as a musician with the Four Temptations, had been acquired (along with everything else Paramount) by Gulf & Western Industries. Like so many corporations, G&W saw the kinds of profits Warner Communications and the CBS Record group were raking in and wanted a piece of it. They hired Tony Martell away from CBS and began looking for partnerships to make hit records and lots of money.

"Bob Krasnow had a deal with them," Gibson recalls of the record-industry veteran who would go on to head Blue Thumb and Elektra Records. "Artie had a deal with them, Michael Lang had a record label. Every single shark hit Tony Martell up for a deal, and they got these great deals."

Ripp made a deal that gave Gulf & Western Industries the rights to distribute his records in the United States and Ampex to distribute his tapes domestically. He made another deal with Phillips to distribute his records and tapes internationally. He used that money to capitalize his operation and pay for production of the dozen records that he contracted to make over the course of the year.

The first record on Ripp's new venture, Family Productions, was by a country-rock artist named Kyle. The album was called *The Times That Try a Man's Soul*. The title was an apt metaphor for the whole Gulf & Western experience.

Family was one of a baker's dozen of record companies under the G&W corporate umbrella. Unfortunately, as he took on the mantle of the company presidency, Martell's son started fighting what ultimately turned into a losing battle with leukemia. Needless to say, Martell became preoccupied by more pressing personal concerns than selling records. He entered the Gulf & Western Building at roughly 9:30 each morning, went straight to his huge twenty-fourth-floor corner office. He would say good morning to his secretary, lock his wooden double doors, and not come out again until the sun was sinking behind the Hudson River.

❊ ❊ ❊

Lang took the tape he borrowed from Mazur to California with him when he went out to visit Artie Ripp, who had relocated to the sunnier climes of Los Angeles. Lang and Ripp were up late talking when Lang remembered he had brought the demo for Ripp to hear. He presented it to Ripp.

"I've got a tape that I think is interesting," Lang said. "It's not my personal taste. I don't really understand it, but maybe it will strike a chord with you. What do you think?"

They popped the tape into a player and Ripp listened.

"Did the kid who's singing play piano?'" Ripp asked.

"Yes," Lang replied.

"Did the kid who's singing and playing the piano write the melody?"

"Yes"

"Did he also write the words?"

"Yes."

"Great! How did you get the tape?"

"It's just something that wound up in my hands, but he's been turned down by every record company. Nobody wants to sign him. Nobody is interested in a singer/songwriter/piano player, or this particular one."

Ripp, however, was interested. He heard what Mazur heard, what the other record company A&R people were missing, what Lang almost heard. He thought, "This is somebody who will be an important talent, that the world would say, 'I love this guy!' He wrote a unique kind of lyric. His poetry and his reflection upon life and the life experience— he wasn't just writing 'I love you, you love me, let's go play on the corner.' He was really writing like a painter, a poet, a playwright. He engaged me. That was enough."

"I really find this is a guy with some extraordinary talent, as a musician on the piano and vocally. He writes great lyrics and melodies and sings his ass off. I'd like to sign him to my label and I'll give you an override," Ripp told Lang, offering him financial incentive for having been good enough to bring him the tape. "Who is his manager?"

"His name is Irwin Mazur and he's in New York City."

Artie Ripp reached for his telephone. It was one o'clock in the morning California time. "Do you have his phone number?"

"Yeah," says Lang. "You're not going to call him now?"

"Of course I'm going to call him now!"

"But it's four o'clock in the morning in New York!"

"Weren't you just telling me that he's been turned down by every record company in New York? The manager's knocking on every door in New York and they're saying 'fuggadaboutit'? This kid is waiting for my phone call. He's waiting for someone to say 'I love Billy Joel and I want to sign him. What do you want?'"

So, at four in the morning in the Long Island home of recently unemployed record man, soon to be father, and artist manager Irwin Mazur, the phone rang.

"Whaddya want for the kid?" he heard as he groggily picked up the receiver. "This is Artie Ripp. Michael Lang played me Billy's tape. I think he's great. I'd like to sign him to an album deal. I'll guarantee you an album, I'll guarantee you a single, and I'll give you a monthly amount of money for Billy so that he can focus on one thing: writing songs and getting his act together as a performer."

"I want an album budget," the now-wide-awake Mazur told Ripp, trying to convince himself he wasn't dreaming.

Ripp responded, "Don't play it for anybody, don't talk to anybody, I'll meet you in front of the Gulf & Western Building on Tuesday."

The basics of the deal were firmed up over the phone, transcontinental, in the small hours of the morning. Mazur waited until morning before he called Billy.

"You wanted a record deal in thirty days," he told his client. "I got it for you."

CHAPTER 7

THE THINGS I DID NOT KNOW AT FIRST I LEARNED BY DOING TWICE

Within the course of about a month, Billy Joel went from potential suicide to solo artist. The deal points to Billy's naïveté and Mazur's desperation. It gave away all the things an artist lives on—publishing rights, copyrights, and royalties. "I didn't know what I was signing. But I probably would have signed anything to get that deal," he recalls.

"I was only twenty and it's so easy to take advantage of a musician. I didn't know what was going on . . . I didn't know anything about publishing or monies that were owed to me."

At this stage of his career, Billy would have happily been through with being the performer, however. As a member of a band, his songs contributed to the whole, but he didn't relish the role of a singer/songwriter, let alone front man. Instead, his whole plan was to write great songs and record them so that people he regarded as better singers and performers could hear and "discover" his songs for their records. He began to compose in earnest for his debut. "The record company gave me a piano," he said, in the blush of the new deal, "so I'm writing a lot of new things."

With the advance, and the promise of a monthly stipend, Billy had something he had not had before: a steady income. With this, his romance with Elizabeth heated up and took a new complexion and direction. "One day, the ultimate shit goes down," Gentile remembers. "I got home from work and I thought the house got ripped off. Jon got home right after me. He had already been home, but he went to the police station to make a report. One was a kidnapping report. Elizabeth was gone. She and Billy took everything. The stereo, the TV set, all this shit that they could have bought. I mean, there was no reason to take the toaster."

So Jon and Elizabeth's marriage finally reached its endgame. Billy, Elizabeth, and the Smalls' young son, Sean, moved to a place in Oyster Bay.

In concert in the early years of his solo career, Billy was as much a stand-up comedian as a performer. His best material in 1971 was musical impressions of favorite stars like Ray Charles and Joe Cocker. But now his brief was to take this batch of songs he'd been crafting over the course of the past year, since Attila was vanquished, and make the best possible records of those songs that he could. He needed to become the best possible Billy Joel, the artist he had contracted to be.

"As you sign a record contract," Billy says, "you go through this change, because as soon as you put your name on the paper, you're an artist. The record contract says, 'Billy Joel, herein referred to as the artist,' and automatically you become an artist just by signing."

Billy went to record the album with a bunch of very strong songs, certainly a quantum leap from the songs he had written for the Hassles and far more musical than what he wrote for Attila. The album contained some truly great songs that wouldn't get their due for another decade, like "She's Got a Way" and "Everybody Loves You Now." Then there are some remarkable compositions that, while not great, at least indicate a major rising talent. There's the suicide note he left Mazur, "Tomorrow Is Today," couched in a quasi-gospel setting. There's a song thanking his sister for being a good listener, "Why, Judy, Why." Then there's the epic "You Can Make Me Free," a 6-minute track that got slashed in half on subsequent releases of the album.

Billy recorded the album on Ripp's new home turf in Los Angeles. The experience in the studio had to be a very different one for Billy. In his previous forays into the recording studio, with the Commandos, the Hassles, and even Attila, Billy filled the role of an essential cog in a well-oiled machine—the keyboard player, songwriter, and vocalist in an established band that would play (with the exception of Attila) more than a hundred shows a year. Everyone knew their parts.

Recording his solo debut was closer to the sessions he played for

Shadow Morton or for advertising agencies. The main difference was that in the Morton and jingle sessions, the people in charge ran down the songs for Billy. On his own record, it was up to Billy to run down the songs for the people with whom he was recording. Ripp hired some of the best LA session men. Larry Knechtel, who had played bass with everyone from Elvis to the Monkees and had just finished working with Simon and Garfunkel; drummer Rhys Clark, who was a favorite of Ripp's and had worked on the Kyle record; Sneaky Pete Kleinow, whose pedal steel had graced records by Joni Mitchell and Joe Cocker, to name but a few; and guitarist Don Evans, who had contributed to Bobby Bloom's big hit "Montego Bay" a year earlier—all played on the sessions, while Ripp produced, attempting like all producers to commit some magic to tape.

"The studio itself is a sterile, non-reverberant, non-responsive box filled with a whole bunch of wires and glass and microphones and so on," Ripp says. "It isn't like performing live, onstage, with an audience . . . There's getting arrangements for the song nailed. The performance of the arrangement becomes the next matter—you have to have the singer get a performance that you really love, so that the artist says 'I really love that.'"

Saying "I really love that" to recordings of his songs has never been an easy matter for Billy Joel. Because of that, working in the studio couldn't have been a comfortable experience for him, especially the playback. "It's not easy for me to listen to myself," he would maintain even after three decades of success. "I'm not objective about my work. So the fact that I said 'This can come out, this is pretty good,' means I can live with it."

"Billy needed to play and sing at the same time," Ripp continued about the process of recording the album. "Because he's singing, you have a piano microphone that's picking up his voice, so doing overdubs on that really generally doesn't work. You have to hit it as a live performance in the studio, which has its good points and its bad points. You can overdub the harmonies, but you can't overdub that lead vocal . . . Ultimately, you have to have this musical erection and orgasm that you have to get to, and everyone else has to hit it at the same time if you're really going to get that magic."

"I think of myself as a piano player and songwriter," Billy concurs. "My singing is all tied to my piano playing. I do all my vocals live while I'm playing, which results in leakage between the vocal and piano mikes. There's never the total separation you'd get with a first-rate mix, but that's become an aspect of my sound, a distinctive trait. And if I must overdub sometime, I'll literally sit at the closed piano and pound my fingers on the lid. Guess the piano bone is connected to the throat bone."

They took the title for the album from the lyrics in the biting, scathing "Everybody Loves You Now," Billy's version of *Look Homeward, Angel*—"Ah, you know that nothin' lasts forever / And it's all been done before / Ah, but you ain't got the time / To go to Cold Spring Harbor no more." It was Billy's way of saying you can't go home again—Cold Spring Harbor was a community due north of Hicksville on Long Island Sound, across the inlet from Oyster Bay, where Billy was now living.

While Billy was in LA making the magic that became *Cold Spring Harbor*, Elizabeth and Jon's divorce became final. After recording (both he and Mazur left the mix-down and mastering to Ripp), Billy and Mazur came back to Long Island, Billy back to his new place in Oyster Bay, funded with his living expense "allowance" from Family Productions.

"I'm living in a beautiful little hamlet called Oyster Bay on the North Shore of Long Island," he said at the time. "We do a lot of fishing here. And an unhealthy amount of drinking. But then, that's my idea of the good life."

Elizabeth was attending Adelphi University, where she was working on a business degree. With the album in the can and the promise of more to come (the contract was for ten albums), Billy, Elizabeth, and Sean found a new home in Hampton Bays, an area analogous, in Billy's mind at least, to the Hicksville of the Hamptons.

"I remember taking the ride out to the Hamptons," says Gentile, "so Jon and Elizabeth could work out their differences and Jon could see Sean on the weekends. Jon gave his green Datsun to Liz and Billy. They would deliver Sean on weekends when Sean was not in camp. Sean was one cool little kid. The Entertainer always called the car the green pickle, funny considering Billy was the one in a real big pickle.

"At that time, Billy had found an abandoned rowboat and started to sand it down like it was his first, putting it back together. It's no bullshit that the cat has a great love for the sea, and has had it way before he became a star."

❄ ❄ ❄

While everything seemed to be looking up at last for Billy, the situation at the Gulf & Western Music division was getting worse by the day.

"Gulf & Western's record holdings ran on automatic pilot," recalls the company's publicist, Howard Bloom, "or would have, if anyone had designed a device that could carry companies without leaders through their daily routines. Alas, no one had. The company was headless . . . and seemingly mindless as well . . . This HQ of tunes was a most peculiar place. There were no staff meetings—ever. There were no lists of the records we were putting out. No one gave us any sense of what to do from day to day. Heck, there wasn't even a list of the names and addresses of our fourteen labels . . . The presidents of the labels seemed elusive, as if they'd been invented by some lowly staffer on LSD."

One of those seeming LSD illusions, Ripp was ensconced in his LA studio/office, trying to make hits out of his records. While working— or attempting to work—the Kyle record, with the help of Sandy Gibson doing publicity and her husband John promoting the record to radio, Ripp began to put the finishing touches on the Billy Joel record.

"It all of a sudden struck me, I made this fantastic deal with Gulf & Western, a deal that, from a business point of view, had never, ever been done in the record business," he says. "The unfortunate thing was, I get the Kyle record on the country stations, I get it on the FM stations, and I get it on the top pop stations, and there are no records in the stores for weeks. I now recognize that basically the guys running the record company, they're sitting and having a drink and eating peanuts and pretzels.

"This was the same company that put out the soundtrack from Elton John from a movie called *Friends*. I think it was the first album that shipped platinum and came back double platinum. They took back that many returns with counterfeits. They presented the G&W president with platinum and gold records and so on, and it was a total farce.

"When I saw that, it made me so depressed, I said, 'I got myself in a platinum coffin with diamond studs.' That's the box I got myself into with Gulf & Western."

The people around Ripp began to notice his change of mood and attitude. Family's director of publicity, Sandy Gibson, remembers, "Artie started totally flipping out. He was mixing the same record for like two years. The joke about Artie was, if he was at a bar and somebody asked, 'What kind of drink do you want?' he would hold his head and go, 'Oh! Oh! Oh!' How could he decide a mix when he couldn't even decide what cocktail he wanted?"

However, to live up to his end of his deal, and keep his advance money coming in, Ripp had to keep the distribution sluice primed with Family Productions albums. He had to finish mixing and mastering Billy's album and get the record out.

"The strangest thing occurred, that I didn't discover until later on," Ripp concedes. "The machine that I mixed the master to was running slow. The studio second engineer, rather than running a speed test on every single time we were running a session to make sure the machine was running at 15 IPS, he didn't do that. So I don't know whether every single cut or some cuts wound up being recorded on a machine that was running slow, so that when you put it on a machine that ran at normal, proper, spec speed, it had this little speed-up to it. People said that I speeded up the record. I didn't speed up the record. This was almost like Murphy's Law operating, that if anything could go wrong, everything would go wrong."

This same technique, recording music at one speed and playing it back at another, had been used for years—albeit to a greater and more conscious extent—by novelty artists like Ross "Dave Seville" Bagdasarian and Sheb Wooley. On the tracks mastered with this "unchecked" combination of machines, the music was speeded up and Billy's voice came through about half an octave higher than it would have had the tapes been mastered properly.

"But at the end of the day," Ripp maintains, "it didn't sound that weird because Billy sang high to begin with. It wasn't like he was a baritone. Nor was he a soprano." And so, late in the summer of 1971,

Ripp delivered the album to the musical Titanic that was the Gulf & Western record division. It came out that fall.

When he finally heard the record, Billy thought he sounded like one of Bagdasarian's characters, the Chipmunks. He played the new album for his friends and was so upset with how his voice sounded that he smashed the LP against a wall.

CHAPTER 8

I BRING TO YOU MY SONGS

While Ripp never doubted the brilliance of both the material on *Cold Spring Harbor* and the performer who made the album, he also knew that, for so many reasons, the album had as much chance of becoming a hit as the artist had of becoming Miss America. The present already a lost cause, Ripp decided he had to build for the future.

"How do I establish Billy in the minds of everybody—journalists, radio, music-business people, and the public," he asked, "knowing that somewhere along the line, Billy will make the right record, have a smash and be a big star?"

The answer was as old as the music business: Put the artist on the road. Throwing good money after a loss, Ripp underwrote a tour that kept Billy on the road well into the spring of 1972.

"I sent Billy out on a European tour and a U.S. tour where he would meet the press, meet the radio people, meet the retailers, meet the public, get the experience of performing," said Ripp. "They put together a band I financed, and he and his manager, Irwin, went out on the road.

"I tried to get Billy to appear at the showcase at this college booker convention in Kansas City. They wouldn't let him appear at the showcase. So I rented a club in Kansas City, printed up a thing that looked like the *Hollywood Reporter* called *Family Scandals*. In it, there were stories about the Stones and this one and that one, and interlaced in it were stories about my artists, like Billy Joel. I also gave it to retailers to give away. We put an invitation to the showcase at the club we rented, along with a copy of *Family Scandals*, under every hotel room door in Kansas City, where we knew all the college bookers were staying. We wound up getting a room full of bookers to see Billy, and we created a college tour."

"Touring made zero economic sense," Mazur says of sending his relatively unknown artist out on the road, an expensive and dicey proposition even under the best of circumstances, "but it was the only way we could get people recognizing who Billy Joel was."

The shows primarily involved opening slots for a variety of acts. Some of these support positions were totally apt, like opening for the epitome of bar bands, the J. Geils Band, and the pure, Beatles-inspired pop of Badfinger. Other billings were wildly inappropriate, like pairing Billy with progressive rockers Yes.

For Billy, these must have been unnerving days. The bulk of his experience as a musician had been as part of a band, usually a band with another person as the focal point of attention, like John Dizek. In those bands, Billy's role was to play the keyboards, mostly the organ, and sing background. While he'd taken the forefront in Attila, they'd done perhaps a dozen shows all told. He'd also worked as a solo piano player in various venues, but they were small audiences and he was there mostly to test out his material as opposed to his personality. Now he was being called on to sell both.

"They'd like to present me as a dynamic, electric personality," he said. "Well, onstage I get it on pretty well, but otherwise I'm about as sparkling as warm beer."

"During those early days of being on the road with him as a solo artist," Mazur adds, "I had to get him up from behind the piano and start getting him to the front of the stage with the microphone and being the character that he was. I worked very hard with him to help him develop the confidence to do that."

One of the by-products of keeping Billy busy was that he didn't have a chance to notice just how poorly the record was doing. It flew below the radar of the charts, most of radio, and the major music press like *Rolling Stone* and *Creem*. Even so, after the record had been out for three or four months, it became evident that something was not right.

"Traveling across the country on the first promotional tour," Billy recalls, "I didn't see the album in stores or hear it getting airplay . . . By late that spring things had become intolerable, the whole promotional tour was a rip-off."

"I literally lived on the road for six months, and I had a band together and nobody got paid. Cigarette money, you know, and sometimes we'd get meals taken care of, but mostly we paid for our own food. After six months, we were going, 'Hey, what's going on? Aren't we going to get any money?' I was told, 'Oh, it's all promotion.' And I found out there was a lot of money that went by [in gate receipts]."

One of the major stops on the tour was the Mar y Sol festival in Puerto Rico. A three-day gathering at the beginning of the spring of 1972, it had the aura of a tropical Woodstock, albeit with a more diverse set of talent—Brubeck played a set, as did Herbie Mann, with a band that featured incendiary guitarist Sonny Sharrock; the Mahavishnu Orchestra, Alice Cooper, and Emerson, Lake, and Palmer also performed. As with Woodstock, the festival took place on a large field with a stage, and it also rained a good portion of the time.

This would be the biggest potential audience Billy had faced. As a defense against his lack of confidence as a performer, Billy had developed a set of impersonations of other singers. Many recall him doing impressions of Joe Cocker, Ray Charles, Paul McCartney, and Stevie Wonder that were so spot on that people often found themselves doing a double check to make sure it really wasn't them.

At Mar y Sol, the rain-soaked area in front of the stage was devoid of people. The promoter walked into Billy's tent and told the band and crew, "Either you go on or you get out. We don't care if it's raining."

Billy and his people got set up, hoping to not get electrocuted. Everybody was in their tents or under some kind of shelter, away from the performance area. Billy sat down at his piano and started to play a little, just to check the sound. Mazur leaned over from backstage and said, "Billy, do 'The Letter.' Just start with that and maybe we can get some people to listen."

Billy kicked into his impression of Joe Cocker's *Mad Dogs and Englishmen* version of the Box Tops chart topper. As soon as he got out "Gimme a ticket for an airplane," the audience started to peer out of their tents to see if Cocker had made an unbilled appearance on stage. Soon ten thousand people started rocking to Billy Joel and his band. Before Mar y Sol, nobody had ever heard of Billy Joel, outside of the New York area, and even there, nobody cared about Billy Joel. But as the sun broke through the clouds at Mar y Sol, Billy Joel had the place reeling and rolling.

"My wife was on the stage with me," says Mazur. "It was a moment I'll never forget. He had that crowd in the palm of his hands. He had never had that kind of command of an audience before. That was the first moment that he took command of the stage."

"We did really well," Billy recalls. "We got three encores. My road manager kept running back, saying, 'They want you again, they want you again.' I said, 'What? Are they crazy? What's going on? It must be the heat.'"

Don Heckman of the *New York Times* saw the show. "The first real excitement was generated by Billy Joel's gospel-tinged rock band," he wrote. "Building up a charge that was reminiscent of the work of the old Leon Russell–Joe Cocker combine, the Billy Joel group brought some life to what had been a generally dispirited environment."

Heckman was not alone in his enthusiasm for the young performer. People from Columbia Records, some of whom were aware of Billy, saw his set. One had also been at the Kansas City college booker convention showcase. When Billy came back to New York for a showcase at the legendary club Max's Kansas City, even more people from Columbia were in attendance.

Max's Kansas City was a small but elite club on Park Avenue South in New York, catty-corner from Union Square Park. In the back room at Max's on any given night, one might find Andy Warhol and David Bowie talking art and Candy Darling offering his/her services to the cute young males in the place. In the main room, young performer's showcased their material. Many careers were made at Max's. Certainly it was a mainstay of the Velvet Underground in their early years. Bruce Springsteen opened for Bob Marley at Max's. The Velvet Underground, the Troggs, and Johnny Thunders and the Heartbreakers all recorded seminal albums at Max's. Billy was supposed to be there for a couple of nights but did only one of them.

"It was one of the first outings on the *Cold Spring Harbor* vibe," Gentile recalls. "He had a grand piano, a pedal steel player, a bass player, a guitar player on this tiny stage. They really fucked up. He was set to play two nights. Vinnie Lopez was there that night looking for a gig. He'd just been let go by Springsteen [he had been the E Street Band's drummer on their first two albums]. Billy bailed on the last night of the thing. He said he had throat problems."

Even so, Billy was beginning to enjoy a buzz in the business. The people who had seen him at these showcases were impressed.

"People at Columbia Records, people in the record industry were starting to say, 'Did you hear this *Cold Spring Harbor* record?'" Ripp marvels. "Did you hear this guy, Billy Joel?'—despite the fact that the record was not a hit."

As the European release of *Cold Spring Harbor* loomed later in 1972, Ripp's European distributor, Phonogram, thought it would be a nifty stunt to put Billy back together with his long-estranged father. At the time, Billy thought his father was living in Germany. He felt pretty sure that he still worked for General Electric.

As it turned out, it took Phonogram a little longer to find Howard than they had hoped, because Billy was a country off. They found Howard living in Vienna, Austria. As Billy got ready to end his European adventure and head back home, the record company contacted him. The telegram announced that they had found his dad.

Since Billy was on his way home, and it would be just about as easy to reunite father and son in the States as it would be for Billy to stay in Milan and do it there, the record company flew Howard to America for the reunion. Billy knew his dad as soon as he saw him. Howard resembled nothing so much as a bald image of his son.

The meeting was somewhat strained. What do you say to the man who abandoned you nearly twenty years earlier? How do you explain the need to leave to someone who was just a child when you left? Eventually, they did talk, and Billy found his father wasn't a monster; he was just another guy trying to pursue happiness in his own way.

One of the bombshells his father dropped on him at this meeting was that he had remarried. He and his new wife, Audrey, had another child, so now Billy had a half brother, his father's son from his new life in Europe. Charles Alexander Joel was seven at the time, the same age Billy was when Howard left Hicksville. Billy was in his twenties, just a little bit younger than Howard had been when he left.

The youngest Joel scion would live his father's dreams. By the time he was in his twenties, Alexander would become both a noted classical pianist and the conductor of the Vienna Volkesopera.

§ § §

There were other places besides Long Island and the New York metropolitan area that were hip to Billy Joel. He was also a known entity with a following in Philadelphia. One of the shows Billy played on the *Cold Spring Harbor* tour was a contest-winners-only event sponsored by the Philadelphia album rock station, WMMR, at the city's Sigma Studios. In addition to the select studio audience, anyone could hear it on the station's live broadcast of the event. During the course of the show, Billy introduced a new song he had written but, in his current state of record company limbo, had yet to record in the studio. Playing that song, "Captain Jack," in that venue proved to be a pivotal moment in Billy's career.

"'Captain Jack' was a 'look-out-the-window' song," Billy noted. "I wanted to smack people in the face and say, 'Whatever you have to do to escape your own life by chemical means is useless.'"

Billy had been down the drug road before. He also knew people who continued to travel it, like Gentile. He saw what the drugs could do to people.

The song also painted as bleak a portrait of growing up in the affluent suburbs as anything before LA Punk hit nearly a decade later. "It's about coming out of the New York suburbs," Billy said, "but in my travels I have seen a lot of the same suburb all over the country. The song is sort of brutal, but sometimes it is good to be brutal and offend people—it keeps them on their toes."

The live version of the song from the show started getting requests and made the WMMR rotation, where it stayed. Soon it spread to New York. People began to talk about it.

"Clive [Davis, president of Columbia Records] invited me to a bash hosted by his friend, Abe Somer, a big-time LA music lawyer," says Walter Yetnikoff, another Columbia executive who would follow Davis into the president's suite. "Everyone was singing something about 'Captain Jack will get you high, Captain Jack will get you high.' Who the hell was Captain Jack?"

Other members of the press followed Heckman's lead and started to write about this phenomenal performer and songwriter. "If you go back in his career to his first album," says Howard Bloom, who ran the Gulf & Western Records publicity department in the '70s, "which the public didn't pay any attention to, the press did, and the press took him to their heart. Billy started out with the press in his favor. I saw the clippings he had gotten before 1973. Billy was no longer with us. Artie Ripp still was, but Billy wasn't."

Part of the reason that Ripp was still there but Billy wasn't revolved around the continuing problems at Gulf & Western. Records weren't being distributed. No one could buy them even if they wanted to. The company was hemorrhaging money. It was trickle-down economics in reverse—the record company didn't have money, and they couldn't pay the artists.

They spent half a year on the road and came home with nothing.

Artie Ripp was in deep trouble, and he knew it. His "platinum coffin with diamond studs" was being lowered into the ground, and the mourners were getting their shovels ready. Needless to say, Ripp couldn't make his own ends meet, let alone those of the artists, managers, and employees, for whom he, as the boss, was responsible. Suddenly, Billy's allowance (and therefore Irwin's allowance) stopped coming. Unable to keep things afloat on Long Island, and unwilling to trust pursuing their money across a continent via long-distance phone lines and the mail, they moved to where the money was, theoretically. At the very least, Ripp and his checkbook were there, though none of them could have known how empty the latter was. Billy, Elizabeth, and Sean, along with Mazur, his wife, and very young son all relocated to Los Angeles, in order to get the business resolved.

"We all moved," said Mazur, who still lives in LA as of this writing. "We were so broke we didn't want the check to get lost in the mail. We had to stay close to the money. We all picked up and moved to LA. That is where the record business was. It was easier to be broke in LA than to be broke in New York."

"Billy and Elizabeth were living—it was called the Howard Johnson Inn, but it wasn't a real Howard Johnson or anything—right next to the freeway," Sandy Gibson recalls. "It was like the Cold Water exit of the Ventura Freeway. Those cars were in their window. It was a horrible situation."

Billy, Mazur, and Ripp found themselves in a no-win situation. Gulf & Western wouldn't or couldn't sell records. Ripp was handcuffed to the deal but was attempting all of his best legal Houdini maneuvers to extricate himself. In the meantime, Ripp says, "I had to figure out how I was going to pay my bills. How was I going to support the artists I made contractual commitments to, personal commitments to? I was trying to figure out how to get out of this mess. I went from wonder-boy genius at Kama Sutra and Buddha to making an absolutely extraordinary deal with Gulf & Western. Now I had to make a deal to escape from Gulf & Western."

It cost him a fortune, but eventually Ripp extricated himself from the Gulf & Western deal, liberated himself from his golden coffin with diamond studs. In so doing, he went from being one of the shining stars of the record business to becoming a glorified independent producer with his own imprint and no one place to distribute his wares.

"I took on something like two million dollars worth of liability, didn't have any more money coming in, because now I was no longer delivering records to Ampex and Phillips," he laments. "Rather than being able to make an overall label deal, which gave me an overhead contribution as well as production and promotion capital, I now had to place artists at individual labels."

One of the artists he had highest hopes for was Billy Joel.

❀ ❀ ❀

Meanwhile, Billy had grown tired of broken promises and lies. He needed money to support himself, Elizabeth, and Sean. Not only were they still living on the highway in a room that sounded as if the cars were actually driving through it, but the holidays were quickly approaching. He decided that the waiting was completely nuts and went out to make some money the best way he knew how, playing the piano. He found a couple of piano bars that were looking for a musician.

"Billy says he's not going to record for Artie, says he'd sooner go out and get a job," recalls Sandy Gibson, who was still on Artie Ripp's payroll, such as it was. "He'll play in a piano bar. I drove Billy to interviews at piano bars. He didn't even have his license yet. He was like twenty-three, twenty-four years old. I drove him to a place in the Valley. At this point—we're talking the end of 1972, beginning of 1973; it was in '73 that he was Bill Martin at the Executive Lounge—it was hysterical. Billy would get out, he'd play the piano, and the bartender or the club manager would say, 'Oh, mmmm, that was pretty good. Sure I'll hire you.' He decided to take the Executive Lounge because it was easier to get to from Malibu."

In December 1972, Bill Martin made his debut at the Executive Lounge. "I went through the *Godfather* thing, where Pacino turns hard," he says. "It was like, 'I don't want to be a rich man or an empire builder, but I'm not gonna get *ripped off* any more.'"

So former rock and roll recording artist Billy Joel started playing standards and favorites for tips at a bar in the Valley. "The characters that Bill Murray and Steve Martin do, I was doing too, only people didn't know I was kidding," he says. "They thought, 'Wow, this guy is really hip!'"

It took Billy back to his Echoes days, in a way. Far from the experience of anything he had done since his bands went all original, he was back to playing covers—back to, as Fats Waller put it so long ago, finding "out what they want and the way that they want it and" giving "it to them just that way."

"If somebody asked for a Sinatra song, I would get into doing a whole put-on Sinatra thing. I'd be having a blast and they would think I was really into it."

The bottom line in this exercise was the bottom line. The better he read the crowd, the more money found its way into the brandy snifter that sat in front of him on the piano.

"What you're doing in a piano bar basically is playing for tips, so you try to pick out what will get bread out of the audience. Is this guy Italian? You play the 'Godfather Theme' or something like that. Is this guy Irish? You play 'Danny Boy.' You try to get those five dollar bills in the brandy glass."

The adventure went on for half a year, during which Billy gathered raw material for the next album that he hoped to make. For all intents and purposes, he *lived* the song "Piano Man." Most of the characters in the song were real—Davy from the Navy and Paul, the real estate novelist, hung out there regularly. John at the bar worked there, of course. The waitress practicing politics was Elizabeth (who turns up in a similar role in the later song "Zanzibar").

In the meantime, other forces were at work. Artie Ripp was aggressively trying to sell this phenomenal young songwriter whom he had signed to an iron-clad contract, while at the same time Irwin Mazur was trying to find a new home for his management client.

"It's disgusting," Sandy Gibson sums up the situation. "Billy's living on the Freeway. I know there's a better life for me, too. So my ex-husband and I get courted by Atlantic Records and they hired both of us. Now we know we're leaving town, so I say to Billy, 'You live in my house. You can pay what we pay, pay our mortgage payment.' We had an acre and a half in Malibu, five miles from our closest neighbor. Our mortgage was $219. So Billy and Elizabeth were living in my house in Malibu. I was living on Park Avenue, courtesy of Atlantic Records."

Billy, of course, was hunkered down nights at the piano bar. And suddenly this little bar in the Valley begins to see some heavy customers, drinkers more likely to frequent the hotel bars in Beverly Hills than piano joints in the Valley.

"After a while, the music business in LA knew I was there," Billy says. "They knew who I was 'cause I'd played the Troubadour as Billy Joel and I'd played in LA a couple of times, so there was interest. I didn't want them to know . . . but toward the end of the gig, they'd heard I was playing in this piano bar and they'd come down and say, 'Why don't you play your own stuff?'"

It wasn't his favorite way to make a living, but he knew in his heart that it wasn't going to last forever. He had already made four albums, he would make more. This was a way station.

"I've never given myself more than two seconds of self-pity," he says, "ever since I realized that the piano-bar gig is something a lot of people have to do for years and maybe their entire lives. And they're happy to have the work."

CHAPTER 9

A GOOD REPUTATION LAYING ON THE LINE

While Billy was working the crowd for tips in the Valley, two guys were walking down Santa Monica Boulevard toward Doheny Drive of a mid-winter evening. One wore a short, dark ponytail, the other was impeccably dressed, looking every inch the successful record company president.

"Most of the components are cool," Artie Ripp told A&M records president and co-owner Jerry Moss, "but what's this ninety-percent clause? You sell ten and pay me on nine? Jerry, that was when 78s broke. They don't break anymore. You sell ten, pay Billy and I on ten."

"Well, that's not the way we do business," the unflappable Moss said as they turned the corner at Doheny, his LA cool a sharp contrast to Ripp's New York street aggressiveness.

"I'm not signing with A&M records, thank you very much, if that's your position," Ripp responded, burning that bridge for Billy Joel.

Fortunately, there were other interested parties for Ripp's artist. One was Atlantic Records. By this time, Sandy Gibson was head of publicity and John Gibson was doing promotion (and Billy, Elizabeth, and Sean were renting the Gibsons' Malibu A-frame while the Gibsons lived in an apartment on Park Avenue, courtesy of Atlantic president Ahmet Ertegun). From New York the Gibsons lobbied for the label to sign Billy.

"Eventually," Ripp says, "we wound up having Ahmet Ertegun, Jerry Wexler, and Jerry Greenberg at my home. Billy sat down and played a whole bunch of songs."

So the owners and head of A&R from perhaps the most happening label at the time sat in a living room listening to Billy play. Billy was equal to the occasion, doing a great job. He knew he'd written some terrific tunes. "I was playing songs," adds Billy, "in a way that conveyed the whole band arrangement. And Jerry Wexler said, 'You play too much; stop playing so much.' I thought, 'We're going to have a problem here, because that's my piano style.'"

He played them one of the key songs he had written over the course of the last year. Called "Piano Man," it was a commentary on his stay at the Executive Lounge, his observations of his regular customers and the people who worked there. Wexler had some critical thoughts about that, as well.

"You know, it's kinda like 'Bojangles,'" Wexler opined after listening to it. "If 'Bojangles' wasn't written, you probably wouldn't have written that, right?"

Ripp braced himself for the explosion. As an occasional writer, and certainly someone who had made his living dealing with artists and writers over the last decade and a half, he knew that Wexler might have been trying to be amusing but that the artist heard him say, "You ripped that song off, didn't you?"

"I didn't steal it," Billy said adamantly. "'Mr. Bojangles' is one thing, 'Piano Man' is another thing. It's a similar structure, same chord progression. That's it.'"

Despite the differences of opinion, Ertegun, Greenberg, and Wexler agreed that Billy needed to be an Atlantic artist.

"In conjunction with Billy's lawyer, I negotiated a deal with Atlantic, a fabulous deal, an *unheard of* deal," Ripp recalls. "It wouldn't get me back my half million dollars that I had invested in him with advances to him, etc., but at least it gets him with a record company that believes in him and has the resources to make an artist a star."

While Ripp was meeting with A&M and Atlantic, Irwin Mazur was not idle on his client's behalf. When Billy had torn it up at the Mar y Sol festival, scouts from Columbia Records were in attendance. They filed reports about this guy who came pretty much out of nowhere and set the soggy festival on fire. The reports reached Kip Cohen, who was the head of the A&R department at Columbia. His secretary, Becky Mancuso-Shargo, had been in the audience at the Kansas City showcase for the college concert bookers a year or so earlier, and she actually had a copy of *Cold Spring Harbor*. When Billy's name started getting bandied about, she waxed enthusiastic to Cohen.

Cohen, using standard operating procedure for an A&R exec, found out who managed Billy and called Irwin Mazur, telling him, "Clive Davis would like to meet with you."

"Great!" said Mazur, seeing his fortunes rise again.

"Can you meet him at the Beverly Hills Hotel?"

"Sure."

So Mazur's wife drove him down to the Beverly Hills Hotel, and there, in the lobby, in front of the fireplace, he held a confab with the president of Columbia Records.

"I made Janis Joplin a star, I made Santana a star," Davis held forth. "Billy belongs with them on Columbia Records. Billy is a Columbia artist, not an Atlantic artist. He belongs with Bob Dylan and Bruce Springsteen. Atlantic is a nice company, but that's not who he is or where he should be.'"

"I agree with you," Mazur said. "I *want* Billy on Columbia Records."

"Great," said Davis. "Get out of your contract."

"I don't think it's going to be that difficult, Clive," Mazur said. "I've talked to Artie about it, and he's frustrated with Gulf & Western."

"Well, Artie and I don't talk," said Davis.

"You don't have to talk," Mazur replied. "I don't screw anyone that's straight with me, and he's always done the right thing. So we all have to get our heads together and do this thing the right way, because I'm not leaving anybody behind."

While Mazur recalled Davis touting Columbia as the company of Bruce Springsteen, he did it with the gift of hindsight. It's important to note that, at the time of their Columbia debuts, Bruce and Billy were both Columbia Records rookies, the albums coming out within months of each other during the course of 1973. Billy's *Piano Man* actually showed more commercial spark than Bruce's *Greetings from Asbury Park, N.J.*, which sold fewer than 30,000 copies. *Piano Man* had already gone gold by the time Bruce's *Born to Run* really broke him to a wide audience.

There still seem to be casual music fans who confuse Bruce and Billy, which is, after a fashion, understandable. They're both singer/songwriters, and they both write often complex songs. Both come from working-class, suburban homes with a certain level of "dysfunction"—Bruce forever at war with his father, Billy forever missing his father. Especially since *Born to Run*, when Roy Bittan joined the E Street Band, the piano work on Bruce's and Billy's records (and in their concerts) have had a passing, over-the-top, classically influenced gestalt. They both were heavily influenced by '50s and '60s R&B, Bob Dylan, and Phil Spector. Bruce once described Spector's Ronettes' record "Baby, I Love You" as "the sound of universes colliding."

But Bruce and Billy have very different approaches. For one, Bruce's lyrics are paramount. His songs, like most in rock, are built from the words up. Billy's are built from the melody up. The Beatles occasionally worked this way, "Yesterday" being a notable example: Paul had the melody but the first words were placeholders. When he sang it initially, the song went, "Scrambled eggs, scrambled, scrambled, scrambled, scrambled eggs . . ."

❊ ❊ ❊

Mazur brought the idea of recording for Columbia Records to Billy, who must have been staggered by this sudden embarrassment of opportunities. "I wanted to be on Columbia Records," he has said, "because it was Bob Dylan's label. In the late '60s and '70s the much hipper label was Atlantic. They had all the great rock and roll bands. Columbia was more high-toned, but they had Bob Dylan."

Now Ripp had two problems and one trump card. He had a handshake deal with Ahmet Ertegun to sign Billy to the amazing deal he had negotiated with Atlantic. But Billy wanted to sign with Columbia. Either way, the company would have to make Artie Ripp happy as well.

"Clive has a secret meeting with Irwin Mazur at the Beverly Hills Hotel" says Ripp. "Then he finds out from his lawyers that I have an ironclad contract and there ain't no way to break it. You wanna say Artie Ripp had a very strong contract? There was nothing wrong with it, man. If there was something legally wrong with my position, Columbia records and Billy Joel would have had me the fuck out of there in a day.

You think Clive Davis wanted me there? Or wanted to pay me?"

Billy, however, was insistent. Clive had sold him on Columbia, where he could take his place among the Dylans of the recording industry. Atlantic was cool, but Columbia was class.

"Well, it's too late," Ripp argued. "I've made a deal with Ahmet."

"I don't want to be with Atlantic," Billy said.

Unable to change Billy's mind, Ripp was forced to go into negotiations with Columbia for their new artist. His first order of business was to make sure the deal was as good or better than what Atlantic had offered. His second order of business was to make sure that he and Michael Lang (who still had a contractual override on Billy) were taken care of. Then, of course, he had to call Ahmet.

"I have to take my handshake back," Ripp told the dapper Turk who ran Atlantic. "The artist doesn't want to be with Atlantic. Clive had a secret meeting while we were negotiating, and Billy told me, 'I want to be on Columbia Records.' I have no choice, Ahmet."

Ertegun replied, "How much money is it going to take?"

"It ain't about that," Ripp explained. "It's not like they've out-bid you. It's more like they've out-personalitied you. Billy is convinced that he should be on Columbia Records with Clive Davis."

Eventually Ahmet put away his checkbook and conceded this artist to Clive Davis.

There was more to it, however. Elizabeth had started graduate business courses at UCLA, and Billy trusted her, as his lover, as well as an astute businesswoman, implicitly. After looking at the situation, she had pointed out that Columbia, spearheaded at the time by Walter Yetnikoff, had a much more formidable international presence.

Elizabeth realized that by getting Billy signed to Columbia rather than Atlantic, they would be "able to sell Billy's records at PXs across the world," says Sandy Gibson. "Also, his publishing became so much more valuable. Atlantic didn't have nearly the world penetration as CBS, with their distributors across Europe—and she made the right decision."

Billy Joel became a Columbia recording artist in the spring of 1973. This suited Artie Ripp just fine.

"My deal with Columbia was ten original Billy Joel albums, plus the best-of," he says. "Anything that came from those albums was part of my deal, and my deal wasn't based on years. My deal was based on ten original studio albums. You're not going to give me back the half million dollars I have in, you'll pay me this royalty, you'll pay Billy his royalty, you'll pay him, his producers, and Michael Lang his override from my royalty.

"I'm the bad guy who has the contract that couldn't be broken. I get twenty-five cents a record, okay. Billy didn't have to pay it to me. The record company pays it to me. And that only happened if Billy sold records."

Billy didn't want anything to do with Artie Ripp anymore, though. While all of Billy's records through the '70s and most of the '80s had the Family logo on them, when he went in to record his next album, it was produced by Michael Stewart. The only album he had previously produced was his brother John Stewart's *Lonesome Picker Rides Again*, the follow-up to his classic *California Bloodlines*.

"Basically," Ripp says, "I stepped out. I was no longer his producer.

"I was successful before I ever met Billy Joel," he adds. "Kama Sutra, Buddha were successful record companies."

Ripp's record-business savvy shows in the way his fortunes grew through the good offices of William Martin Joel. Ripp figured he had spent close to a half million dollars developing Billy. Estimates place that twenty-five cents an album he continued to get for many years courtesy of Billy's first ten albums (before he was finally bought out) as garnering Ripp in the neighborhood of $20 million.

CHAPTER 10

SING US A SONG, YOU'RE THE PIANO MAN

The *Billboard* Top 10 Pop Singles chart for the week of November 2, 1973, was an eclectic mix of music, to be sure, ranging from the Motown soul of former Temptation Eddie Kendricks's "Keep on Truckin'" to Jim Croce's posthumous declaration of identity "I Got a Name" to the bubblegum, teen-dream stylings of the DeFranco Family's "Heartbeat—It's a Love Beat."

A year and a half earlier, fellow Long Islander Harry Chapin had breeched the Top 30 with a story ballad about driving a taxi, aptly called "Taxi." Columbia felt it appropriate to launch their Long Island singer/songwriter with a similar song. So on November 2, 1973, Columbia released Billy Joel's musical telling of his adventures playing at the Executive Lounge, "Piano Man." The album of the same name followed a week later.

Many people, both in radio and the press, found the song similar to the way Jerry Wexler had heard it—that is to say, "derivative" at best, plagiarism at worst. While people who knew of his Long Island legacy called him on being a Harry Chapin-style balladeer, more musically savvy people (like Jerry Wexler) caught on to the fact that Billy told his tale over the same chord progression as Jerry Jeff Walker's hit song (via the Nitty Gritty Dirt Band) "Mr. Bojangles," which had broken the Top 10 in 1971 and was still a popular radio recurrent. Coincidentally, "Piano Man" also had the same progression as Bob Marley's "No Woman No Cry," actually more of a keyboard-oriented song, and many other popular tunes, basically a D chord with a descending bass-line.

That Columbia picked the song for his first single came as a shocker, even to Billy. He had a self-image and reputation as a melodist—such as he had a reputation at all—and despite the keenly observed lyrics, even he found the melody to "Piano Man" a bit bland and repetitive, though he would never have admitted that to Wexler. The song becoming a hit surprised him even more. However, these criticisms, even Billy's self-assessment, miss what makes the song so musically brilliant for a Top 40 hit. In an audacious move on Billy's part as both a composer and a performer, and on Columbia's part for recognizing that the subtle difference could put the song over, "Piano Man" is a *waltz*, one of a handful of Top 40 songs in that meter during the rock and roll era.

"Piano Man" the song was one of the newer compositions that Billy recorded for *Piano Man* the album. Much of the material on *Piano Man* dated back to *Cold Spring Harbor* and even before. While later in his career, Billy allegedly threw away older songs because they felt "stale," some of the best material on *Piano Man* were songs written for *Cold Spring Harbor* but not, for one reason or another, recorded.

"Some of the things on *Piano Man* are old," Billy confessed at the time. "'Captain Jack,' 'Billy the Kid' and 'Travelin' Prayer' are two years old. The rest of it comes from about six months ago . . . I'm not sure what I was aiming at with this album. I guess they're just songs."

"Captain Jack" was the song that had really brought Billy to the attention of the big record companies, with people singing the Chapinesque ballad of suburban depravities at Columbia Records parties, thanks largely to the excitement it generated in Philadelphia. "Travelin' Prayer," a pop-grass, on-the-road-again song, featured ace session banjo player Eric Weissberg, himself having earned his own gold record with "Dueling Banjos" the previous winter.

"Billy the Kid" might have been the most interesting song on the album. Featuring heavy orchestration, the song had overtones of modern American composer Aaron Copeland and spaghetti-western scorer Ennio Morricone. It demonstrated that Billy had more about him musically than his Beatles fixation, and lyrically it drew an interesting, if somewhat jejune, parallel between what made a teen outlaw in the Wild West 1800s versus what made one in the suburban late 1900s.

Of the newer songs, "Ain't No Crime" presaged another of Billy's issues, his nascent problems with alcohol, as the song is about a death-dealing hangover.

"I wrote 'You're My Home' for [Elizabeth]," Billy says. "It's corny, but true. I didn't have any money to give her a present, so I said, 'This is for you.' And she said, 'Does that mean I get the publishing rights?' That's when I started thinking about her getting involved in management."

"I don't make my songs for any audience," he would later realize. "I make my songs for me. I know that may sound self-serving, but I can't second-guess an audience."

If there was one major unsatisfying aspect of the *Piano Man* album, it was the fact that it had a studio sheen. In retrospect, Artie Ripp—who made the same error on Billy's debut (perhaps, in the long run, a worse error than the one that happened in the mastering)—realized the problem: "It took time for Billy to find a band that was his band, that was as extraordinary as he was and weren't really just studio cats. At the end of the day, *Piano Man* was a studio cat record."

As far as Columbia was concerned, it got the job done. To the credit of the promotion department of the record company, they continued to work the single for nearly six months. "Piano Man" finally entered the charts on April 6, 1974. It peaked at #25 in the *Billboard* Hot 100 but rose to #4 on the Adult Contemporary chart. It was followed by a couple of somewhat less successful singles: "Travelin' Prayer," which peaked at #77 in the Hot 100, and "Worse Comes to Worst," which topped out at #80. For his first time out of the gate after the false start of *Cold Spring Harbor*, this was pretty good. However, even four years later, Elizabeth Joel claimed that the album, which had gone platinum by that time, had netted Billy less than $8,000.

In 2004, more than thirty years after the record came out, a New York radio station polled its listeners to compile a list of the 104 most important events in the history of rock and roll. Billy recording "Piano Man" came in at #75.

As *Piano Man* caught fire, Billy fired his manager, Irwin Mazur. Not that Mazur had much hold on him. Ripp and Michael Lang had been chipping away at Mazur's ties to Billy, contractually and psychologically.

"Michael became a confidant of Billy's," Mazur recalls, regarding the intrigue in Billy's camp. "I think when the train really started rolling, everybody started whispering in Billy's ear."

"By the time it came to interest by Columbia in Billy," claims Sandy Gibson, "Artie already had bought out most of Irwin's share . . . Irwin was absolutely no match whatsoever for Artie . . . Artie had wheedled everything away from Irwin by that point."

"Artie made a nice financial deal with me so I wasn't out on the street, so to speak. That was good," says Mazur. "I had no royalty participation. Artie had the royalty participation. Artie just gave me a flat 'I'm going to pay you a half million bucks over the next three years' or something like that. All I had was my pride in seeing my dream realized.

"At this time, Elizabeth Joel stepped in and said, 'I am now the manager.' After eight years of blood, sweat, tears, and everything else, she became the manager. At that time, management contracts weren't worth the paper they were written on. Artie made a deal with me. My stomach was ripped out of me and my heart was broken."

Elizabeth was a shrewd businesswoman. She had studied for a masters degree in business from the UCLA School of Management and had begun to know the ins and outs of the music business. However, she also knew that she was too inexperienced at that point to do the job on her own, so Caribou Management was brought in. Caribou Management already managed Chicago, another successful Columbia band.

Because they already had relations with Columbia, and another hit group on their roster, Caribou had a certain amount of leverage they could exert. The company's principles, Larry Fitzgerald and William Guercio, knew the people in promotion whom they needed to call to get things done for their artist. They also had a great deal of experience in the studio, since they owned their own recording facilities. This left Elizabeth the time to start chasing other loose ends of Billy's business, particularly his publishing and copyrights, which were strewn all over creation.

"Elizabeth would sit in the lobby of somebody's office for twelve hours until they talked to her," Gibson recalls of Elizabeth's quest to get back the publishing rights on some of Billy's songs. "But they got a lot of the stuff."

Beyond the changes in the Billy Joel team, there were also changes at Columbia. Billy's champions at the company, Clive Davis and Kip Cohen, got caught up in the corporate bloodbath.

When the A&R person and executives who brought an artist on board at a record company either move on or get fired, that artist is often referred to as "an orphan." The corporate parents who contracted to guide the artist's steps through the company leave that artist in the hands of whoever follows them, and the level of sympathy and understanding of the artist on the part of the foster executives can vary widely and wildly. Many a career in the music business has fallen to executive turnover. Nevertheless, although he was out of it creatively, Artie Ripp had a vested interest in Billy Joel succeeding at Columbia.

"Clive Davis was executed out of the company at that point," Ripp recalls. "Charles Koppelman took Kip Cohen's place as head of A&R. Walter Yetnikoff became the new head of the company. Fortunately, Walter and I knew each other from the time he started as a lawyer, and I knew him in International [the department Yetnikoff had run just before becoming president], and so on. I made sure that Billy performed at the Columbia convention so that everyone at the company could be touched by this guy's power and magic as a performer, musician, singer, songwriter, and so on. Everybody got it."

Not only did the new regime at Columbia "get it," so did the press. While Billy has had a rough-and-tumble relationship with the press during his career, in the early years it was more like a love affair, especially with the trades. The music-trade magazine *Cashbox* named him "Best New Male Vocalist" for 1973. *Music Retailer* named him "Male Artist of the Year." And *Stereo Review* gave *Piano Man* "Album of the Year" honors.

The hits, the good notices, the awards led to a better class of gigs. Now, instead of opening for other acts at smaller venues, he could headline. He even managed to sell out some bigger houses as the marquee act, including Carnegie Hall and Lincoln Center's Avery Fisher Hall in New York, Massey Hall in Toronto, and the Kiel Opera House in St. Louis. After a decade of playing professionally, Billy Joel's career seemed to finally be heading in the right direction.

"When I was drumming for Henry Gross," said Gentile, who was in the road band for Gross just before the latter hit the big time for a short while with the gold record "Shannon," "we opened for Billy in—are you ready for this?—Allentown, Pennsylvania. Billy had just released *Piano Man* and was starting to sell out two-thousand, three-thousand-seat theaters. He was so fucking thrilled that finally his piano could be center stage, he didn't have to move it from side stage to center stage to play—or, depending on who he was opening for, he sometimes had to play side stage. I walked in there before the show and I said, 'Where's that fuck, Billy Joel?' And he popped his head up from behind the piano. He was just sitting there. He looks at me and says, 'Bruce! What are you doing here?'"

§ § §

Another popular concept in the music business (and in baseball) is the sophomore slump—the idea that the artist has a lifetime to write the first album and months to write the second. In Billy's case, it was as if *Cold Spring Harbor* had never existed. In fact, many who were unaware of that inauspicious debut would regard *Piano Man* as his debut.

Billy released *Streetlife Serenade* on October 11, 1974, less than a year after *Piano Man* came out. Again, it was produced by Michael Stewart. Again, it featured some of the best studio players in Los Angeles at the time—both Crusaders bassist Wilton Felder and renowned session bass player Larry Knechtel, for example.

Like *Piano Man* before it, *Streetlife Serenade* was also recorded at Devonshire Sound in North Hollywood. However, Billy was beginning to build a team who worked with him in the studio and continued on the road, particularly engineers Ron Malo and Brian Ruggles.

In retrospect, Billy found the album had interesting musical ideas but nothing to say lyrically. He tried to inject some classical piano work into the title track and called out the fakes and phonies on the album's hit, "The Entertainer."

"'Piano Man' was me," he concedes. "'The Entertainer' wasn't. The things I write have a seed of personal experience, but my life isn't interesting enough to have every song be about me."

"The Entertainer" did, however, address issues that had *caused* the real-life situations in "Piano Man." "I was talking about the cold, hard business of records," he said. "The rock star as god—I hate that."

"I have a real cynicism about this whole star thing. I don't think I'm so special—I just do what I do."

The new album differed from *Piano Man* in a number of ways. On a few cuts, Billy started trying out his recently acquired synthesizer, adding that texture to the piano, but there was not nearly as much orchestration, and there was certainly nothing as strong or pronounced as "Billy the Kid." The songs included a bit of homebrewed ragtime ("The Root Beer Rag," after one of his favorite soft drinks), a couple of ballads, and a country-esque ode to his roots, "The Great Suburban Showdown."

"I like to be as eclectic as possible," he says. "I don't like to stick in one bag, because then you become, 'Oh, he's the guy who does this . . .' I like different kinds of music, whatever's good. I don't want to limit myself to writing in one vein."

"I never do the same thing twice," he adds. "To keep me interested, there always has to be something new, something different."

The single version of "The Entertainer" performed respectably if not spectacularly. It peaked at #34 in January 1975. A month earlier, the album had topped out at #35.

In addition to getting only limited radio play, Billy played very few dates in support of *Streetlife Serenade*. He did make a couple of guest appearances, most notably singing "Twist and Shout" at Rutgers with Bruce Springsteen. But the album was not doing much to further his penetration into the hearts and minds of rock fans.

One of the songs on the album was a snide shot at his current home, about the people in Los Angeles who came for the fame. "Los Angelenos" had a cynical quality and showed that Billy was beginning to feel a bit homesick. He came from New York, after all, and until he had moved into the motor inn and finally the Gibson A-frame in Malibu, he had never lived anywhere else. What he discovered in LA was that the living at the time was relatively easy. The California sun was seductive, and it kept Billy seduced for more than three years.

He started work on his next album pretty soon after *Streetlife Serenade* hit the streets. The new album became a series of false starts. Fitzgerald and Guercio initially tried to put Billy together with Elton John band members Dee Murray and Nigel Olsson, with Guercio in the producer's chair. The chemistry wasn't right and the music never gelled. Then they went back to the Michael Stewart approach of finding the best studio guys in LA to play on the tracks, but Billy didn't like the results of that, either.

"I was with Caribou Management," Billy explains. "Very 'West Coast' and we were not 'tuning into each other.'"

So Billy decided to dissociate himself from Caribou, and along with that decision came the realization that nothing was holding him on the West Coast but inertia. He also began hearing horrible things about the place he still thought of as home. This was the mid-'70s, when New York City was in danger of becoming the first major municipality to go bankrupt, default on its bonds, not be able to pay its teachers, police, and firemen, and sink into an ocean of financial despair. It was an era of high crime and low expectations in the greatest city in the world.

"When I was in LA, there was all this anti-New York sentiment, especially by ex-New Yorkers—they are the *worst*," Billy recalls. "It bugged me, and when I heard New York was going down the tubes, I said, 'I'm going back to see this; it looks like the place to be, to write about.'"

So Billy, Elizabeth, and Sean packed up what they wanted to take with them and headed back to New York, with Elizabeth and Sean going on first. Elizabeth set up the household about an hour out of the city in the exurban Orange County town of Highland Falls, New York.

Billy arrived a little later, traveling by bus. He walked into the new house and was so happy to be back after his three years in the sun that he went right to the piano and wrote "New York State of Mind." One of the perks of the move back to New York was that Billy felt that he was where he belonged, where he could stay. He finally took on the effects of permanence that had eluded him in LA, like getting a grand piano for his home. He insisted that he and Elizabeth spend the night of its arrival sleeping beneath it.

Billy was home.

❀ ❀ ❀

Billy had missed many things while in Los Angeles, but the thing it took him longest to realize he was missing was a band. From junior high until perhaps a year prior to his move to LA, he had belonged to a band, been part of a band's sound, participated in the gang/ensemble/political body that created the frission only a band can provide.

The internal workings of a rock band are a microcosm of sociology. Each band, like each person and group of people, is unique; each has a singular personality. Change a member and the band changes. A good example of this is one of the groups Billy shared the pop spotlight with throughout his career, Fleetwood Mac. Begun as an offshoot of John Mayall's Bluesbusters (another interesting study in how personnel changes lead to personality changes), they were conceived as a blues band led by Peter Green (who wrote the Santana hit "Black Magic Woman") with the stellar rhythm section of Mick Fleetwood and John McVie and two other guitarists, Jeremy Spencer and Danny Kirwin. When Green's drug-induced paranoia landed him out of the band (and eventually in prision and an asylum), his replacement, keyboard player Christine Perfect (soon to become Christine McVie), began to move the band away from the straighter blues orientation. Spencer left to join a religious order, and Kirwin and the band parted ways as well, opening the door for Bob Welch, who took the band even further in a pop direction. When Welch left to test the waters as a solo artist, he was replaced by a pop duo from Los Angeles, Lindsey Buckingham and Stevie Nicks. This solidified the band's pop orientation, and a decade after spinning off as a hard-core British blues band, Fleetwood Mac had morphed into one of the most successful pop/rock groups of all time.

While Billy realized that he had now taken on the mantle of Billy Joel, songwriter, when it came to making his albums—his initial idea in recording was the creation of very public songwriter demos, after all—he missed this dynamic personally, musically, and professionally. As Ripp realized—too late—Billy was a band guy with a solo career.

"Billy rejected the first recording of *Turnstiles* because he wanted his own band that he was going to tour with to be on the album," said Jerry Schilling, a member of the Memphis mob that surrounded Elvis, who joined the Joel team around this time as road manager. "William Guercio, who was producing, had the top session players in the country on the album."

Schilling met with Billy and Elizabeth during the latter stages of Schilling's relationship with Caribou. He wanted to see how the music business worked outside of Elvis's considerable sphere of influence. So one night over drinks in Las Vegas, he mentioned this emerging curiosity to a booking agent friend of his. The agent told him that he just might know of an opportunity. He set Schilling up to meet with Guercio, Fitzgerald, and their associate Howard Kaufman.

"So we kind of hit it off and they said, 'We want you to meet somebody,'" Schilling recalls of his first meeting with Elizabeth Joel. "This New York lady comes into the room. I'm from Memphis and she's asking me all these questions. Finally, in my naïveté I just said, 'Are you asking me if I mind working for a woman?' And she said, 'That's exactly what I'm asking you.' I said no, and she says, 'Alright, we're going to Colorado tonight.' So we flew to Denver, drove up to Boulder and wound up at Caribou Ranch [Guercio and Fitzgerald's studio]."

Unfortunately for Schilling, there still was no album to tour. On Billy's earlier albums, he used the band the producer wanted. Now, the combination of the disappointing reaction to *Streetlife Serenade*, two Top 40 singles under his belt, and just having more experience and confidence as a recording artist gave him license to set out to get what he wanted musically. "Michael [Stewart] felt comfortable in the studio with those musicians," Billy says of his producer on the first two

Columbia albums, "whereas the live band is a lot hotter, and a lot harder to record in the studio."

Back on the East Coast, Billy began the task of putting together the Billy Joel Band, an entity he could tour with, record with, and despite his nominal position as "the artist" whose name appeared on the cover of the album, experience the personal and musical dynamics with.

The core of the band came from an existing Long Island group, Topper. Billy had worked previously with bass player Doug Stegmeyer. Stegmeyer introduced him to the band's drummer, Liberty DeVitto.

"Liberty used to work with Mitch Ryder," Billy noted. "He is a real Italian rocker. He's got tons of energy and is the group's comedian."

Guitarist Russell Javors, also from Topper, joined the band as well, along with sax player Richie Cannata. Together, they began to work on the set of songs that had not gelled to Billy's satisfaction at Caribou Ranch. Initially they got their feet and feel by playing a short club tour. Then they brought themselves and the songs into Ultrasonic Studios, about 7 miles from the Joel family Hicksville homestead, in Hempstead. Billy produced the sessions, and not only did he use his road band to cut the record, he used his live sound engineer Brian Ruggles to record the basic tracks of that band.

"Billy looked at it as a band," Schilling says. "He didn't look at it as Billy Joel. He always, back then in those foundation-building years, considered it a band, and the band had input and the lighting guy had input. Billy wrote the songs, but the band played them.

"He still has the same drummer, Liberty DeVitto. I remember Billy saying to me, way back then, 'We gotta put Liberty into the rider!'" Schilling laughs over this music-business joke about the addition to a live-venue contract that could include anything from a platter of macrobiotic food for seventeen to a bowl of M&Ms with all the green candies removed. "And I guess Liberty's still in the rider."

Turnstiles finally came out in May 1976. Among the people on the cover, going through the titular turnstile is Sean Small, Elizabeth's son. The album is packed with songs that have grown into Billy Joel standards—indeed, some of the songs the rest of his work would be gauged against. Not that *Turnstiles*, even in retrospect, was Billy's most successful album, but it well might be his most successful collection of songs, and that had been Billy's goal to that point. He wanted his albums to sell his songs. In one of his life scenarios, Billy is a songwriter who became an accidental recording artist. "Say Goodbye to Hollywood," for example, was covered by Ronnie Spector backed by the E Street Band in the early '80s.

"I heard Ronnie in my head as I wrote the lyrics!" Billy says. "It was wild! And to have Miami Steve Van Zandt and the E Street Band back her up was the best. God, that made me truly happy."

"I was moving back to New York and I was really happy to be getting out of LA . . . The first year I was there, I was kind of seduced by the nice weather, the palm trees and the views from the Hollywood hills, the Pacific Coast Highway and all that stuff. That wore off after about a year."

"New York State of Mind," the bluesy torch song for Billy's home state that came pouring out of his piano as he got home from his cross-country bus trip, was covered by Barbra Streisand and then virtually every saloon singer and lounge artist out there. The list of great vocalists who have carried the torch on this song include Tony Bennett, Shirley Bassey, Mel Tormé, Carmen McRae, and Diane Shuur. Even fellow Long Island club rat Leslie West, who went from the Vagrants— one of the bands that would play Mazur's club—to relative success in Mountain, recorded a version of it. But it was the first cover, Streisand's, that stands out in Billy's mind.

"I thought, 'This is one of the greatest woman singers ever, doing . . . me? Me?'" Billy says. "I really loved it, though, because it kind of finally made me legitimate in this business to my mother."

Then there are songs that have become classics in Billy's own hands. One of the main recurrents from the album is "Angry Young Man," a song in which the lyrics juxtapose the pragmatic with the political, the mainstream with the radical, while the music fuses everything from Chopin to the Who, with a synthesizer solo in there to boot. Ironically, Billy casts himself as the middle-of-the-road voice of reason.

"'Angry Young Man' was written about his tour manager before me," Schilling maintains. "Billy told me that was who it was about . . . If you listen to the words, it really describes the guy. I heard stories from the band. Not that he was a bad guy, he was just a little different."

Then there's the epic "Miami 2017 (Seen the Lights Go Out on Broadway)," an apocalypso of a song that fuses stadium rock with an almost theatrical sensibility—a musical *Twilight Zone* episode. "When I got back to New York from LA," Billy explains, "the city was on the verge of bankruptcy . . . It was an apocalyptic vision."

With all this going for it, *Turnstiles* still sold poorly, peaking at #122, nearly one hundred positions worse than *Piano Man* and a slide of eighty-seven positions from the #35 reached by the disappointing *Streetlife Serenade*. In the contemporary music business, Billy probably would have been sent to the minors or at least given his waivers so another company could see what they could make of him. However, the music business of the '70s still had the notion of building careers, and while the Columbia management that had signed him was no longer in power at the company's 52nd Street headquarters, the current management believed nearly as strongly in the potential of Billy Joel. It was a belief that would prove well founded by the end of the next year.

CHAPTER 11

SHE'S NOBODY'S FOOL

As 1976 waxed on, Billy found himself in a strange place professionally—for the first time since even before his days with the Hassles, he was without management. He had a self-produced album coming out. He, Elizabeth, and Sean had moved out of the house in Highland Falls to an apartment in Manhattan. One day, late in the year, he casually asked Elizabeth if she would manage him, not just as a buffer for the Guercios and Fitzgeralds of the world, but for real.

"The very next day," he muses, "there were phones and shelves and typewriters and secretaries in our apartment."

Having Elizabeth manage him made tactical sense. She understood him as a person and as an artist, had known him for the part of his career that really mattered, from the Hassles on. She had the business acumen and had been in de facto charge of Billy's career pretty much since he had fired Mazur and signed with Columbia Records.

"She's the person who hired me, actually," recalls road manager Jerry Schilling. "Then I met with Billy up at Caribou Ranch after that. I found Billy fascinating. He is one of maybe the most intelligent artists I've ever worked with. He has this persona that he's presented on purpose of this street guy and he doesn't know anything about the business. Bullshit! Billy is brilliant—I learned that—and he was smart enough to not act like it. That is probably one of the reasons—maybe fifty percent of the reason—that Elizabeth was such a great manager, because Billy realized what he had to do business-wise to get across his artistic side."

The persona the pair presented was an exercise in subterfuge. It worked well. Billy played his part as the streetwise rock artist, but Elizabeth's role was even more deceptive. In rock and roll, even at the major label level, a pretty face will get you a long way, both as an artist and into the executive suites. Elizabeth Joel had the executives at Columbia licking their lips like predators before a kill. It often turned into a case of the hunter getting captured by the game.

"I was regarded as Billy's girlfriend," she recalls, "a twenty-year-old with long hair in a miniskirt."

The element they missed was that, beyond the sexy exterior and flirtatious demeanor, Elizabeth Joel was smart and well educated, a shrewd and subtle negotiator, and she didn't miss much.

"She was a good manager for him," Sandy Gibson, still a friend of Billy and Elizabeth's at the time, recalled. "She ran a tight ship, she made sure they got paid, she was on the bus all the time. They made a lot of money, an unbelievable amount of money. She made certain allies who would play ball with her, who she's still friendly with today. There were certain women in publishing or women in the marketing department. She found her people who would help her and managed to overcome. She was focused, focused, focused, and she brought him to the top, top, top. They bought the house on East Sixty-second Street. It had a swimming pool. They hit the big time together."

Billy and Elizabeth called their new management company Home Run Systems, and it could be used as a model for anyone putting together a home-based business, at least in its early years. Billy described it back then, in the mid-'70s, as "a mom-and-pop operation." Beyond everything else, it meant a new level of togetherness for them.

"I could never understand how Paul McCartney could have his wife, Linda, onstage," Sandy Gibson mused. "I finally got to ask her, and she said that sometimes it was the only time she could be together with her husband. You have to get into the thick of it, otherwise you're an outsider. That's the story of Bruce Springsteen's first marriage. They weren't together."

Despite the poor sales of *Turnstiles*, or perhaps because of them, Billy embarked on his most ambitious tour to date. For one thing, it was his first really long and intensive tour, well thought out and well booked. It also marked Billy's first tour as a headliner.

"For years," said Billy, "we were the opening act for the Beach Boys and the Doobie Brothers . . . Nobody wants to see the opening act. They want to see the headliner . . . You couldn't go up there and do 'Piano Man' because the crowd came to hear 'Help Me Rhonda,' so I would say something outrageous, or do my Joe Cocker imitation—anything to get attention—and then we'd do 'Jumpin' Jack Flash.'"

"He came to my room one night and said, 'I'll, never, never be an opening act again,'" recalls Schilling. "And he never was. It cost him some money that we needed at the time, but he had the courage to do that. Billy was courageous enough to be willing to give up work if he had to be a secondary artist, when he couldn't afford it. We would play, like, Pine Knob in Detroit. He was on the stage and there would be no lights. He's not on the marquee. He's in the middle of 'New York State of Mind' or 'Angry Young Man' and people are walking in. He would just be crushed."

Needless to say, the tour was done on a shoestring, a condition Elizabeth was familiar with, having gone through all the years of living in motel rooms off the highway, sharing living quarters with the members of her husbands' various bands. Conversely, having worked most of his adult life with Elvis, this sort of egalitarianism was new to Schilling. "There was no class distinction in how we lived, which wasn't great anyway," he said. "We had a bus with twelve bunks on it. But it was a band."

On the *Turnstiles* tour, Billy's relationship with Columbia was put to the test. To accommodate the "no opening act" dictum from the artist, new and less lucrative venues were played, with the result that the tour lost money. A lot of money. It was up to Elizabeth Joel to try to get tour support from Columbia Records president Walter Yetnikoff. Fortunately for Billy, as Schilling observed, "Probably no manager worked Walter Yetnikoff better than Elizabeth Joel."

No doubt this was because of all the lip-lickers at Columbia Yetnikoff was the boss wolf, the biggest wolf of them all—even his Yiddish name, the nickname that most of his close associates got to call him, Velvel, means wolf. Yetnikoff's peccadilloes and appetites were legendary. After becoming president of the CBS music division in the wake of Clive Davis's firing, Yetnikoff transformed into an id out of control. He had a bevy of blonde beauties that he referred to as his "shiksa farm" (*shiksa* is Yiddish for "non-Jewish woman"). There can be little doubt that Yetnikoff saw adding Elizabeth to his flock as a tasty possibility.

"Billy Joel," Yetnikoff writes in his autobiography, "was struggling. Billy paid little attention to the business side of his creativity. His copyrights were scattered and his career had stalled with the release of *Turnstiles*. His then wife and manager Elizabeth called to say he was trying out new material on the road. Would I come to a concert? I did. I spent more time watching the audience than evaluating the music. I let the audience, a better gauge than me, do the evaluation. They loved what they heard.

"'I love it too,' Billy told me backstage, 'but we're canceling the rest of the tour.'

"'The material is developing beautifully,' I said. 'Why do that?'

"'No support money. Elizabeth called Columbia for another eighty thousand dollars and they laughed.'

"'Tell her to call again tomorrow morning. Take my word for it, no one will be laughing.'

"Billy got the money, the tour went on and the record came out."

With the additional tour support, Elizabeth sought to exploit and develop some other avenues, especially Billy's international visibility. Ripp had sent him to Europe on a sort of scattershot tour, and at that particular time and under those circumstances, that had to be enough. Now, however, Billy was recording for Columbia Records, and Columbia had a strong international division, strengthened even more because that had been Yetnikoff's bailiwick before he took over the whole shooting match. Billy started making noise in Australia, so the tour took him there for the first time.

"CBS down in Australia really believed in Billy," Schilling notes. "In Australia, we went down and did about three days of press."

Elizabeth's wisdom can be found in many things on this tour, not the least of which were the venues. Across the United States, Billy played at all the best showcase clubs—places like the Bottom Line in New York, the Cellar Door in D.C., and the Ritz in Memphis. These were not great places to make a lot of money, as they accommodated hundreds rather than thousands of people, but they were intimate, and they were designed to present an artist in the best light to the media. At the Bottom Line, for example, the paying customers sat up front, but they sat at long tables. The press and media sat on a raised platform behind these seats, at smaller, round tables where they could schmooze and be schmoozed. This made clubs like the Bottom Line great places to make contact with an audience and win over the press and radio.

"Before *Turnstiles* there was that cooling-off period, but he still had that 'Captain Jack' thing," says Schilling. "He had some underground following from place to place. That's why he could play some of the better clubs like the Bottom Line and the Cellar Door. It was a hit-and-miss time. We didn't sell out all the little clubs we'd play. The Bottom Line sold out, of course. I can't remember some of the other ones, probably because we didn't do that well."

In addition to shows at showcase clubs, Billy was booked into dozens of colleges and played Carnegie Hall. "By the end of 1976, there was a buzz on Joel," says his longtime booking agent, Dennis Arfa. "The venues he played were hand picked. Sometimes he played in rock 'n' roll rooms, but we also wanted the Carnegie Halls to show that side of Billy, to build that class image which is very much a part of Billy."

New York Times music critic John Rockwell very publicly made Arfa's point when he reviewed Billy's first Carnegie Hall show: "Hearing Billy Joel at the 1971 Puerto Rican Pop Festival, one realized that this young, unknown pianist-singer had great potential. Hearing Billy Joel at Carnegie Hall . . . a concert he once described as 'one of my dreams,' one knew that this artist was fulfilling all that promise as a musician and a star."

❧ ❧ ❧

Perhaps the best idea Elizabeth had while managing Billy was hooking him up with Phil Ramone. After a couple of false starts on *Turnstiles*, Billy wound up self-producing the record, with help from his live engineer Brian Ruggles and from Bruce Botnick, who was something of a studio celebrity due to his work with the Doors. Billy and the band had worked through a lot of the material he had written for his next album already, and the time had come to think about actually recording it.

One thing the *Turnstiles* experience taught Billy: The job Stewart and even—though he would be loath to admit it—Ripp did as producers was a lot harder than it looked. Billy didn't want to face it again. This probably didn't upset the powers at Columbia too much. Billy needed a hit album, and Ramone had just won a Grammy and helped sell more than half a million albums for Paul Simon with *Still Crazy After All These Years*. Elizabeth brought in several candidates, including Ramone. Billy and Ramone clicked right off the bat.

The ageless Ramone had begun his music career as a violin prodigy, but by 1961, he'd already engineered several jazz records, including albums by John Coltrane and Dr. Billy Taylor. He opened up his own studio, A&R, in New York, and by 1964 he had already won the first of the eight Grammy awards he has earned to the time of this writing, that first one for engineering the epochal Getz/Gilberto album that introduced audiences to the timeless samba "The Girl from Ipanema." By 1976, he had already produced albums for Quincy Jones, Burt Bachrach, Phoebe Snow, and the 1975 Grammy winner for Album of the Year, *Still Crazy After All These Years*, with Billy's fellow Columbia artist Paul Simon. This was clearly the kind of magic that Billy needed.

"I got a call from his wife at the time, Elizabeth, and she asked me to meet with Billy," Ramone recalls. "Several producers were being considered. We had lunch, I went to his Carnegie Hall performance, and I said what I felt. I said, 'I listened to all your albums, and truthfully I think they are too glitzy, too shiny, and they don't represent what I saw when I saw you perform in Toronto and what I saw at Carnegie Hall.' Obviously, I said the right thing."

Ramone had said the magic words, the very thing Billy wanted to hear, that his records needed to capture the energy and power of his live shows. Now, at last, he had a concrete reason why his shows worked and his albums didn't from someone the music industry respected. Ramone seconded Billy's feeling of "Love me, love my band. These guys go out on the road nine months a year. They know the material better than anybody."

Not only did Ramone want to try and catch the live lightning of Billy Joel in concert in a studio bottle, he wanted to do it with Billy's band. Ramone was downright enthusiastic about the idea, and particularly about working with Billy's drummer, Liberty DeVitto.

"The first time I saw Liberty was at a record company preview, many years ago, where they showcased some of the artists," he recalls. "I saw Liberty play with Billy Joel and I went crazy. I just thought, 'What a great musical animal.' I met him about a year later when Billy and I talked about making music together. I said to Billy, 'You know, I'd really love to have your band. I think it's got a driving energy I haven't heard in the studio in a long time.' Liberty brought something to the sessions. He could play heavy-duty, straight rock 'n' roll, and he could play very sensitively. I call him a 'song drummer.' He knows when to stay out of the way of a lyric and yet keep the beat hard and heavy."

"Phil liked my guys right off the bat," Billy says. "He heard them play the songs and said, 'Don't play any different than you play on the road—be the rock and roll animals that you are.'"

So with a crop of new road-tested songs and five previous solo albums under his belt, Billy Joel and his band pulled into Ramone's A&R recording studio at Seventh Avenue and 51st Street in New York City. This time the whole vibe in the studio was different. "We did songs in five takes instead of fifteen," Billy said. "[Phil] was one of the guys. We'd throw around ideas, kick the songs around, try them different ways. And get them right. Sometimes we'd throw pizza at each other."

"Everybody at the label loved him and was determined that he should have a hit record," Ramone recalled, "but he'd been here five, six years and nothing big had happened . . . We talked about the hit— we were aware of that. And we decided there was nothing we could do about it other than make the music count.

"Billy and I became real good friends. There was a real unity between the band and me, a great cohesion. I went on the road a lot with him and understood what performed well and what didn't per- form well. It's funny, every time we made an album, he'd go out on the road and the new stuff never got applause—not until it was a hit."

❦ ❦ ❦

Jimmy Bishop walked into Irwin Mazur's office at CBS Music in Los Angeles. Bishop was the head of April Blackwood Music, one of the music-publishing companies under CBS music. CBS Music had hired Mazur shortly after Billy had cut him loose, and by 1977 Mazur had spent four years running the West Coast creative operation for the company with a fair degree of autonomy. Bishop had brought Mazur an advanced acetate copy of the new Billy Joel album, fresh out of the studio.

"You had something to do with this kid, Billy Joel?" Bishop asked.

"Yeah," said Mazur. "I think so."

Together, they listened to the acetate test pressing of Billy's new album, *The Stranger*.

"He wants a lot of money," Bishop told Mazur.

"What's a lot of money?"

"He wants $250,000."

"If you don't give him $250,000 for this album, I'm going to fucking go rob a bank and buy it myself."

And so Billy Joel re-signed with CBS music publishing in advance of *The Stranger* coming out.

CHAPTER 12

I CAN FINALLY FIND OUT WHAT I'VE BEEN LOOKING FOR

Even though, officially, he hadn't graduated with the rest of the class of '67, in 1978 Billy Joel was invited to attend the ten-year reunion of his class from Hicksville High School. He had to send his regrets for the evening, however. Billy couldn't make the February 18 party due to a previous engagement on that date. That night he was on national TV, playing "Just the Way You Are" for a live audience in Rockefeller Center's Studio 8H during the broadcast of NBC's late-night stalwart, *Saturday Night Live*. That week, the song had just reached its peak on the *Billboard* pop singles chart at #3. The week was just one of the capstones of a remarkable year for William Martin Joel, a year that would see him go from cult favorite to bona fide star, whether he liked it or not.

The album market that Billy's first Phil Ramone–produced record, *The Stranger*, was released into was the best of times and the worst of times for a singer/songwriter. Disco had begun to bust through the dam of the underground and had become an inundating force in popular music, led by three Australian brothers who had also developed a cult following as singer/songwriters earlier in their career—the Bee Gees. Their contributions to the soundtrack to *Saturday Night Fever*, coupled with the film's popularity, made the music from that film the most prevalent sound of 1978. The Gibbs brothers' work—their hit "Staying Alive," younger brother Andy's "Thicker than Water," and their production of Samantha Sang's "Emotion"—literally surrounded "Just the Way You Are" as it worked its way up the charts through that winter.

"Just the Way You Are" itself was something of an anomaly for

Billy. Usually he struggled over his songs, facing down the piano—the vicious beast with eighty-eight teeth, as he referred to it when writing songs—and a blank piece of paper for lyrics. This one just bubbled up into his consciousness one day.

"I was in the middle of a meeting with someone, and 'Just the Way You Are' popped out of my head," Billy says, describing the song's genesis. "I said, 'I gotta go home right now and write this song.' I just stopped the meeting."

Despite the immediacy of the song, it nearly spawned a war in the studio, and definitely generated some projectile pizza. The "rock 'n' roll animals" didn't think the song was rock 'n' roll enough. Drummer Liberty DeVitto was particularly adamant. He told Billy he thought the song was down there with Neil Sedaka's "Laughter in the Rain" on his own personal wimp-o-meter. "Everybody was down on it and thought it was too goofy and sappy," Billy recalled. "Liberty didn't even want to play on it. 'I'm not Tito Puente!' he said. 'I won't play that oily cocktail lounge cha-cha/samba crap!'"

Even after they recorded the song, there was some question as to whether it would make its way onto the album, or get buried on the B-side of another single, or perhaps not even get released at all. They were playing the song back in the control room at Ramone's A&R Studios when one of the background singers on the album and a previous production client of Ramone's, Phoebe Snow—who had had a Top 10 hit with the Ramone production of her debut album and its hit, "Poetry Man"—walked in. She was accompanied by Linda Ronstadt, herself possessed of three Top 10 singles at the time.

They said, "You've got to put that on the album!"

Billy replied, "Yeah? You think so? We didn't like it that much."

They pleaded with Billy to put it on the album. "I'm going to listen to what women say!" he laughed in retrospect.

"Just the Way You Are" became a milestone and a millstone for Billy. As a pop recording artist, he got from it the kind of success the powers at Columbia always knew he was capable of generating. It stayed in the Top 10 for most of the winter of 1978. It set up three more singles from *The Stranger* for Top 20 success. The song grew his fan base exponentially.

But the band had had something as well. Billy and the band self-identified as rockers. This song smacked of the Executive Lounge, and would, indeed, become a lounge standard, though how bad is that when the saloon singers who have recorded it range from Frank Sinatra to Shrek? It would also become a popular wedding song. It was such a pretty song, and its sentiment had the true trait of great pop music—anyone could relate to it. Who doesn't want to be told that they're loved just the way they are?

Like it or not, the song had a lasting brilliance to it. The art was revealed in several ways. There's the arrangement. Where previous Billy Joel albums were rife with orchestral riffs, there wasn't even a smack of strings on this one, just a hint of a synthesizer buzzing behind electric piano. Jazz great Phil Wood's sax work, especially his solo, is epic. Then there are the little barbs in the lyrics—lines like "What will it take 'til you believe in me the way that I believe in you."

"That edge of anxiety," Billy said, "made it a more meaningful song."

In 1978, though, the music scene had become dynamic to the point of instability. As music for the dance floor took over the airwaves in America, in England anarchy ruled, musically and every which way. The punks had set everything old to flame, gleefully pogoed around the fire as the bloated pop and rock of the era burned to the ground, and then set about rebuilding popular music in their own stripped-down, loud, snotty image on the ashes.

While the impact had yet to smack American popular music upside its complacent head, the people who wrote about it, the frontier taste-makers, were all for the great pop music overthrow. Suddenly the gentle poetics of Billy Joel and his ilk, even with the subtle lyrical "edge of anxiety," fell totally out of critical favor. On the basis of just this one song, critics began saying that Billy had aspirations of becoming "a crooner" and, worse yet, a middle-of-the-road performer. Thus began a war between the press and Billy Joel, with repercussions of it lasting through the writing of this book.

"People who think it's me," Billy said of the song, "are misled. Live, we do harder rock 'n' roll."

Nor was the criticism limited to the critics. "'Just the Way You Are' was a big hit," Billy mused. "[My father] called me up and said, 'You've written better songs than that.'"

Another thing the critics jumped on was Billy's classical training, which started to come back to haunt him. Critics would actually accuse him of being classically trained: "'He studied piano,'" Billy said. "I had never realized that one of the prerequisites for being critically acclaimed was not knowing how to play your instrument."

This was the flip side of the egalitarian, more-forgiving nature and lower expectations of rock players that Billy found so exciting at the start. But it was also indicative of another element in the critical communi-ty—Billy had gotten popular without their permission. As Howard Bloom observes, "If you go back in his career to his first couple of albums, which the public didn't pay any attention to, the press did, and the press took him to their heart, because the press works on a very sim-ple basis: 'If I can make you a star, I have demonstrated my power. This pleases my ego to no end. If you already are a star, and I haven't made you a star, then I can demonstrate my power by destroying you.'"

If quality means withstanding the test of time, though, the critics, including Howard Joel, were wrong. As soon as the song was eligible, in 2004, it became one of the titles in the Grammy Hall of Fame. It has been recorded by more than one hundred different artists ranging from reggae star John Holt to firebrand Cuban jazz saxophonist Arturo Sandoval. Billy's own version remains a staple on pop radio.

❦ ❦ ❦

In May 1978, Billy had three songs from *The Stranger* in the *Billboard* Top 100 singles chart. "Just the Way You Are" was joined by "Anthony's Song (Movin' Out)" and "Only the Good Die Young." The latter song helped spice up Billy's reputation and album sales by generating a teapot tempest with the Catholic Church. With lyrics like "You Catholic girls start much too late," "You got a nice white dress and a party on your con-firmation, you got a brand new soul and a cross of gold," and "You never counted on me while you were counting on your rosary," the song's alleged "anti-Catholic" sentiments led to many radio stations banning the tune. One of those stations was Seton Hall University radio station

WSOU, but as one of the student disc jockeys pointed out, "It wasn't the song so much as the comments that followed it."

"I didn't have trouble with the Catholic Church," Billy said, highly amused by the controversy. "The Catholic Church had trouble with me!"

"When I wrote 'Only the Good Die Young,' the point of the song was not religion but lust! 'Come out, Virginia! I'll tell you anything you want to hear!'

"The minute they banned it, the album started shooting up the charts."

The fourth and final single from the album, "Always a Woman to Me," put the record over and spurred even more controversy. Suddenly not only was Billy too musical and anti-Catholic, he was a misogynistic chauvinist as well. Billy's exasperation with the oh-so-politically correct organizations that leveled these charges and the media that reported them began to escalate.

"They missed the point," he railed. "I was saying that if a woman like Elizabeth enters the work force and is aggressive, she's called a bitch; if a guy is aggressive, he's called ballsy. I'm saying like, 'You're just as good as me, if not better.' She can compete with me on that level, but it doesn't mean she's not a woman."

Like many of the best albums, especially of that day, the best songs were the ones you had to dig for. Songs that weren't singles on the album remain some of Billy's best, particularly "Vienna" and the epochal, theatrical "Scenes from an Italian Restaurant." "Vienna" was written about tracking down his father and discovering his half brother. "Scenes from an Italian Restaurant" was an even more complex piece musically, lyrically, and psychologically. On a musical level, it was a suite, similar to the "Golden Slumbers" medley on side two of the Beatles' *Abbey Road*. On a lyrical level, it was a further exploration into Billy's musical exegesis of *Look Homeward, Angel*, yet another in a long line of songs that said you can't go home again.

"It was actually three different songs that I sewed together," Billy explained. "One song was called 'The Italian Restaurant Song,' because I wrote 'bottle of white, bottle of red.' Another song I wrote, a little piece of a thing called 'Things Are Okay in Oyster Bay.' I was living in Oyster Bay and it was one of the first apartments I ever had.

It was like a hippie crash pad, but I really dug it. [The song was] this cutey-pie little tune, not worth anything. So, then I needed to get from the instrumental section and I recognized we're going somewhere with this. We're going to [this other] song called 'The Ballad of Brenda and Eddie.' It was sort of my ode to the king and queen of the high school."

In the end, Brenda and Eddie try to go back to the Parkway Green to discover that the gang had moved on: "The king and the queen they went back to the green, but you can never go back there again . . . Couldn't go back to the greaser, best they could do was pick up the pieces."

Ironically, in the wake of *The Stranger*, Billy was discovering that success as well as failure made it hard to go "back to the green." In a little over a year, Billy had gone from a marginal cult artist whose minor hits were two years behind him to a ubiquitous voice on radio, a frequent face on television, and a regular presence in the press. For better or worse, he had become a star, subjected to all that status involved. For example, going to Yankee Stadium for ball games, now that he could afford good seats, was problematic. With all the people asking him to sign this and that, he disturbed the other fans who couldn't care less that Billy Joel came to the game, especially when people stood in front of them to get his signature. For similar reasons, Billy was upset. All he wanted to do was enjoy the game.

"I try to go back to Long Island and just talk to people, but they talk to me like I'm superhuman," he marveled. "I try to say, 'Hey, give me an hour and I'll get as drunk as you.'"

From 1977 to 1985, *The Stranger* was the best-selling Columbia record ever, until Bruce Springsteen's *Born in the USA* eclipsed it. Although it was kept out of the #1 of the *Billboard* 200 Albums chart by the ubiquitous *Saturday Night Fever*, the album spent six weeks at #2, and would stay on the Top 200 for two and a half years. To date, the album has sold more than 10 million copies in the United States.

"Basically," Artie Ripp adds, "when *The Stranger* finally came out, that changed the whole Billy Joel world, but that wasn't until 1978. '75 was *Piano Man*. Even that was five years from the time I signed him."

Of course, Ripp was one of the major beneficiaries of Billy's new popularity. The ten million copies of *The Stranger* earned Ripp $2.5 million. His investment in Billy Joel paid off at last.

❀ ❀ ❀

Another reason for the album's success was Billy and the band touring furiously behind it. With the phenomenal success of the record, Billy had made a quantum leap in that direction as well. Where he wasn't even selling out some of the clubs on the *Turnstiles* tour, with *The Stranger* tour Billy found himself playing arenas and stadiums across the country. Again, he found the scale of these shows staggering. "There are acres of bodies, moving like wheat," he said. "It looks like Iowa."

In addition to the quality of the venues changing, other things about the Billy Joel backstage were changing. Despite both Liberty and Billy being married, there were always girls backstage. In addition to the inebriating liquids that helped lubricate things backstage, there was now a sizable call for Colombian marching powder. Billy was certainly not alone in these sorts of backstage antics. In the days before AIDS, and even in the days after, there would always be drugs and groupies. Ian Dury had it right when he wrote "Sex and Drugs and Rock and Roll."

The tour took Billy to Australia in April 1978. The final show in Sydney would be the last on the tour. After three years as Billy's tour manager, Jerry Schilling had decided to move on. The Sydney show also would be Schilling's last as Billy's tour manager. Schilling had also decided that, rather than just fly home with the band, he would take a short vacation and spend some of the money he had earned during more than nine pretty solid months of touring. Being in this part of the world gave him access to areas he'd never seen before, so he planned an extensive trip through the South Pacific. His itinerary had him traveling through Bali, Indonesia, Hong Kong, and Japan. To get his visas, he had to take a number of vaccines, including a cholera shot. As the tour pulled in to its final show, a performance at the Sydney Opera House, Schilling started running a 104-degree fever. The cholera shot had worked—he had cholera.

"Now, I never missed a gig, but of course the last gig, I'm deathly sick and I can't go to the show," he recalls.

Late that night, he was sweating through his sheets in the hotel when the lights and all the power in his room went out. Shortly after, his phone rang. It was the band's sound man, Brian Ruggles, on the other end.

"Jerry, we've got a problem."

"What do you mean we have a problem?"

"Billy's got into a fight and he's in jail."

"Oh my god!"

Schilling hung up the phone and threw himself out of bed. He got dressed in a big hurry in the pitch-dark room, wearing mismatched socks, shirt buttons askew, shirttail out of rumpled pants, hair all akimbo, flushed with fever. He ran to the elevator. As the elevator door opened on the lobby, he was greeted by the sound of music.

"There's the promoter, Billy and everybody singing 'Volare,'" he laughs. "It was all a joke.

"I have to say, I never felt as part of, and had as much fun as that year I spent on the road with Billy and the guys."

By March 5, 1978, as Billy kicked off the European leg of *The Stranger* tour in Amsterdam, the album had peaked at #2. Toward the end of the year, *The Stranger* had gone multi-platinum. As he had moved from cult artist to star, from clubs to arenas, Billy had also moved up in status at the Columbia Records annual company convention. He had attended these previously as a promotional priority. In 1978, he attended as one of the year's key moneymakers. At the show, he ran into an old acquaintance who was now working in the company's publishing department.

"While I was working for CBS," recalls Irwin Mazur, "*The Stranger* had just gone platinum, and there was a convention down in New Orleans. I hadn't seen Billy in a couple of years. I just saw him, and we hugged each other, and he said, 'You motherfucker!'"

CHAPTER 13

EVERYBODY'S ALL EXCITED BY IT

When *The Stranger* tour ended in the middle of April 1978, the album itself had already peaked in sales but was just starting to gain momentum on the radio, with two of the four singles only beginning to break. Billy found himself in a pop-music maelstrom of the best but most dangerous kind. He finally had a certifiable, undeniable hit album and a song on its way to becoming a standard.

As Billy and his band pulled into A&R Studios again, he had the enervating task of following this hit album with another one that would be just as successful. Phil Ramone was again in the producer's chair as the musical ideas and pizza flew.

"When I come up with a melody, it's not calculated. It's like an erection: it happens."

"*52nd Street* was a much different album than *The Stranger*. It had a harder edge to it, although there was still orchestration on it."

A great deal of the difference sprung from the idea of writing for a band rather than for himself and a bunch of studio musicians. He had just spent nearly a year with the band; he knew them, knew their capabilities, and could write for them, as he had written for his own vocal and pianistic abilities for years, and for the singular needs and visions of Attila, the Hassles, and the Lost Souls before that.

"I am not a virtuoso pianist; I'm a piano player," he stressed. "A lot of times I write on the piano, but I mean for it to be translated to the guitar. On the *52nd Street* album we had a really good guitar player [Steve Khan] so there was a little less piano because I wanted to feature him."

Success in music can work two ways, and that largely has to do with the way artists regard their fans. If the artist perceives the fans as liking the hit but not the art, that artist will recreate the hit. If the artist perceives the fans as people of taste, demonstrated by the fact that they like the artist, that artist will continue to grow and hope to take the audience along.

For Billy, that was not a question. He was too restless not to at least hope his audience would come along. For his next project, he found himself exploring a lot of different avenues. The first single, "My Life," was a lyrical declaration of independence, albeit musically it bore a passing similarity to "Anthony's Song (Movin' Out)" from the previous album. It featured Chicago singer Peter Cetera on backing vocals.

"I wrote that one thinking about a young person leaving home," he says, "It's kind of a mutual 'see you around, don't let the door hit you in the ass.'"

The song rode the wave of anticipation and excitement in the wake of *The Stranger*, going gold and hitting #3 on the *Billboard* Pop Singles chart.

One song featuring great guitar work over piano was "Big Shot," the album's second single. The video, a performance, showed off some of the band's dynamics, with Billy even getting up from behind the piano to do some strutting, posing, and preening à la Rolling Stones front man Mick Jagger. The song itself, however, was a possible indicator of problems that lay ahead: "It's about anybody who's ever had a hangover," Billy declared. "I did a lot of personal research for that song."

Columbia followed this with the album's last hit, "Honesty," a ballad even more overwrought than "Just the Way You Are." Nonetheless, the song offered some insight into how Billy writes. "My music and lyrics aren't written at the same time. I always write the music first. A lot of times I write bail-out lyrics, just to carry along a melody while I work on the real lyrics.

"My drummer, Liberty DeVitto, will sometimes make up dirty lyrics and we use those until it gets to the point were I say, 'Uh-oh, I'd better write real lyrics for this or I'll get up onstage and sing Lib's words.' I can just see getting up on stage and going [singing] 'Sodomy, it's such a lonely word . . .'"

"Though the two have to fit together, for me the language is really secondary . . . It may take me a year to figure out why I wrote some of the songs I did, why I said some of the things I said and what I really meant."

Pop music had gone in another unexpected direction in 1978. Along with *The Stranger*, one of the other big albums of the year was Steely Dan's *Aja* (also featuring Steve Khan), which similarly spawned four singles. While not calculated—like Billy, the band had already had a couple of minor hits and several acclaimed albums of similar material—the audience reaction to the jazzy sophistication of this music seemed almost a reaction to the one-two punch of punk and disco. They even took the liberty of employing bona fide jazz musicians for the record rather than using the usual session suspects; Wayne Shorter took a solo on one tune, Joe Sample and Don Grolnick played piano on others.

Billy also took the opportunity to stretch his Brubeck influences, not so much rhythmically as harmonically, expanding the musical palate that he laid on the crowd. In this way, listeners had to dig into the album for the best songs on *52nd Street*. Three of them, "Half a Mile Away," "Zanzibar," and "Rosalinda's Eyes," fortified Billy's band in the studio with a who's who of outstanding contemporary jazz players, like trumpeters John Faddis, Randy Brecker, and Freddy Hubbard, vibes maestro Mike Mainieri, percussionist Ralph MacDonald, guitarists Eric Gale and David Spinozza, and saxophonist Michael Brecker. Most of the horn players feature in the soulful, swinging big-band section of "Half a Mile Away."

The music to "Rosalinda's Eyes" had a Latin jazz feel, but the lyrics were Billy trying to come to grips with his parents. He always had a fantasy about finding love letters his father wrote to his mother. He described the song as what he imagined one of them might say.

"Zanzibar," on the other hand, inadvertently dealt with another aspect of Billy's youth—his love of sports and drink. He had the music (as almost always) and he even had a title he liked for the music, Zanzibar. But he couldn't figure out what he wanted to say about Zanzibar. He went to Ramone, once again at the helm of the album.

"Oh, it sounds like a great place," Ramone said.

Billy thought Ramone was talking about the country Zanzibar. "Well, what do you think when you hear that word?"

"I think of all these guys sitting around watching TV in a bar," Ramone replied.

"'Zanzibar,' oh yeah, a sports bar. This is a song about a sports bar. Thank you, Phil."

Out came a lyric about watching four-time heavyweight champ Muhammad Ali box, Pete Rose playing baseball, and Billy waiting for a sign to "steal second base" with the waitress.

The album came out toward the end of October 1978, a little over a year after *The Stranger*. This time there was no *Saturday Night Fever* to keep him off the top of charts, and by the second week of November, *52nd Street* climaxed its eight-week ride at #1 on the *Billboard* 200 Albums chart.

✿ ✿ ✿

While the altitude atop the charts was fine, the ride up there was hardly a smooth one. The hit single "My Life" engendered the first in a long line of plagiarism suits tendered against Billy. A songwriter in Reno named John Powers accused Billy of stealing his song "We Got to Get It Together" for "My Life."

Billy couldn't believe it. He knew that he had written the song. He knew that he had never heard of or met John Powers. Powers claimed that he had sent the song to Columbia Records, and although it had been rejected by them, Billy must have heard it there.

The suit brought out the pugilist in Billy. He was ready to take it to the judge. He was ready to murder the guy. Fortunately, cooler heads prevailed. They pointed out that it would be far cheaper to negotiate a settlement than to litigate. Sure, it wasn't fair, but neither was life.

Elizabeth had retained Ina Meibach, one of the very few successful women music-business attorneys at the time, to look after Billy's legal matters. Meibach was one of those "certain allies who would play ball with her" that Sandy Gibson described. They made up Elizabeth's power base. They decided to negotiate with Powers, paying him $42,500 but not admitting liability.

This was not good enough for Powers. On the one hand, he ran advertisements inviting people to compare the songs. Then, when Billy went off on him in the pages of *Playboy*, Powers sued him for defamation. It took until 1988, but the case was finally dismissed. In the decision, the judge wrote: "The reader should be put on notice that many, if not all, of Billy Joel's statements will be nothing more than his opinions. His sought-after opinions as a leading songwriter should not be chilled by litigation unless he's lying outright."

Billy found the suit unsettling on a number of levels. Primarily, he regards his songs as his children, and suddenly "My Life" had the taint of the bastard. "'My Life' [is] a song that turned sour for me . . . just like some of your kids turn into bums," he said.

"Some of them grew up to be doctors and lawyers," he adds about his songs as his babies, "and others grew up to be drug addicts and dropouts. But I love them all for different reasons."

"I give birth to these songs. I go through labor pains with these songs . . . It's horrible—until you finish."

"Everything I've done is different. The proof is that some people thing I'm a balladeer, others think I'm a rock 'n' roller, still others think I'm the 'piano man.' . . . Yes, critics have said I write . . . in cold blood. I don't . . . If it's commercial, it just happens to be commercial. If you don't like my music, fine. But don't question my motives."

On another level, Billy had remained fairly accessible to young, aspiring songwriters and musicians. The Powers suit had changed that. "Now I see somebody coming at me with a tape, it looks like a subpoena."

❀ ❀ ❀

The *52nd Street* tour began in late September in New Haven. The first leg of the tour ended with five nights at New York's Madison Square Garden in the middle of December. Billy and the band took a month off for Christmas and New Years. Then they spent much of the rest of the winter playing throughout Europe.

On February 15, 1979, the National Academy of Recording Arts and Sciences gave out the 21st annual Grammy Awards. "Just the Way You Are" won two of the little gramophone statuettes; it was named both Record of the Year and Song of the Year.

Less than a month later, Billy joined a small army of CBS artists and executives on a musical excursion to Cuba, for an event called Havana Jam, though to those who where there it has become otherwise known as "the Bay of Gigs." The idea of spending some time in Havana appealed to Billy. He saw it as a way of getting closer to his father, who had gone to college there. "My father had lived in Cuba, so I was interested for that reason," he said. "We were told it was just to bring American music to the Cuban people."

While CBS was fairly tacit about it, the goal of the show was more than diplomatic. CBS hoped to put out a film and album of the event. And indeed they did, releasing a double album of the concert that featured Kris Kristofferson and Rita Coolidge, Stephen Stills, Weather Report, and several all-star jazz ensembles, along with Cuban artists like the large jazz ensemble Irakere, which featured sax great Paquito D'Rivera and trumpeter Arturo Sandoval and was led by noted pianist Chucho Valdez. They all gained their first exposure to most American audiences via these albums and shows.

Billy, however, was the biggest star on the bill, the headliner. Allegedly unaware of CBS's great plans for the show as a media event, he was less than happy when he found out. He refused to cooperate with the production of the album and the film of the event. He is not on either the video or the two albums that chronicled the experience, despite the fact that he had the event's top billing. "I'm not down here on some capitalist venture," he said. "I'm here to play music for these people."

The entourages were kept pretty small, just the musicians and key management people. In the role of performer, Coolidge was there with her husband, Kristofferson; as a manager, Elizabeth Joel also made the trip. They were the only wives allowed. Part of this was so that the Cuban officials in charge of the event could keep things manageable. They did, however, want to show off the country. They took the artists to the floor show of the famed Tropicana Hotel, a holdover from pre-Castro times for the tourist trade that still flourishes on the island, despite America's refusal to participate. During the show, commenting on the sexy outfits on the dancers and the lack of marital company, Liberty DeVitto asked, "Hey, is it horny in here or is it me?"

The concert that the artists were down there to play was, for Billy, like a plunge into a great unknown. He and the band weren't sure whether anyone would know anything in their set. Nor did they want to get involved in politics. Stills had gotten into a Spanish rap on socialism that had received a lukewarm response, at best, from the Cuban audience (even though most of the people in that audience were the families of high-ranking Cuban officials).

Billy was afraid of a similar response. It's not like a lot of American rock and roll got played on the state-sanctioned Cuban radio stations; apart from everything else, he felt unsure about how the music would go over with an audience who didn't know the songs. What he didn't realize was that the Cubans can prevent the importing of many things American (as the Americans disallow such Cuban products as cigars), but they can't block radio signals, and young Cubans could listen to the American rock coming out of Miami. The audience definitely knew the music.

John Rockwell made note of this as he wrote up the historic event for the *New York Times*: "Mr. Joel's presence at this three-day festival of Cuban and American popular and jazz musicians—the only American pop performer here whose career is in full tide—lent the proceedings a legitimacy they might have otherwise lacked. And he drew the most fervent response of the entire festival."

The Cubans loved him. "We listen to him on radio," one said. "But now here's Billy. This is the most important thing to happen in twenty years."

The tour continued through twenty-four more American cities during April, resuming in May in Honolulu as a way station on the route to several shows in Japan and Asia. As Billy was becoming a bigger draw through his hit recordings, he found himself playing bigger venues. While at one time he held forth saying, "Big halls are rip-offs for the artists and the audience," like so many artists who once held that opinion, he was forced to play big halls anyway. So now his show had to grow, and as a performer, so did he, taking on the lessons that dated as far back as when Irwin Mazur had managed him.

"Because we're doing bigger rooms, the guys who do my sound and lights wanted me to get up front more," he said.

With the growing cohesion in the band, and Billy actually working the stage, the show got better and better. As a solo artist, Billy was one of the earliest acts to conceive his art for a recording and then take it live, one of the first few artists who became known mostly through his records and then developed a live following. Now that the band was several years old and tight, his live reputation grew as well. There was more to a Billy Joel concert than just playing the hits. It had become a show.

As they became tighter in the musical sense, the band also became looser and more confident. Where the joke the group played on Jerry Schilling when he had his bad reaction to the cholera vaccine might well have come from Billy, the band, particularly DeVitto, got in their fair share of yucks, too.

"I sat down at the piano one show," Billy recalls, "and I did the whistling intro for 'The Stranger.' I'm in darkness and the spotlight slowly comes on . . . Gradually each member of the band is spotlighted and they turn to face me. Each of them is wearing a black paper eye patch or a moustache, their teeth blackened. I blow the sensitive whistling in front of twenty thousand people, the romantic mood of lovers cuddling close shattered . . . Humiliated, I plunge into the song and discover the keyboard is stuck together with long strips of adhesive tape. The gentle, melodic intro sounds like I'm walking across the keys in snow shoes."

Toward the end of the tour, Billy played a benefit concert for Charity Begins at Home. The organization, started by Billy, gave funds to organizations on Long Island that needed help to, in turn, help others. Dozens of agencies that support the poor, hungry, disabled, elderly, and abused on Long Island have benefited from the charity's largess.

As the organization's name said, though, charity begins at home. Now that Billy was beginning to see the rewards for his years of hard work, he was able to improve the lot of his mother and sister.

The charity continues to thrive as this book goes to press. During the holiday season of 2004, a New York City rock station raised more than a half million dollars for the organization with an on-the-air auction.

The Joel residence on Meeting Lane in Hicksville. *(Photo by Hank Bordowitz)*

Billy and his mom, Rosalind, share a moment at the dedication of the Billy Joel Cold Spring Harbor Park in 1991. *(Photo from the collection of Bruce Gentile)*

Representing Long Island: The Lost Souls play Flushing Meadows at the 1965 New York World's Fair. *(Photo from the author's collection)*

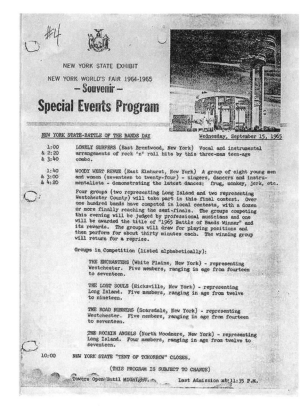

#4

NEW YORK STATE EXHIBIT

NEW YORK WORLD'S FAIR 1964-1965
— Souvenir —

Special Events Program

NEW YORK STATE-BATTLE OF THE BANDS DAY   Wednesday, September 15, 1965

1:00   LONELY SURFERS (East Brentwood, New York) Vocal and instrumental
& 2:20   arrangements of rock 'n' roll hits by this three-man teen-age
& 3:40   combo.

1:40   WOODY WEST REVUE (East Elmhurst, New York) A group of eight young men
& 3:00   and women (seventeen to twenty-four) - singers, dancers and instru-
& 4:20   mentalists - demonstrating the latest dances: frug, monkey, jerk, etc.

          Four groups (two representing Long Island and two representing
          Westchester County) will take part in this final contest. Over
          one hundred bands have competed in local contests, with a dozen
          or more finally reaching the semi-finals. The groups competing
          this evening will be judged by professional musicians and one
          will be awarded the title of "1965 Battle of Bands Winner" and
          its rewards. The groups will draw for playing positions and
          then perform for about thirty minutes each. The winning group
          will return for a reprise.

          Groups in Competition (listed alphabetically):

                THE ENCHANTERS (White Plains, New York) - representing
                Westchester. Five members, ranging in age from fourteen
                to seventeen.

                THE LOST SOULS (Hicksville, New York) - representing
                Long Island. Five members, ranging in age from twelve
                to nineteen.

                THE ROAD RUNNERS (Scarsdale, New York) - representing
                Westchester. Five members, ranging in age from fourteen
                to seventeen.

                THE ROCKIN ANGELS (North Woodmere, New York) - representing
                Long Island. Four members, ranging in age from twelve to
                seventeen.

10:00   NEW YORK STATE "TENT OF TOMORROW" CLOSES.

          (THIS PROGRAM IS SUBJECT TO CHANGE)

Towers Open Until Midnight.   Last Admission at 11:35 P.M.

The Hassles (from left to right): John Dizek, Jon Small, Richie McKenner, Howie Blauvelt, and William Martin Joel. *(Photo from the author's collection)*

The Hassles (from left to right): Billy Joel, Richie McKenner, Jon Small, John Dizek, and Howie Blauvelt. *(Photo from the author's collection)*

The Rock House, home of Jon and Elizabeth Small, Billy Joel, Bruce Gentile, Tom Davis, and the cream of Long Island rock. *(Photo by Hank Bordowitz)*

TONITE

THE **HABIT** & THE **GRASS MANAGERIE**

SAT. NITE

THE ★ **HASSLES**

THE ★ **HABIT**

★ **HAPPINESS-ISS**

★ **MYNDS EYE**

EVERY WED. NITE
Teenagers Sun.
Afternoon 2 to 6 P.M.

MYND'S EYE

Coming May 29th **THE SMUBBS**

GOLDEN PHEASANT DISCOTHEQUE
248 Union Blvd., West Islip—MO 1-9717

Coming! Saturday Nite! To the Golden Pheasant on Union Boulevard in West Islip, New York! United Artists recording artists the Hassles! Pictured standing, left to right: Billy Joel, Jon Small, Richie McKenner, John Dizek in fur, bassist Phil Marden, who replaced Howie Blauvelt in the last days of the Hassles, sitting. *(Photo from the collection of Bruce Gentile)*

Conquering the world with volume: Billy and Jon Small as they looked in Atilla. *(Photo from the collection of Bruce Gentile)*

Billy and Jon Small as they looked some thirty years later at Jon's fiftieth birthday party. *(Photo from the collection of Bruce Gentile)*

"There's a place on the stage for a very young man": Billy the Kid performs. *(Photo by Richard Aaron/Starfile)*

"I'm soooo tired. Someone peel me a grape?" Billy reclines on a hotel divan. *(Photo by Steve Joester/Starfile)*

Billy Joel, entertainer, on the *Turnstiles* tour, 1976. *(Photo by Karen Ragozzine)*

"My very own Tchotchke Award!" A bearded Billy shows off his Grammy during the 1981 presentations at Radio City Music Hall in New York City. *(Photo by Chuck Pulin/Starfile)*

Beauty and the Beast: Billy and Christie look so happy together.
(Photo by Vinnie Zuffante/Starfile)

Christie Brinkley, Alexa Ray Joel, and Billy watch a horse-jumping competition in the Hamptons during happier days. *(Photo by Brett Lee/Starfile)*

Billy, the band, and the cast and crew take a break during a video shoot. *(Photo by Danny Chin/Starfile)*

Who sez we can't dance? Billy gets down with his bad self during his show. *(Photo by Steve Joester/Starfile)*

Frank thinks, "If he only knew." Billy and his soon-to-be-erstwhile manager Frank Weber answer questions about Billy's upcoming Russian concerts at a press conference at the New York Public Library. *(Photo by Vinnie Zuffante/Starfile)*

Alexa Ray meets the werewolf: Billy introduces his daughter to Walter Yetnikoff, president of CBS Records. *(Photo by Ron Pownall/Starfile)*

The piano was trashed in the USSR. Not by me, though there *were* all those bottles of Stoli . . . Christie Brinkley and Billy donate to the Hard Rock Café in New York City the electric piano he threw off the stage in Moscow during a fit of pique. *(Photo by Chuck Pulin/Starfile)*

Pop music stars comparing notes: Daryl Hall, John Oates, Cyndi Lauper, and Billy talk tunes. *(Photo by Bob Gruen/Starfile)*

Billy Joel, Paul Simon, Mick Jones, and his new Foreigner bandmate, Johnny Edwards, backstage at a 1991 benefit for the preservation of Native American tribal lands in the Hamptons. *(Photo by Bob Gruen/Starfile)*

Billy and Jon Small compare notes with their mutual ex-wife, Elizabeth, at a party for Jon's fiftieth birthday. *(Photo by Bill Grieco; from the collection of Bruce Gentile)*

Billy and longtime sound man Brian Ruggles at Jon Small's fiftieth
birthday party. *(Photo from the collection of Bruce Gentile)*

A long way from the Rock House: Billy and
Bruce Gentile at the dedication of Billy Joel
Cold Spring Harbor Park, 1991. *(Photo by
Bill Grieco; from the collection of Bruce Gentile)*

The plaque for Billy Joel Cold Spring
Harbor Park, dedicated in 1991.
(Photo by Hank Bordowitz)

Brother Ray brings Billy into the Hall: Ray Charles inducts Billy into the Rock and Roll Hall of Fame at the annual dinner in 1999. *(Photo by Bob Gruen/Starfile)*

Jammin' with Billy, Paul McCartney, and Dion
at the Rock and Roll Hall of Fame induction in 1999.
(Photo by Bob Gruen/Starfile)

Billy and Judy Collins party with Bob Dylan
at the Whitney Museum in New York City.
(Photo by Vinnie Zuffante/Starfile)

Billy with artist and paramour Carolyn Beegan
at the Songwriters Hall of Fame ceremony in
1999. *(Photo by Chuck Pulin/Starfile)*

I'm a shameless fan: Garth Brooks congratu-
lates Billy on his Award of Merit backstage
at the American Music Awards ceremony in
1999. *(Photo by Vinnie Zuffante/Starfile)*

Billy parties with his soon-to-be bride Katie Lee at the China Club in New York after the 2003 Tony Awards. *(Photo by Dominick Conde/Starfile)*

DOESN'T MATTER WHAT THEY SAY IN THE PAPERS

Late in the winter of 1980, ads started appearing in the music-business trades with Billy in jeans and a leather jacket, in a field tossing a rock in the air, looking every inch the hood he had wanted to be as a teen. The legend said, "Hey—I got a little something for ya." In the lower-left corner was a picture of his new album, showing Billy in the same out-fit getting ready to toss the same rock at an enormous picture window.

Thus Columbia chose to announce the release of the newest Billy Joel album, *Glass Houses*, in February 1980. The album came out on the heels of the 22nd Grammy Awards on February 27, 1980. Once again Billy took home two of the trophies, an Album of the Year statuette and a Best Pop Vocal Performance, Male, both for the *52nd Street* album.

The experience of having won four Grammys and landing two multi-platinum albums had not been all Billy had hoped it would be. For one thing, of the seven hits from the two albums, three were bal-lads, a much higher percentage than he recorded in that genre. That had led to what Billy felt was a misperception of his work.

He recorded *Glass Houses* to disabuse both the press and the public of this image. It was Billy's effort to chuck some rock—hence the cover—at the public perception that he was a middle-of-the-road bal-lad singer.

But it was more than that. When Billy took the band into A&R Studios once more to lay tracks with Ramone, he had several other things on his mind. In the wake of his successes of the last couple of years, his live show had moved from relatively intimate venues to are-nas. To answer that, Billy had brought guitarist David Brown into the band on lead guitar. This allowed him to record *Glass Houses* with the notion of adding some coliseum-strength material to his shows—both in terms of the music and in terms of the sound. Steve Khan had allowed him a little more guitar leeway on *52nd Street*, and the addition of David Brown to the band on lead guitar offered him that much more.

Beyond that, the record reflected the state of pop music, brought into his home by his teenaged stepson Sean (whom he thanks "for the inspiration" in the liner notes). Any complexity in pop had largely caved in on itself by the time Billy was in the studio making *Glass Houses*. The songs and the relative starkness of the recording reflect that.

So, in addition to the "usual suspects" of pop radio like the Eagles, when "You May Be Right," the first single on *Glass Houses*, started working its way up the charts to #7 in the spring of 1980, it was also competing against newer blood like Blondie. The music on *Glass Houses* was at once Billy's reaction to the growing New Wave and his answer to it.

This became even more evident in the spring when the second single started climbing through the likes of Gary Numan's "Cars," Rocky Burnette's "Tired of Toein' the Line," and Lipps Inc.'s "Funkytown" (along with more generic fare like Bette Midler's "The Rose" and Olivia Neutron Bomb's "Magic"). That tune, "It's Still Rock and Roll to Me," became Billy's first single to top the *Billboard* Hot 100 Singles chart.

It was the song's bridge that threw gasoline on the flame war that had erupted between Billy and the press: "It doesn't matter what they say in the papers, 'cause it's always been the same old scene. There's a new band in town, but you can't get the sound from a story in a magazine aimed at your average teen."

The press responded in kind. "It's Still Rock and Roll to Me" was voted the worst song about rock and roll ever in a *Rolling Stone* critics poll. "The song is an out and out attack on the press, so why shouldn't it try to get even?" Billy wondered, amused. "I don't sit around and play footsie with the press, especially *Rolling Stone*. I have a running battle with them. I don't know when it started, but I know I'm not about to let it drop . . . I kind of dig it."

"'It's Still Rock and Roll to Me' wasn't against punk rock," he added. "I thought punk rock was healthy for the music business, which had gotten bloated."

"I thought about doing an album [during the '70s] called *The Age of Jive* and taking a pot shot at everything. But I'm no F. Scott Fitzgerald; I [was not] gonna be the conscience of the seventies."

"Sometimes a Fantasy," with a video that hinted at phone sex and lyrics that more than hinted at masturbation—the first line is "Oh, I didn't want to do it, but I got too lonely," which led Billy to admit, "What else could the song be about?"—didn't even raise eyebrows less than three years after Virginia had sparked a controversy with the Church. Consequently, it broke the Top 40, but just barely, peaking at #36.

The mid-tempo "Don't Ask Me Why," however, gave ammo to the people who were accusing Billy of going "middle of the road." The track did top the Adult Contemporary chart, while breaking into the pop Top 20. Even the Latinesque track had its experimental fillip. "In the midsection of the song 'Don't Ask Me Why,' there are fifteen pianos overdubbed on top of each other," Billy noted.

The closest thing to a ballad on the album was "C'Etait Toi," and it was also one of Billy's biggest musical misfires, by his own admission. "I don't think we'll ever play that song again. Although I like that song musically, I did it in French, and I don't even speak French, so I really made a mess out of that. It's not really a crowd pleaser, not even in France."

Despite the "bad press," *Glass Houses* spent six weeks at #1 on the *Billboard* 200 Albums chart. It quickly sold the 1 million copies required for platinum status in the United States. It also won the American Music Award for Album of the Year.

✿ ✿ ✿

By 1980, Billy was a cottage industry: The machine that Elizabeth had set up to manage his affairs was thorough and efficient. It had five separate divisions, but in all of them, the primary product was Billy Joel:

* Home Run System Corp. was the management company that represented Billy. As Billy became a larger draw, they also decided to take chances on some other acts, including the Australian band

the Sports and former Artful Dodger keyboard player Eric Troyer, who would have success as a sideman for artists ranging from Gene Simmons of Kiss to adult contemporary star Celine Dion.

* Impulsive Music/Joel Songs represented Billy's music publishing interests, which, with such enormously successful records, were sizable.
* Billy Joel Tours took tour production—how the show was staged, including the sound and lights—in house.
* Home Run Agency took Billy's concert booking in house as well.
* Roots Rags Ltd. created all Billy Joel merchandising material, from T-shirts to ties.

For her part, Elizabeth Joel was beginning to get tired of the music business at this point. She had helped to build Billy into one of pop music's most successful entities over the course of the last four years. But except for the fact that she was married to the career she was managing, it wasn't what she primarily wanted to do. In fact, her waning interest in the management company might have signified the beginning of her waning interest in her marriage to Billy.

"At this point, Elizabeth and I are only involved in the creative aspects of management," Billy said. "Elizabeth is no longer so much in the forefront."

As Elizabeth began removing herself from the business, her brother, Frank Weber, had begun to fill many of the gaps. She had brought him aboard from a position in marketing with a military electronics firm on Long Island. Initially both Weber and his wife were against the idea, but Elizabeth persisted. "She said Billy's business had outgrown her ability to handle it, there were so many people—lawyers and accountants—involved," Weber recalls.

Billy's instincts told him that this might not be such a hot idea. "I had questions about somebody's brother coming," he said. "Because she had brought Frank in, I thought it would help preserve the marriage by having someone . . . handle the management and the business for me and her to have . . . another agreement."

As part of the deal that kept the marriage together, Billy signed an agreement that split his and Elizabeth's assets evenly.

By 1980, Weber was with Home Run full time and slowly began taking on more and more of the business of Billy Joel as Elizabeth's interest continued to wane. He was joined by people like Jeff Schock, who began to help market Billy. Rick London, Weber's brother-in-law, took on much of the accounting.

Weber took his job very seriously, saying, "When you are working with managing someone's career, you are dealing with his life so it is not wise to make arbitrary decisions. We offer the choices."

Ironically, even with three multi-platinum records under his belt, millions of miles on the road, and a war chest full of songs, Billy was far from wealthy. "People think I've got this multimillion-dollar mansion," he said at the time. "I paid $300,000 for it, and it wasn't even money up front; I've got a mortgage. I'm not a multimillionaire. Frankly I'm not sure what I'm worth . . . I honestly don't know and don't ask.

"That's why I have lawyers and managers to keep it fairly distant from me."

That distance would come up to bite him on the ass before very long.

✿ ✿ ✿

The *Glass Houses* tour, Billy's fourth extensive and extended tour in as many years, played throughout Israel and Europe during the early days of the spring of 1980, and played throughout the United States until late into the summer. In June he played another five sold-out nights at Madison Square Garden in New York.

On the occasion of those shows, *New York Times* rock critic Robert Palmer saw fit to take some pot shots at Billy: "He has won a huge following by making emptiness seem substantial and Holiday Inn lounge schlock sound special . . . Yes, Mr. Joel has written some memorable pop melodies. Yes he's an energetic, flamboyant performer. But no, this listener can't stand him . . . He's the sort of popular artist who makes elitism seem not just defensible but necessary."

Around the same time, Billy and Elizabeth were turned down for an apartment in New York's venerable Dakota, the fortress on the corner of Central Park West and 72nd Street where former Beatle guitarist John Lennon had lived and in front of which he would be gunned down by a deranged fan later that year. Other celebrities living there at the time included Roberta Flack, Lauren Bacall, and Gilda Radner.

"I was turned down for an apartment at the Dakota because I was an admitted drug user," Billy said, amazed. "In an interview I did a long time ago, I admitted I once smoked a joint before going onstage. That came up in the meeting with the Dakota board—these bankers and lawyers. We're looked at as undesirables—addicted to drugs and sex orgies. In truth, we happen to be duller than those bankers."

The board admitted this was part of the reason, along with the problem of "groupies," like the fans of John Lennon who hung out outside the apartment's gate, and "a growing feeling that there are already enough celebrities and not enough families in the building."

Billy was so upset by both the Palmer article and the piece in the *Times* about the Dakota board that he ripped up both onstage during the Garden shows.

However, Billy and his team realized that articles like these were symptomatic of a larger issue—how Billy was perceived. He had become a superstar in a similar way that his Long Island elder Rodney Dangerfield had—with no respect. For Rodney, however, it was part of the act. For Billy it was a problem.

As he and Columbia could afford the best, they took this problem to the most successful spinmeister in the music business at the time, Howard Bloom.

"I was an expert at taking people who had a deep, fundamental, profound validity that the press was missing," Bloom explains, "discovering that validity in every way I could, and demonstrating that validity to the press."

Through his company, the Howard Bloom Organization, he had successfully launched or transformed the careers of artists ranging from funk phenomenon Prince to blue-eyed-soul stars Daryl Hall and John Oates to heartland rocker John Mellencamp—in the latter case, a transformation that included a name change from the stage name John Cougar to his real last name.

Bloom had already had professional contact with Billy Joel, albeit indirectly. Shortly after Billy had dissociated himself from Artie Ripp,

Bloom had become the head of publicity at Gulf & Western's music division. The press Billy had garnered for *Cold Spring Harbor* was in the files he had inherited.

"Ten years after I had worked at Gulf & Western, Billy came to me, with the following problem: First the press had loved him, then there had been a huge gap," Bloom explains. "Then he came up unexpectedly in the press and became a major hit-maker. The press doesn't like it if you become a major hit-maker without them. Their ego investment is no longer in building you; their ego investment is now tearing you down. So the press was tearing Billy down.

"The archetypal article was one in the *Los Angeles Times* by Robert Hilburn. It was a full, two-page spread with two face-to-face reviews. Basically it was saying that this is why I love, and you should love, this artist on the right-hand page, and on the other page was this is why you should hate this artist. Now, the artist you were supposed to love was Bob Seger. The artist you were supposed to hate was Billy Joel.

"I had to tell Billy's story at length to people. I had to take them to lunch and spend three hours talking to them, and so did Elaine Schock. In fact, the first person I had to convert was Elaine. Elaine was my publicist on the case, and Elaine was part of the press clique—publicists felt that they couldn't be good publicists if they couldn't be part of that clique. What they didn't realize was that they took on the same viewpoints as that clique, and they hated certain of their clients—Elaine hated Billy Joel. She didn't want to work with him. She hated him because she was supposed to. She was supposed to hate what Robert Hilburn hated. It took me three months to convert Elaine to Billy Joel."

"I thought I was so cool," Schock says almost sheepishly. "I mean, *Billy Joel!* So, Howard had to turn me into a convert, because I had been on 'the other side' . . . He was able to change my mind completely. And once I was converted, I stayed."

In the early part of pleading Billy's case to influential writers, Bloom and Schock appealed to one thing they knew writers had in common, a very basic thing. Writers tended to be literary. Writers understood what separated good writing from bad writing. Most music critics, rather than coming from a music background, more often came from a literary background.

"As writers, one of the first things they look at are lyrics," says Bloom. "They judge artists, to a large extent, by the lyrics. Well, Billy Joel is one of the finest lyric writers of the twentieth century. In reality, though I love Bob Seger, and there's no reason ever to put Bob Seger down, if you compared the lyrics of Bob Seger to the lyrics of Billy Joel, it took only two and a half minutes to see that Bob Seger is an ordinary lyricist and that Billy Joel is an extraordinary lyricist. So I showed Elaine, literally, how to take one page of Billy Joel lyrics and one page of Bob Seger lyrics, lay them down next to each other, and let a person who has gone to college as an English major take a look at them. There's no contest, even though you have to spend three to four hours explaining, even though you might have to do that explaining for two years straight.

"Well, once Elaine got it, she went to Bob Hilburn. Elaine had come from California with [*Rolling Stone* editor] Jim Henke, so she knew Bob and the California clique. I knew the New York clique. Between us, we turned them around.

"Now, when I explained to Billy what I wanted to do at the very beginning, he glowed. He loved it."

Schock, as it turned out, would become a far more intricate (and intimate) part of Billy Joel's organization than even she realized. "I met my first husband, Jeff, at a meeting at Howard's, and as we were going over the plan, I thought Jeff was writing down what our publicity plan was. He was actually drawing my legs. I looked back and it was like, 'What!?' That was my first encounter with Jeff and the Billy Joel management team at that point, which included Jeff, Rick London, and Frank Weber."

Schock, however, was unavailable at the time, and in fact living with Henke. This gave her a major edge in reaching rock tastemakers. "Timothy White [author and frequent *Rolling Stone* contributor at the time] had already written this story 'The Angry Young Man,'" she recalls. "Billy hated that story. He was like, 'Everybody hates me, blah, blah, blah.' I said, 'It's because they don't know you.' We made a plan. My best friends were *Rolling Stone* editors, journalists, et cetera. I was living with the music editor of *Rolling Stone* at the time, so I knew all the critics. Billy so completely changed my mind that I knew all I had to do was bring him around to all the influential critics. I did that, and he was so charming and smart and so good that he changed their minds, including Timothy White's. I mean, Timothy White became a good buddy of his."

❁ ❁ ❁

In 1981, Billy's contract with Columbia was up. Having spent so much money and time, and then having earned so much money, Columbia wanted to keep him. And so negotiations were begun.

As Elizabeth had backed away from the business and Frank Weber took more and more control of the reins, the team that Elizabeth had put into place was slowly supplanted. One person who went was attorney Ina Meibach, whom Weber replaced with attorney Frank Tannen. By all accounts (including his own) CBS president Walter Yetnikoff intensely disliked Tannen. As Weber and Yetnikoff sat down for initial parlays about the contract, Yetnikoff let Weber know that he would be easier to negotiate with if Weber had a different attorney. On Yetnikoff's recommendation, Weber hired Alan Grubman from Grubman, Indursky and Schindler. Grubman had done legal work for Home Run, but he was also one of Yetnikoff's yes-men.

"I liked controlling Alan Grubman," Yetnikoff declared, "which is why I set him up with some of our biggest artists. In short order, the Grubber was representing Bruce Springsteen and Billy Joel. Dealing with a non-confrontational lawyer made my life easier. I'd never have to worry about Grubman suing me. 'I don't know how,' he'd joke, though I believed the joke."

One of the key negotiating points was the 25 cents that went to Artie Ripp and Michael Lang from every Billy Joel record sold. Up to that point, it had been a recoupable expense on Billy's side of the record-company ledger. "The only way Billy signed again to Columbia was they said, 'We'll pay the quarter to them. It doesn't come from your money anymore,'" says Sandy Gibson. "Artie still gets a quarter from every Billy Joel record sold, as does Michael, but Columbia pays it now, not Billy. And you know who told me this? Tony Martell."

Tony, who had run the Gulf & Western record entity, had returned to Columbia after the demise and dissolution of Gulf & Western. His son, T.J., had passed on after his battle with leukemia. Martell had gone on to become a senior VP at Columbia and even interim president for a time, as well as the spearhead of the music industry's anti-cancer initiative, which he named after his son: the T.J. Martell Foundation.

The negotiations between Billy's machine and Columbia were, by all reports, fierce. During the negotiations, for example, Walter Yetnikoff literally shredded one of Alan Grubman's shirts in a moment of heat. Yet when Grubman, Weber, and Columbia finally brought the deal they hammered out to Billy, he wasn't even concerned with what was in it. He effectively just asked, "Where do I sign?"

At the 1981 Grammy Awards, Billy won Best Rock Vocal Performance, Male for *Glass Houses*. But Billy still hadn't found what he was looking for on a record. "For years, I didn't think our records were up to the standards of our concerts," he said. "They're kinda hard for me to listen to."

To prove the point, he eschewed a studio album as his first on his new Columbia contract, in 1981. Instead, he released a live recording. However, rather than just the standard "greatest hits live" package, Billy opted for something a little different. Throughout the previous tours, he had recorded many shows. Into each show, he slipped in one of the "songs that got away," including songs from *Cold Spring Harbor* that even his more serious fans had never heard. Thus, he was able to compile an album of pre-*Stranger* songs like "Miami 2017" and "Los Angelenos." Two of the songs actually went on to become hits. Even Ronnie Spector, backed by Steve Van Zandt and members of the E Street Band, hadn't been able to make a hit of "Say Goodbye to Hollywood," but the live version finally took the song into the Top 20. Further, a refugee from *Cold Spring Harbor*, the ballad "She's Got a Way," fulfilled a decade-old destiny and finally made the charts, peaking at #23 on the *Billboard* Hot 100 Singles chart.

CHAPTER 15

I CAME HOME TO A WOMAN THAT I COULD NOT RECOGNIZE

While his music career was going great guns, Billy's marriage had hit the skids as the '70s segued into the '80s. Elizabeth had grown tired of the music business and all its accoutrements. "The more he kept doing drugs," says Sandy Gibson, "the more he kept getting pulled away by other women, the less she liked it. She really didn't like the music business."

"Around late spring of 1980, we were talking about a transition for both of us," Billy said. "It was evolving as far back as that. We just slowly, steadily grew apart."

One of the ways he dealt with his growing frustration on the home front was riding his motorcycles. "When you're on a motorcycle," Billy said, "no one can tell who you are . . . so that's a way to get away from it."

Over the years, he had built up quite a collection of them, some rare, some just very powerful. Howard Bloom has gone so far as to describe him as "a motorcycle fetishist. He just loves the hell out of his motorcycles.

"I had a motorcycle back then," Bloom adds. "We used to talk about motorcycling down to the Jersey shore together. Billy would say, 'Oh, yeah, your Honda 550 is a good motorcycle, and those four cylinders are a good idea, but if you really want to apply it right, you've got to get a BMW.' So Billy had a BMW, and he had a bunch of other motorcycles that had a bunch of different riding characteristics."

"A motorcycle," Billy concedes, "is an amusement-park ride. It's dangerous. Everybody out on the road is out to get you ."

At about 5:40 P.M., on April 15, 1982, Cornelia Bynum of Huntington made a turn at the intersection of New York Avenue and West 9th Street in Huntington. Making the turn, she ran into Billy on one of his bikes, a 1978 Harley-Davidson. "You know those roads out on Long Island," Bloom adds. "A lot of them are lonely little roads, very little traffic, lots of trees. Billy was riding along on one of those roads on one of his motorcycles. He went through a green light. A woman coming on the road at right angles to him did not stop for the red light and plowed straight into him."

"I felt absolutely helpless while I watched myself flipping over the car and bang, I landed on my back," Billy recalls. "Right before I hit, I had a flood of images, jumbled-up thoughts. I thought I was going to die and I was pissed off at the car, which looked the size of Brooklyn to me. I thought, 'You can't do this to me, I'm not ready to die.'"

When he realized he wasn't dead, he took inventory. The bike, of course, was ruined. But he found that he was able to get to his feet. It might have been the shock, or it might have been that boxing all those years had inured him to pain—broken knuckles are a way of life for boxers. As he notes, "There's a scar on every single knuckle . . . I didn't realize my hand was hurt after the spill on the bike until I tried to drag it out of the intersection . . . I found that I couldn't and glanced down to see that my left wrist was the size of a grapefruit and my thumb was split open with the bone and all this red junk hanging out. I was plenty upset, naturally, but I just thought, 'Broken wrist. Broken thumb. Need a good surgeon and time to mend.'"

"We were afraid for Billy's life," Bloom says of the immediate aftermath of the accident. "Billy had to be medevaced by helicopter to Columbia Presbyterian Hospital in Manhattan. First we were afraid for his life. Then we were afraid for his hand. I mean, this guy makes his living with his fingers. Without his fingers, his brain has no way of communicating with other people. We were afraid he was going to lose them."

He spent hours in surgery as Dr. David Andrews fixed his wrist and thumb. By the time he was out, it was pretty certain that he would have use of his hand, but to what degree was not known. As the hand healed, it became evident that the surgery had repaired the vast majority of the damage. "Dexterity is not a problem," Billy said at the time, "but stamina may be. As a result of the damage that was done, certain muscles atrophied while my hand was in the cast . . . I still plan to do a two-and-a-half-hour set, and pump the keys to reach the kid in the last row of the arena, but I won't know my physical shortcomings until I have to face them."

"The biggest thing I learned from the accident was that when you think you have all the control in the world, suddenly someone is going to run a red light."

Billy soon found out that he had less control than he thought, and learned another important lesson about the nature of stardom. While stardom had many perks, including the ability to collect motorcycles, there were many downsides as well. When you're a star, every encounter makes you a potential target.

"Not only did she hit him," says Bloom of Bynum, "then she hit him with a lawsuit. And she knew she was wrong. She knew the damage she had done. My understanding is, the woman got out of her car, saw what she had done to this guy, and was beyond apologetic. She was mortified.

"Within two days, her mortification turned totally around. Why? Apparently, she went to consult with a lawyer, and the lawyer, in all probability, said something like this: 'You don't realize, you just hit the jackpot. This is a star. If you sue a star, the star has to settle with you. The star has to settle in order to keep the story out of the papers. The star can't afford to be the subject of tabloid headlines for the next year and a half while the trial goes on if you accuse him of hitting you, so I strongly advise you to accuse him of hitting you, so we can hit him with a seven-million-dollar suit, and he'll settle for, let's say a million and a quarter.' So that's exactly what the woman who hit him did."

And, as the lawyer hypothetically predicted, Billy, fuming, settled out of court.

To add further insult to the injury, rumor had it that his insurance company told Billy that if he ever rode his motorcycle again, his policy on his hands would be canceled. Whether or not that was the reason, the accident put him off his iron horses. He never got back in the saddle again, at least in public. Not that it would, as things turned out, keep him out of trouble on the roads.

Elizabeth had ridden the wave with Billy. She'd caught it when he was but a teenager (and she not all that far into her twenties), having his first whiff of rock and roll success. She rode it through the trough that saw them living penniless in southern California, with the Ventura Freeway running through the window of their motel room. She rode into the crest of the wave as *Piano Man* segued into *Streetlife Serenade* and into *Turnstiles*, and his career finally exploded when she took charge from *The Stranger* through *Glass Houses*. And now, after riding the wave for more than a dozen years, she was tired of it. She no longer had the taste for the lifestyle of rock and its roller-coaster thrills, and she had outgrown it.

Billy, on the other hand, seemed to be enjoying the sex and drugs and rock and roll, and increasingly the sex was not with Elizabeth, who had also lost interest in the drugs (if she ever had it to begin with). "There was cocaine traveling in Billy's circle," Bloom says discretely. "Here's a person I love, and here's a person I think has more than an intellect. Intellect is very raw and useless stuff unless it's combined with emotions. Billy had that combination of emotion and intellect. And he had that creative inspiration that makes you an artist. So, to see somebody that I loved, for all these reasons, stoned and surrounded by people who were stoned, was not a pleasant thing at all."

Shortly after he left the hospital, in the summer of 1982, Billy and Elizabeth split up. The divorce was not easy, as it had to be done on several levels. The personal level is never easy. Getting a divorce is like having a root canal. Sure, it hurts like hell before it happens. But the actual pain of it happening is something else again, compared with dealing with the extended course of cleaning out the infection, packing it off, and the rest of the treatment. A root canal can take weeks— a divorce can take years.

"It really shook me up when my marriage didn't work out," Billy said. "I was one of those people who intended for that to last forever, like with swans. But I found out that we're not swans, we're people."

Ultimately, Billy accepted the divorce and, with a certain resigned equanimity, said, "She's a good friend and I hope not to lose that."

But Billy and Elizabeth had more than just civil issues to sort out. They were also business partners, and for many of the same reasons she wanted out of the marriage, she wanted out of the business. "If it were up to her, she'd rather be in museums all over Europe," Sandy Gibson explained. "She didn't want to talk to Walter Yetnikoff, really.

"She tried to do everything honorably. I could say she's stern, I could say she's a stick in the mud sometimes, but she is *honorable!* She didn't want to screw him. They made money together—you take your part, I'll take my part. Of course, she was also his wife. She was going to get a big part, but so what? He had the rest of his career."

Billy tried to do things honorably too at first, though naïvely. His attorney in the divorce was a lawyer Elizabeth had introduced to him. "I think what had happened, Elizabeth handed me a . . . contract, and I sat with [attorney] Ron Williams and he explained what every paragraph meant."

The attorney made no effort to abridge the decree, and Billy wound up owing Elizabeth half of not just everything he had made previous to the divorce, but on all future earnings from intellectual property created previous to the divorce. He agreed to pay Elizabeth $3 million for her anticipated share of the pre-1984 song copyrights.

"I shouldn't have gotten married," Billy said in retrospect. "She said we either had to get married or our relationship was over, so I said, 'OK.'"

In the meantime, Elizabeth's brother Frank, who had been consolidating power at Home Run for the past three years, was suddenly in a quandary. With his sister out of the picture, what would Billy do about management? "[Elizabeth] was bored with the business, tired of hanging out backstage," Weber recalled. "They had a spat and Billy told me, 'It has nothing to do with your gig.'"

"Elizabeth suggested several other managers he could have," says Sandy Gibson. "And I guess the family suggested Frank."

On the face of it, if Billy could get past the fact that Frank was the brother not just of the person he'd replaced in the Hassles, but his ex-wife as well, Frank would have seemed a natural to take over for Elizabeth. He had, for all intents and purposes, been running the business aspects of being Billy Joel for the previous three years. He knew where everything was, in terms of the books and the players.

While Elizabeth had called on him to help, apparently there was more sibling rivalry then revelry between Frank and her. Frank started pointing out to Billy mistakes he claimed she had made. Frank accompanied Billy when he got his Haitian divorce. And he sued his sister for monies he claimed she owed him from their deal when he came on board.

"Elizabeth's brother is a dog," opines Gibson. "The first thing they did was turn around and sue Elizabeth. They got at least twenty-five percent of the money she earned. She had to stay by the phone. In New York City, you have to go to court, and if you miss the phone call, you only have three hours and they'll start without you. She spent a year or two by the phone until that was finally settled. They were so mean to her. Man, did her own brother sue her."

CHAPTER 16

A FOOL WHO'S NOT AFRAID OF REJECTION

After two months of recovery, Billy was ready to try his rebuilt hand. He spent a good hunk of the summer of 1982 at A&R Studios with his band and Phil Ramone. After more than half a dozen years of working together, the Billy Joel Band had become quite a cohesive unit, based on the idea of a power trio—with a twist. Where the traditional power trio—like the Who or Billy's beloved Led Zeppelin—consisted of bass, drums, and guitar, Billy took the guitarist's role in his band, and in creative terms the guitarist took the role that the occasional keyboard player would in the Who—overdubs and ornamentation.

"We have a trio called the Mean Brothers, which consists of me, Doug on bass and Liberty on drums," he explained. "We always lay down the basic tracks. Then the guitars and horns come in and do their thing. The Mean Brothers have their own satin road jackets with Doberman pinschers on the back."

His time in the hospital and recovering must have been, for Billy, an unusual period for reflection. Howard Bloom might be overstating things when he calls Billy one of the finest lyricists of the twentieth century, but certainly he ranks along with Pete Townshend and Bruce "The Thinkin' Fool" Springsteen as one of rock's first tier—especially when you consider that he regards lyrics as secondary to the music. With the set he recorded in the wake of his accident, he showed a quantum leap in his willingness to tackle new topics.

"The album," he half joked, "opens with four songs about, respectively, unemployment, guilt, pressure and war—The Four Horsemen of the Apocalyptic American landscape."

This was serious stuff. It took a lot out of Billy to write it, but ultimately he was very satisfied with the results. "When I was through with the album," he said, "I thought that it was a very American album. I thought that it was about growing up behind some kind of curtain or barrier. It struck me that nylon is a very American material, and it stuck."

Once again, he faced off against "the big black beast with eighty-eight teeth." *The Nylon Curtain* might have been his most decisive, if derivative, victory against it. Musically, it's his most Beatles-inspired album, with nearly every song having a post–*Rubber Soul* twist. He fuses string quartets (a favorite George Martin/Beatles affectation) with synthpop, contrasts the Leninisms of "Allentown" with the Lennonisms of "A Room of Our Own," and the McCarthyisms of "Goodnight Saigon" with the McCartneyisms of "Scandinavian Skies." Musically, it was something he might have had in the back of his mind since that sad day in 1970 when the Fab Four announced they would play no more.

"He loved the Beatles so much," said longtime friend Bill Zampino, who would become his road manager, "that after they broke up, he'd say, 'It's a shame that you can't hear more songs from the Beatles. Maybe I'll write myself one to cheer me up,' and then he would."

With its musical complexities and lyrical depth, *The Nylon Curtain* may well have been the hardest thing Billy Joel had created as a solo artist. "I feel like I almost died making *The Nylon Curtain*," Billy said. "The thing you don't have control over is writing—you have to pull it out of yourself, stretch yourself . . . You pace the room with something like the dry heaves, having no control over the muse, horrified that it won't come. You're always in the desert looking for the oasis, and all that's out there with you is the piano . . . You have to lay your guts on the table and go through them eleven times on an album. Fifty thousand packs of cigarettes later, you start getting it."

The most evident reflection on his recent mishap, hospitalization, and recovery was the song "Surprises," which even he says was written as "I tried to remember . . . what was going through my mind at the time of the accident."

The Nylon Curtain will stand as a document of its time, one of the few early-'80s albums that took the Walter Cronkite approach to its lyrics: It didn't make the news, but it did report it. Most of the editorializing was done on the musical level. For example, while "Pressure" dealt lyrically with all the input of daily life in the twentieth century, the tension level was heightened dramatically with the edgy combinations of strings and synthesizers.

"We used a lot of the panning and phasing that I loved on albums like *Electric Ladyland* and lots of exotic touches layered on top of layers. For the tag line of 'Pressure' we laid six synthesizer tracks over each other and then we got four Russian balalaika players from Brooklyn to come in, after they'd done some orthodox wedding, to play from the charts we gave them . . . They spoke in broken English. They didn't know me from Adam!"

While Billy claimed the album eschewed politics, two of the songs were strong statements of the human toll of the waning days of the Reagan era. Less a political broadside than, for example, Michael Moore's film *Roger and Me* would be some seven years later, "Allentown" nonetheless took a hard look at the human devastation that the downsizing, deporting, and dying of American industry could wreak on a community that had largely counted on one industry for survival—in this case, the rust belt, especially in Pennsylvania's Lehigh Valley.

"Allentown is a metaphor for America," Billy said. "It sounds like Jimmytown, Bobbyburg, Anytown . . . I tried to write the song 'Levittown' before I tried to write 'Allentown,' but it didn't sing as well."

In the wake of the song, 16,000 citizens of Allentown petitioned him to play there on his next tour. On the tour, he played Lehigh University in neighboring Bethlehem—it was the biggest venue in the area—for more than 6,000 fans. Before the show he got the key to the city. "I just wrote a song," he demurred on accepting the honor. "I'm not Thomas Edison. Let's not blow this all out of proportion."

"Allentown" was not an easy song to write. Not that Billy couldn't place himself in the role of an unemployed person without much hope for the future. He had been there. So, with the closing of manufacturing plants throughout Long Island, had many of his old chums. It was just hard to see America in these kinds of terms. "It was literally the fifth time I sat down to write it," he said, "and it became a song about the solitary anguish of unemployment and the current climate of diminishing horizons."

As with most of his songs, it started out as a musical composition. He set out to musically reflect the multiple facets of the area. The area, which sits in a valley in the foothills of the Appalachians (as the chain of mountains starts to do its cartographic morph into the Poconos and Adirondacks) combines great natural beauty with heavy industry, a working class, and some of the more renowned universities on the East Coast.

"I like the straight-force piano resonance in 'Allentown,'" Billy says of the musical composition itself, "an Aaron Copeland–influenced arrangement of major sevenths that's percussive and stirring. Gives me goosebumps it's got so much classic, shoulder-to-the-wheel Americana in it . . . I started writing that ten years ago while hitting the circuit of colleges in the Lehigh Valley."

While it wasn't a "hit" per se, "Goodnight Saigon" also attracted a fair amount of attention for its look at the human toll of the Vietnam conflict ten years after the fall of what became Ho Chi Minh City. "I wasn't trying to make a comment on the war, but writing about the sol-dier as a person."

He knew many of them. Lots of people from his area of Long Island didn't even wait to be drafted. They joined up hoping to be sent into the conflict.

Although he had evaded and avoided the draft, there were many survivors of Vietnam among the people with whom Billy had grown up. When he decided that was what the song would be about, he went to them and started to draw them out on their experiences in the war. Initially there was great reticence, but ultimately he got a picture of what it was like—a far different one than Hollywood had to offer. Frank McCarthy, president of Vietnam Veterans Against Agent Orange, wrote that the song was the first that actually expressed the experience of soldiers who'd lived through the war. The song further inspired California congresswoman Barbara Boxer to co-sponsor legis-lation to compensate Vietnam vets for Agent Orange disabilities.

The album pleased Walter Yetnikoff. While he recognized that the subject matter might be a tough sell, he respected both the growth it displayed and Billy's serious convictions. What he didn't respect was the first cover, a picture of a body under a bolt of cloth.

"I wanted the album jacket to look like a book cover," Billy said, "the latest novel from Ludlum or Michener . . . CBS wanted my picture on the front, but I'm sick of my face."

In typical fashion, Yetnikoff called Billy to tantrum on him over the cover art.

"I'm not having it," Walter said.

"What's wrong with it?" Billy asked.

"Everything. What's that body doing on the floor? And why is it covered with a *shmata*?" asked the CBS head honcho, slipping in the juicy Yiddish word for "rag."

"That's the Nylon Curtain."

"That's the Nylon *Shmata*. If you want to throw away your album because of a stupid cover, just call it *The Nylon Shmata*."

"I thought the cover was artistic."

"You want arty-farty, Billy, or do you want sales?"

Both Billy and Walter wanted sales. Columbia changed the cover, and both men got their way. The nylon *shmata* went away but wasn't replaced by Billy's wise-guy-falling-asleep-in-class visage. Indeed, with a reverse letterbox effect, it did look like a book cover, the sun setting on cubistic rows of identical houses, a suburban vision couched as a post-industrial (nearly Soviet modern) nightmare. The album sold, eventually moving more than 2 million copies in the United States alone. It reached #7 on the *Billboard* 200 Albums chart and earned a 1982 Grammy nomination for Album of the Year.

However, *The Nylon Curtain* only had two songs that actually made the Top 40 on the *Billboard* Pop Singles chart: "Pressure," which rose to #20, and "Allentown," which hit a little higher at #17.

The year before *The Nylon Curtain* came out, *Billboard* began to mirror the change in the listening audience, the way that audience listened, and the fractionalization and factionalization of radio itself in the wake of these changes. The music-business trade magazine of record instituted charts that reflected what formats other than pop/top 40/contemporary hits, adult contemporary, and R&B radio were playing. Certainly "album-rock" radio had been around for some time, but now there was a way to prove how well a record was actually doing in that format. It was on the album-rock stations that *The Nylon Curtain* enjoyed its greatest success, with "Pressure" hitting #8, and "Allentown," "Scandinavian Skies," and "A Room of Our Own" all reaching the format's Top 40. Billy finally had certifiable proof of one of his core ambitions. Rock, at least rock radio, had embraced him.

MADE HIS MOVE ON CHRISTIE LEE

After a relatively short tour that culminated with a New Year's Eve performance at Madison Square Garden, Billy found himself back home. Only now the home was empty.

"I just have to get used to being on my own," he said. "I'm dating people, but I don't expect bachelorhood to change my life-style that much. I'm not Errol Flynn; I live quietly and mostly hang out with old friends. I'd make a bad playboy."

On the other hand, if he made a bad playboy, you couldn't tell it by the women he had started dating. His long-stunted rock and roll libido began to exhibit its full bloom in the wake of his divorce. It was the era of the rock star and the supermodel, of Mick Jagger and Jerry Hall, Elvis Costello and Bebe Beull, Axl Rose and Stephanie Seymour, and on and on. Billy joined this fray with gusto. "One of the first relationships I had after I became unmarried was with Elle MacPherson when she first came to America . . . We used to go for walks and I had to lift up my arm to hold her hand . . ."

He decided to take a vacation, and seeing as it was the middle of winter in New York, he booked a cruise to the Caribbean, where he could get some sun, relax, and perhaps plan his next move. As the old Yiddish saying goes, man plans, God laughs. Before he even set foot on the boat, he met supermodel Christie Brinkley.

Brinkley was dealing with some heartache of her own. Her longtime flame, Oliver Chandon, of the Moet et Chandon Chandons, had recently been killed in a car-racing accident. Like Billy, she took the cruise to get away and get some relaxation and perspective. They met at the airport as they waited for the plane that would take them to the ship's port of debarkation.

"I saw her getting on a plane to go to this island in the Caribbean," Billy recalls. "I said, 'That's Christie Brinkley!' I recognized her immediately and tried to get her to recognize me."

This act of "trying to get her to recognize" him demonstrated a quantum leap from the Billy Joel who once claimed he had only two friends in high school. Billy Joel approaching a supermodel showed that, despite protestations to the contrary, he was beginning to be comfortable with at least the perks of being a superstar. While he couldn't go to Yankee Stadium anymore, he could realistically approach a famous and beautiful woman without a surety of being shot down.

It turned out that she was on the same plane as Billy because she was going on the same cruise as Billy. Billy discovered this when he ran into her again several days later. This time—shades of Virginia Callaghan—she did notice him because he was doing the thing that made him most notable, making music.

"I started playing a piano in a lounge," he recalled. "There were these three women who started watching me. It turned out to be Elle MacPherson, Whitney Houston, and Christie . . . Whitney was this annoying sixteen-year-old model who kept telling me 'Let me sing' and I kept telling her to shut up."

Eventually, on that cruise he hooked up in the aforementioned relationship with MacPherson. However, that evening when he finished, he and Brinkley started talking. Billy was smitten. Christie, still on the mend from a tragedy, was not ready to enter into anything.

"We were friends first," Billy says. "I was nuts about her, but it took her a while to reciprocate."

"[Billy was] a strong support for me," Christie adds. "It's his heart and soul, you know, that made me want to marry him."

Billy was overjoyed. When they started dating seriously, several months after the cruise, he and Christie would check into hotels as Rocky and Sandy Beach. In the blush of the new relationship, Billy started working on his next album. He called his publicist and adviser Howard Bloom and invited him to brunch to talk about it.

"I met him at the apartment," Bloom recalls, the apartment being

Billy's pied-à-terre in one of the hotels on New York City's tony Central Park South. "We were going to go down to Rumplemayer's. He had this black-and-white marble student notebook. He said, 'The most amazing thing happened to me last night. I have to tell you about it over breakfast.' This was the tale:

"'In Long Island, when I was growing up, I always thought of girls as "broads." You had nothing to talk about, you had nothing in common with them. You just told them anything you thought they wanted to hear in order to score. Girls were there to score. Girls were there basically as trophies, so you could go back to the boys hanging out, the whole idea was that it wasn't sleeping with the girl that mattered, it was coming back and saying, "Hey, I scored. I got that girl last night." But you never talked to them. They were a different species. It's just like they were living on a different planet.' Billy was explaining this. These are my words, not his.

"He said, 'I met this girl. I could talk to her. She wasn't like the broads on Long Island, she was intelligent, and we talked all night long. We talked until four o'clock in the morning. And you know what I did between four o'clock and now?' And he handed me the notebook and opened it. He had a complete album of songs. Billy Joel, the man who used to pace in his music room out in Long Island, in this big house overlooking the water, facing the piano, and agonized by the fact that everything he wrote was derivative, agonized by the fact that he couldn't come up with a song, had written an entire album after he had met this incredible woman, Christie Brinkley.

"The difficulty was that, it was the first time in his life that Billy Joel had been totally derivative. Now, one day I had been with Billy out at the house in Long Island, and he said, 'You have no idea how hard it is for me to write songs. It's a terrible experience. I have to lock myself in a room with a piano, and I pace back and forth, and I'm tortured. And the songs come out of me with such difficulty. And I'll tell you something about my songs, every one of them disappoints me. They're all derivative.'

"When he said that, I went into a little shock, and basically said the kind of things that I was saying to the press: 'Billy, you have no idea what you're doing. Of course it's derivative. Everything is derivative.

Everything has roots, but your stuff is brilliantly original. And here's why.' I don't think there was anyone else around to tell him that in really credible ways.

"So I was shocked, because everything he wrote on that album was a cliché. Obviously there's something about this album that I don't know, that I don't understand, because the album sold four million copies, right off the bat. What was Billy giving to people with 'Uptown Girl'? What am I missing?"

What Bloom seemed to miss was that Billy was practically giddy and so was the album, *An Innocent Man*. The songs he wrote were an homage to all of the pop music he had grown up with. He had tributes to a cappella doo-wop, a note-perfect Frankie Valli and the Four Seasons tribute, and liberal tastes of Stax Soul, Little Richard, Motown, the Righteous Brothers, and the Drifters. It was the Billy Joel rock 'n' roll review, and there was so much joy in the disc, it practically exploded out of the package.

"I decided I wanted to have as much fun as I could have, and I wanted it to *sound* like I was having fun," Billy says. "It doesn't really ape anything. It just *feels* like it. There actually isn't a standard chord progression in the LP. It's musically pretty complex. The challenging thing for me was making it feel so simple.

"On every album I adopt a different sort of character, and the character on this album is sort of a sweet person who is in love and feeling good. It's a guy enjoying the courtship rituals—making out, dating, slow dancing—and the insecurities that go with it—the gamut of passions that come with romance. I wrote ten songs in about seven weeks, which I've never done before. It just came pouring out of me."

The album was clearly the work of someone in love, but more than that, it was the work of a more mature person and artist. Billy was now thirty-four years old. He was eighteen when he had met Elizabeth. This was also the '80s, and the rules of relationships had changed. Technically, Billy was still married to Elizabeth (the divorce wouldn't be final until 1984), and for a while he kept the relationship low key, but the first single off the album, "Tell Her About It," was full of the new rules of romance.

"You should communicate your feelings to somebody you're in love with," he advised "despite the insecurity that brings."

The song topped the *Billboard* Pop Singles singles chart as well as the Adult Contemporary chart. Another of the Adult Contemporary chart toppers, as well as a Top 30 pop hit, "Leave a Tender Moment Alone" was a companion piece to "Tell Her About It." Together they formed a sort of musical yin and yang of songs about relationships.

"You say something really tender and affectionate and a part of you thinks 'I don't believe I said something that corny,'" Billy says, "so . . . you've got to make some kind of humorous comment to cover yourself."

Billy and Christie effectively announced their relationship with the release of the second single from the album, "Uptown Girl." "'Uptown Girl' is a joke song," Billy says. "It's a tribute to Frankie Valli and the Four Seasons . . . It's a joke, but if you listen to it in the context of the album, you get it."

In the promotional video for the song, the titular "Uptown Girl" turned out to be Christie. At the end of the clip, she waltzed into the garage where "downtown" Billy and the band plied their blue-collar trade. Wearing fuck-me pumps and a bouncy skirt, she left the shop with Billy, the overalled mechanic. Thus, to the incredulity of many, Billie Joel and Christie Brinkley became a "public item."

As exuberantly in love as its creator was, much of the album actually was written for the joy of the music. Where *The Nylon Curtain* was rife with Copeland and the Beatles, *An Innocent Man* celebrated the simple pleasures of rock and roll from the time before it lost the "and roll" and simply became "rock," the days of Chuck Berry, the Beach Boys, the Coasters, and (in a more New York state of mind) the Four Seasons. This was the innocence in the title, and it radiated from the title track outward.

"'An Innocent Man' was written to evoke the same kind of feelings that I got when I heard Ben E. King and the Drifters," Billy said. "There's a high note in that recording—this was done in 1983—and I had a suspicion that was going to be the last time I was going to be able to hit those notes, so why not go out in a blaze of glory?"

It also celebrates his past. In a musical way, it was the path back to the green that even Brenda and Eddie, the alpha male and female of his high school days, couldn't spiritually make. Billy could, and he rejoiced in it through "Keeping the Faith."

"The song says I'm not living in the past, I'm celebrating *today*. I'd never have had the fire if I'd never hung out with the wild boys and heard the old music."

❀ ❀ ❀

There's more to being a recording artist than just playing music. There are all the business aspects, the annoying details of meetings and contracts, and, the worst for Billy, photo shoots. Once again, Columbia wanted a picture of the artist on the cover, and this time Billy acquiesced. However, despite the fact that he was going out with a woman who had her picture taken for a living, Billy still did not like the way he looked on film.

"Billy never thought of himself as good-looking at all," Howard Bloom recalls, "so we had a problem with photos. We had an Annie Liebowitz photo shoot, and basically I said, 'If we're going to have a photo shoot, it has to reflect who Billy is. Billy loves his motorcycles, so we're going to do it with the motorcycles. It has to reflect the rebellious aspect of Billy, so we're going to do it with the motorcycles. So we got Annie Liebowitz out, we got the motorcycles out of the garage, we put Billy—not against the house—because I didn't want Billy portrayed as a rich person—that would turn people off. Billy had to be somebody who is like you, so you can get where Billy is, too. Billy has to be a figure that empowers you, not overwhelms you. Not that threatens you. Not that threatens to be the force of your parents putting you back down again. So, the house, no. The motorcycles, yes.

"I got to see Annie's technique. She waited until sunset, when the colors are really, really rich, and the colors are changing, literally, every second. She must have shot sixteen rolls of film of Billy to capture every instant of that sunset and every possible facial contortion that Billy would go through."

The album cover itself was shot on the stoop of a house in New York City, the kind of entranceway that his parents' first apartment in the Bronx might have had. It was the kind of place where doo-wop was born, where Frankie Valli or Dion might have started singing with their friends. The album came out in July 1983.

In January 1984—with the album having peaked at #4 and *An Innocent Man* nominated for Grammy Album of the Year, with "Uptown Girl" nominated for Best Pop Vocal Performance, Male (it had reached # 3 on the Hot 100 and gone gold), and with the title track of the album commencing its climb to the Top 10 and #1 on the Adult Contemporary chart—Billy hit the road with the band for a serious world tour for the first time since his accident. It kept them traveling from January through July, from Orlando to Osaka, with three days at Wembley Stadium in London and finishing off with seven shows at Madison Square Garden.

"When Billy did his week at the Garden, I called up his tour manager, Harry Sandler," says Bruce Gentile. "I told him I was a longtime friend and asked if there were any last-minute gigs available. I ended up on 'cookie duty,' keeping track of all the limos that were to enter the Garden. Coke was the in drug and the band was using heavily. Billy won an award for selling out the Garden the most nights in a row. I carried the award to the limo that was leaving with Roz and her guest. Billy himself never looked better. When I finally got to greet the piano man, Christie was a bit taken by how long I've really known her man."

When all was said and done, *An Innocent Man* sold 7 million copies. The album generated six Top 40 singles, including three that reached the Top 10.

❁ ❁ ❁

Billy Joel married Christie Brinkley, on a 147-foot rented yacht in the middle of New York Harbor, on March 23, 1985. "The reason we're going on the boat is to get away from the press," said Billy. "The wedding is not something we want to go public about. We're not Charles and Di. We don't think of ourselves as royalty. We happen to be working people."

Christie walked down the aisle on the arm of her father. She wore a Norma Kamali satin gown adorned in lace and gold, and held a bouquet of fifty white roses. It was a seven-minute-long ceremony, punctuated by James Brown's "I Feel Good." Bill Zampino was Billy's best man. All through the ceremony, Billy and Christie stared into each other's eyes as if there was no one else in the room.

During the reception Billy quipped, "A lot of people have told me I seem so happy . . . I feel happy. I must have been a real drag at one time."

When Billy had married Elizabeth, she already had a child, and that seemed to be quite enough. Initially they were living catch as catch can, and it just didn't seem kosher to raise a kid in a motel room at the Howard Johnson motor lodge, let alone have more. By the time it did seem feasible, Sean was getting older, as was Elizabeth. With Christie, Billy hoped to start fresh in this regard.

"When I married Christie," he says, "I really wanted to get married and I really wanted to have kids."

It must have been a helluva honeymoon, because nine months later, almost to the day, on December 29, 1985, their daughter, Alexa Ray Joel, was born. "Her name is a feminine version of Alexander," Billy explains, "and I like the fact that Alexa has a particular rhythmic pattern and strong sound."

Billy was about to learn, firsthand, just how much of a change a baby brings to a household. He worked only sporadically, and mostly for charity, during 1986. It kept him off the road for a year, with the exception of playing the first annual benefit show for America's family farmers, "Farm Aid," with John Cougar Mellencamp and Randy Newman. It also kept him out of the studio, with the exception of participating in the fund-raising efforts to help relieve the appalling famine brought on by drought throughout central and eastern Africa, the U.S.A. for Africa "We Are the World" sessions. Beyond his musical philanthropy, he also recorded a couple of songs to add to a "best of" collection. Fortunately, *An Innocent Man* still had legs; the final single from the album, "Keeping the Faith," peaked on the charts in February 1985, fully eighteen months after the album was released.

When the sales of *An Innocent Man* finally started to wane in June 1985, Columbia released *Greatest Hits, Volume I & Volume II.* The two songs recorded for the album came out as singles. "You're Only Human" went Top 10, while "The Night Is Still Young" broke into the Top 40, all without Billy having to tour. It was the rock and roll version of paternity leave.

CHAPTER 18

WHEN YOU'RE COUNTING ON A KILLING, ALWAYS COUNT ME IN

While things were going well for Billy on the home front, he discovered that the three-year layoff had not been good for the band. When he reassembled them and brought them into the Power Station studio in 1986 to begin work on a new album with Ramone, who was once again in the producer's chair, Billy found that his relationship with longtime band members Doug Stegmeyer and Russell Javors had begun to sour. "It got to a point, it became such a big business what we were doing," Billy lamented. "Rather than be friends like we used to be, we became business associates . . . On *The Bridge* album, it came to a head."

In a band, there is that delicate balance between the fact that the people generally enjoy playing together (though in truth, members of some of the best groups in history—Cream leaps to mind—hated each other passionately, but even that passion helped fuel their creativity) and the fact that they are in business together. The band is their livelihood.

Billy's extended honeymoon and then his paternity leave had thrown the equilibrium of the Billy Joel Band off-kilter. The group's stability was further undermined when Billy (allegedly on urging from his new bride) changed the rules of the business.

"Liberty DeVitto was sharing with me and Bobby Graziano at Bobby's Auto Body Shop," says Gentile. "He told us that Billy was majorly fucking up the financial stability of his longtime friends' lives."

Despite the tension, the core band remained the same when they went into the studio to cut *The Bridge*. While Billy would maintain, "The only premise for *The Bridge* when I started was that it not be a concept album," the title itself offered a loose concept that pervaded the album—that of connections, bridges. There were bridges between himself and his new wife, bridges he had to get over to deal with that relationship, ties between people he admired and finding out that the admiration was mutual, bridges between the thirty-seven-year-old rock star and the seventeen-year-old Hassle, bridges between classic and contemporary in rock and roll.

"I realized there's been a lot of connections made on this record. There's a duet with Ray Charles, and Ray Charles is somebody I admired for years and years," Billy admits. "There's a song with Steve Winwood playing the Hammond organ, and I've always admired Steve—for years and years. So there's another bridge."

Winwood, whose song the Hassles had recorded even before he got to record it with Traffic, played the organ solo on "Getting Closer." Charles did a full-fledged duet with Billy on "Baby Grand." "I named my daughter, Alexa Ray, after him," says Billy. "Ray heard about it from Quincy Jones, who is a friend of my producer, Phil Ramone, and sent word that he would love to record with me if I had the right song. I was so excited that very night I sat down and wrote 'Baby Grand.'"

"I found out I could hold my own as a singer," he says of performing a duet with the legendary performer. "I'm not a great believer in my own voice."

One of the songs on the album, "Modern Woman," had already come out before the album was released. Yet another departure from his usual modus operandi, Billy had recorded the song for the end credits of the film *Ruthless People*. "I hated that thing!" Billy exclaimed. Despite this, it hit the Top 10 in the *Billboard* Hot 100 Singles chart.

Another change in his MO, at least as a solo artist, found him collaborating not just on performing the songs but on the writing of a song for the first time since the Hassles had disbanded. On the track "Code of Silence" Billy formed a creative liaison, writing and performing with New Wave chanteuse Cyndi Lauper.

"I had gotten to the last song and I had terrible writer's block," Billy recalls. "Cyndi Lauper was recording downstairs at the Power Station, and she comes up to me and says, 'Bill, what's the matter? You look like you're going out of your mind. You're climbing the walls.' And I said, 'I can't get this song I want to write.' She was great. She got one of those yellow legal pads and said, 'You sit down at the piano and play, and I'll write down the . . . words you throw out.' . . . She ended up showing me this legal pad . . . and the title came out, 'Code of Silence' . . . She actually stimulated a lot of the writing and suggested a lot of things. She kind of pinpointed what should happen on this song."

The Bridge also contains another of those great Billy Joel album tracks, the swinging, big-band-style personality portrait "Big Man on Mulberry Street." Billy recalls, "I had a writing studio down in Soho, in this place called the Puck Building. I had ten thousand square feet where I had all this writing and recording equipment set up . . . Sometimes I would leave the building and walk down to Little Italy, get a little food, wine, a little espresso. The walk I took was on Mulberry Street. And I just kind of invented this character who thought he was Mr. Cool. The character is really kind of a nebbish, but in his mind he's king—the king of Mulberry Street."

The album peaked at #7 on the *Billboard* Top 200. In addition to the soundtrack hit "Modern Woman," the album included the *Billboard* Adult Contemporary chart topper "This Is the Time," a song Billy says tells us to "remember this good time, because we're going to need to remember it when times get tough." It hit the Top 20 in the *Billboard* Hot 100 Singles chart as well.

The bigger hit "A Matter of Trust"—another Top 10 pop single as well as a Top 20 rock track—was written just as "a guitar oriented song that had some grit in it." The song became the headline of many stories written about Billy in the decade following the album.

✿ ✿ ✿

Recording *The Bridge* coincided with Billy's twenty-fifth anniversary as a solo artist. To celebrate, Billy endowed the Rosalind Joel Scholarship for the Performing Arts at the City College of New York, Rosalind's alma mater. It was first presented during one of Billy's master classes, this one not at a college, but at Town Hall in Manhattan, on May 16, 1996. The year also marked the twenty-fifth anniversary of New York FM radio station WPLJ. The station and Sony further endowed the scholarship fund. WPLJ also broadcasted the event live.

In 1986, while he was dealing with making *The Bridge*, another whiff of things to come arrived on Billy's doorstep, this time in the form of trouble with the IRS. He was notified that he owed $5.5 million in back taxes. Both he and his manager felt that, since she spilt the proceeds from their marriage 50-50, and because, as manager, she had fiduciary responsibility to see that these taxes were paid, Elizabeth should foot half the bill. To that end, they held her share of his copyrights as a lien. The problem, however, was not singular—as Billy would soon discover—but systemic.

In the midst of his management settling his financial woes, Billy took *The Bridge* on a tour that kicked off in September 1986 and ran, on and off, until the beginning of August 1987. At this point in his life, Billy included his wife and daughter in everything he did. They could even be seen bopping in the background of the "Matter of Trust" video—well, Christie could be seen bopping. Alexa bopped by extension in a baby carrier slung across Christie's shoulders.

So it wasn't unusual or unreasonable that they should occasionally travel with the band. Christie became quite the backstage attraction. "The band had a bunch of stickers printed," says Gentile, "and they put them on the Anvil cases they put their instruments in. You'd go backstage and you'd see these cases all in a row, all of them with this sticker that says, 'Where's Christie?' 'Where's Christie?' 'Where's Christie?'" The two words were one of the most asked questions backstage during that tour.

Having Alexa on tour presented its own special set of challenges. The environment backstage at a concert can rarely be categorized as wholesome. Dressing rooms become hangouts for groupies, and the riders to the contract often stipulate that the promoter provide a variety of inebriating beverages. This is above and beyond any recreational substances the band might bring on their own. Bruce Gentile recalls that several members of the regular entourage "had all the cocaine in the world on them at all times."

Beyond that, there is electrical equipment and hot lights and a variety of musical instruments all about. It's loud, often smoky, frequently at least R-rated. A buffer has to be set up for the children on board, and the Billy Joel entourage carefully created that buffer. Parts of the backstage area at a Billy Joel concert began to resemble a nursery.

"I went on tour with him a lot and I would bring my family," notes Elaine Schock, who by this time had married Jeff Schock, one of Billy's inner circle. "I think my favorite memory was taking my very little kid backstage and . . . when you went backstage at a Billy Joel concert, for kids it was wonderful. They always took really good care of the kids . . . They had pinball machines back there, and games, and they made sure the kids' ears were covered so they could see the wonderful concert but not become hearing-impaired because of it. Everyone in the band brought their family. Billy made it easy to bring ours. Liberty brought his kids, I brought my kids, Christie and Billy were together, and Alexa was there. All the kids would hang out by the pool . . . It was really kid-friendly."

During the dog days of the summer of 1987, the Billy Joel show, with families and film crew in tow, pulled into the Soviet Union. In 1987, the Iron Curtain was showing signs of opening. The Russians were slowly making inroads and overtures to finally overthrowing communism and becoming members of the world community. The country's leader, Mikhail Gorbachev, had just published a treatise on the subject called *Perestroika*. Billy Joel and his traveling rock and roll road show became the first full-blown Western rock act to tour the Soviet Union. He even footed the $2.5 million it took to put on the six shows, hoping to recover it with a special filmed for HBO, a live album, and a documentary.

Christie and Alexa were with him, as well. In addition to all the other equipment, they also brought along provisions, like crates of bottled water and food.

"I think they were just thrilled to have a rock star from the West— with a big PA system," Billy recalled. "I mean, they applauded the *equipment*."

Among the members of his entourage was Walter Yetnikoff. The CBS Music president was, after all, going to be releasing the album and video culled from the shows. Yetnikoff also thought it would be an interesting opportunity to flex his political muscles and meet with a *refusenik* family (a Russian Jewish family that had been refused an emigration visa so they could move to Israel). But he also attended the shows.

"I went to Billy's big concert at the Olympic Sports complex," Yetnikoff recalled. "Billy rocked. In fact, he rocked harder than the

Soviets wanted him to rock. They told him no encores, but he did seven. He sang 'Back in the USSR,' and the crowd went wild. Fans rushed the stage. American rock and roll ripped up the iron curtain. Billy's nonstop performance so angered members of the Soviet Central Committee that Billy's tour manager, fearing arrest, hid in the men's room after the show. Moscow was never the same."

The shows were a media event. The *New York Times* and many of the other big newspapers from around the world sent reporters and photographers. Nor was it solely an easy show. During one concert, Billy threw an electric piano off the stage in a fit of pique. He shouted to a film crew that shined its lights on the audience, "It's my show!"

"It was a real prima donna act," he said of the incident, "but I have to protect my show . . . People in the audience want to be in the dark. They want to get loose."

He included the incident in the documentary. Another one that happened behind the scenes proved more telling. It reflected the strife that had been running through the Billy Joel Band both making the album and throughout the tour. Billy was over the moon about doing these shows, but others in the group didn't share his enthusiasm. It proved to be an acid test for the band. "It separated the wheat from the chaff," says Billy. "There was no money, everything was difficult. It was a real test of 'how much do you want to play?' . . . I wasn't getting that anymore. I was getting, 'We're into double scale now.'"

While he didn't make his money back from the show, Billy still regards the Russian tour as one of the high points of his musical career. "Ever since we played Russia, everything has been kind of anticlimactic. We felt like we'd hit a pinnacle."

The album that chronicled the event, *Kohuept*, came out in October. It became the first Billy Joel album since *Cold Spring Harbor* not to go gold. It rose to only #38 in the *Billboard* 200 Albums chart. His cover of the Beatles' "Back in the USSR" didn't even make the pop charts and just reached into the 50s on the *Billboard* Rock Tracks chart.

When the double live album came out, the band was still touring on and off, spending part of that month in Australia. They finished the year just before Christmas playing a Homeless Children's Medical Benefit Concert at Madison Square Garden.

$\diamond \diamond \diamond$

After nearly a year on the road, 1988 was, as far as all appearances to the general public, a fairly quiet year for Billy. He turned up in the movies once again, this time giving the voice to the canine version of the Artful Dodger in the Disney animated film *Oliver and Company*. He mostly did it for his four-year-old daughter. He took Alexa to the premier of the film and watched her reaction. She recognized the voice, but it took her a while to make the connection. When she finally did, she looked at her father and told him he was a cute doggie.

The quiet, however, was only on the face of things. Behind the scenes, Billy discovered that the tax problems he dealt with before the tour were just the tip of a very large, deep, and ponderous iceberg intent on scuttling his ship.

"I remember the evening: me and Billy at Fontana di Trevi on Fifty-seventh Street; over fettuccine Alfredo and a river of red wine," Walter Yetnikoff recalls, "him telling me how he had to sell his Manhattan apartment to Sting to buy a bigger house for Christie in East Hampton; me wondering why Billy Joel, whose copyrights are worth millions, has to ditch his Manhattan digs; him telling me he's strapped for cash; me telling him that I smell a rat, that he needs to audit his people; him telling me to mind my own goddamn business; me ordering more wine."

After the evening out with an artist who had been one of his major moneymakers and a friend for more than a decade, Yetnikoff decided not to mind his own business. He told Billy's attorney, Alan Grubman, that something was wrong with Billy's accounts. He suggested to the lawyer that perhaps he should hire someone to audit his manager's books on Billy's behalf.

It was unlike Grubman to say no to Yetnikoff. That was one of the reasons Yetnikoff recommended him to any CBS artists who were looking for new representation. Yet, according to the subsequent suit against him, Grubman wouldn't do it because Billy's manager, Frank Weber, "would fire him as Joel's attorney if he attempted to do so."

At the same time, Billy began minding his own business and took Yetnikoff's advice. He had been the first major celebrity client to hire

Grubman, Indursky and Schindler as his attorneys. In his wake, Bruce Springsteen, Michael Jackson, John Mellencamp, Madonna, and a host of others had become clients of the firm. In the wake of Grubman's refusal to hire someone to audit the books, Billy became the first of his music-business clients to leave. He retained John Eastman, Paul McCartney's brother-in-law and one of Billy's Hamptons buddies. The first thing Eastman did was hire one of New York's leading accounting firms, Ernst and Young, to audit Billy's finances.

When Ernst and Young finished going through the books, the accountants informed Billy and his new attorney that he was worth considerably less than he thought, considerably less than he ought to be. They found what they described as many improprieties. Billy's business dealings had been handled poorly at best, but more likely they had been handled criminally.

According to the suit that was subsequently filed, Weber often "took more monies from the revenues produced by some of Joel's tours and recordings than Joel himself received."

Additionally, Weber had used Billy's copyrights as collateral for interest-free loans from CBS—as non-taxable income. He also invested Billy in things in which Weber had a personal interest, thereby collecting a commission from the investment. Weber also had obligated Billy in a series of high-risk investments, including:

* A real estate deal that made Billy liable for a million-dollar transaction that went belly up in Virginia.
* Investments in oil and natural-gas syndicates.
* Buying a racehorse from Morris Levy (the same Moishe who had hired and fired Irwin Mazur fifteen years earlier) and then "burning" it—that is, maiming the horse and claiming the insurance on it. Billy alluded to this in a diatribe against managers in a *Musician* article offering advice to younger musicians from more experienced ones: "I would never let anyone dictate the direction, timing or nature of my art. The moment someone on the business end starts to make those decisions for an artist, their art starts to take on the aroma of a dead horse."

It was further discovered that Weber overcharged Billy for his music videos. These clips had been produced by a company owned by another Weber brother-in-law, Rick London.

Dealing with the personal root cause of his difficulties in terms of his management and money would be one of the biggest professional lessons Billy Joel would learn as his life slipped from its fourth decade into its fifth. Billy certainly liked having the money but had no idea where it actually came from. His relationship to his finances, in fact, was almost one of antipathy.

"To have to translate what you do into dollars and cents makes it all mundane," he said. "It takes away the magic to see what the gross is and the net is, what the taxes are, to know what you earn . . ."

Like so many artists, Billy would yawn his way through meetings on his finances. "When Frank has tried to take me through the books, my eyes start to glaze over."

Weber had probably come to count on Billy's indifference to his finances. Frank Weber would tell his golf buddies that Billy didn't "even know how much he has to send his mother each month, he's so out of the money loop."

Eastman and Billy brought in ace rock and roll litigator Leonard Marks, who had represented Bruce Springsteen in his suit separating him from his former manager more than a decade earlier. As Marks started to draft his suit, Billy fired Weber as his manager, on August 30, 1988.

"You were right," Billy told Yetnikoff. "The audit was an eye-opener. I was being robbed blind. Now I'm suing. So thanks for the wake-up call."

After the firing, Billy said, "I'm really hurt by the whole thing. As far as I'm concerned it's my third burn. There was Artie Ripp, my ex-wife, now this. How many lives do I have?"

CHAPTER 19

RED FLAGS ARE FLYING

In addition to cutting loose his management, Billy decided that some other fundamental adjustments were called for in his professional life. The Soviet tour convinced Billy he needed to make some changes in the band. This included shedding one of the Mean Brothers. He didn't so much fire bassist Doug Stegmeyer and guitarist Russell Javors as just not invite them to the studio when he began working on the material for his next album, *Storm Front*.

"That was a difficult thing for me to do. I'm a very loyal person. But I essentially think of myself as a writer, and a writer has an obligation to have his music interpreted by different people. It was beginning to get stale," Billy said. "I didn't want to go into the studio and talk about people's deals; I wanted to talk about music. We went the extra mile on this album because we were having so much fun."

Joining stalwart drummer Liberty DeVitto, in Javors's place David Brown became the band's sole guitarist. Stegmeyer was replaced with Schuyler Deale, a bassist who had cut his teeth with another legendary Long Island band, the Good Rats. Ironically, when Stegmeyer subsequently left the band of another generation's renowned Long Island performer Debbie Gibson some years later, Deale took over as the bass player in that situation, too.

"At one time, I wasn't sure if I was going to tour again, but working with this group stimulated that sense of fun again," Billy says.

However, the laid-off band members were a little bit miffed at the fact that their "very loyal" former employer didn't even bother to call them to let them know they weren't invited back. "After thirteen years," said Javors, "it would've been nice to have gotten a phone call." Javors had already started to work with the Carpenters at the time, so he had a fallback position.

Stegmeyer never heard from Billy to tell him he was out of the band, either. He joined Javors in working with the Carpenters, and also played on records by artists as diverse as English pub rocker Graham Parker and jazz fusion pianist Bob James.

"Doug Stegmeyer went through a lot of money because his nose got very big," Gentile says. "You know that Al Stewart song 'Time Passages'? With Doug, I used to parody that song as 'Nasal Passages.' Whenever I would run into Doug, he would come in and ask me, 'Who's got drugs here?' I had to keep reminding him, 'Doug, I'm in the freaking program. I don't do drugs. I don't even drink methadone anymore.'

"Sparks was a bar that Doug hung out at a lot. The Billy Joel Band, at the time, used the place to practice. Sparks was on 25A, down the block from Ruggles's and Stegmeyer's homes in Centerport. The first video performed and shot live from that place, 'Say Goodbye to Hollywood,' was probably one of Billy's first in black and white and shot in such tight quarters. Sparks used to have a commercial on [Long Island rock radio station] WBAB that ended by saying this place is so cool even Billy Joel slept there."

Six years after Billy let him go, in 1995, Stegmeyer committed suicide. "Doug blew his brains out one night," Gentile recalls sadly. "I remember running into a district court judge who tipped me off about Doug and his permanent solution to his temporary problem. Doug was depressed with the biz. His brother told me the news as he cursed Doug's lawyer and Billy. Rumor had it that Billy wanted to own all record royalties from the players he had fired.

"Doug knew the bass guitar like no one else. He was really something special. What a sad loss he was. Everyone was shocked and saddened. I saw a letter in *Bass Player* magazine informing them that they failed to mention Doug's passing. They ended up saying some fine things about Doug. Doug was indeed a great player."

❀ ❀ ❀

During the summer of 1989, as the changes were taking place in the Billy Joel Band, Billy took up Long Island University on an invitation to do a "master class" on his music and the music business. It was the start of something big, and something Billy, the aspiring history-teacher-without-a-high-school-diploma found himself enjoying very much. So much so that he repeated the experience often at universities across the country over the course of the next decade and a half.

"He was asked to do one at NYU," said Elaine Schock, who was still his publicist, now running her own agency, Shock Ink, with Billy as her main client. "I invited press to it, and the master classes took on a life of their own. He did them when he was asked to do them, and they were usually at big, important universities. I'm sure he never got paid a dime for them. Every press person that attended just loved it, and the students seemed to learn a great deal from the class."

People would come out of the woodwork for these master classes, and manage to get backstage. One time, someone Billy went to high school with went backstage and tried to hit him up for a $50,000 loan.

In the final preparations for making his next album, Billy considered the many changes he had made in his professional life, and decided on one more. Along with the changes in his band and his management, Billy determined it was time to get some fresh blood in the producer's chair. He brought in Foreigner guitarist Mick Jones. Born in London, Jones had hits with one of the first bands to rock the classics, Nero and the Gladiators, who took Edvard Grieg's "In the Hall of the Mountain King" into the English charts. After a stint as a studio player and then in the proto-progressive rock group Spooky Tooth, Jones moved to New York to take a record-company gig, settling in Long Island and working with Leslie West before forming Foreigner. By the late '80s, Foreigner had run its course, and Mick settled into the producer's seat, working on Van Halen's *5150* album. Eventually he wound up as one of Billy's neighbors.

"Mick Jones is a songwriter, so there was a good relationship," Billy said. "He's a good musician, a good guitar player, and I thought that would give him a little more insight into what I'm trying to do."

Nor was Jones a slouch when it came to writing hit records. With Foreigner, he had penned or co-written sixteen Top 40 hits. "He has an inside track on a songwriter's problems," Billy acknowledged.

"I don't have as much faith in my abilities as a recording artist or singer or pop star as I should have. I've got to have another set of brains to tell me what they hear."

Changing his producer meant changing the whole method of recording, the whole means of making the album. With Ramone, Billy would go into the studio with rough drafts and half thoughts that became tracks and then songs—leading to placeholder lyrics like "Sodomy." While Foreigner had been known to take more than a year in the studio to make an album, perhaps Jones had learned from that experience. He wanted Billy and his band in the studio, ready to record.

"He wanted me to come with songs already written!" Billy marveled. "And he wanted us to rehearse! I was horrified. What about spontaneity?"

The first single from the album was "That's Not Her Style." This was just toward the end of the time when record companies still made vinyl discs that played on turntables, with long-playing albums that played at 33 1/3 rpm and smaller discs with big holes that spun at 45 rpm. The picture sleeve from the single featured the naked backside of a tall woman. People suspected it was Christie, but Billy insisted "That's not her style." The joke didn't help sell the single or get it airplay. It hit #77 on the *Billboard* Hot Singles chart, though it rose to a respectable #18 on the *Billboard* Mainstream Rock Tracks chart.

That didn't really matter, because the next single, "We Didn't Start the Fire," became one of the most successful that Billy ever recorded. A 4-minute, 50-second stroll through Billy's lifetime, it touches on the key political and cultural points of global history from 1949 through 1989. It was Billy's fortieth-birthday present to himself.

"I turned forty this year. I wasn't bothered by it. But I was wondering how to deal with this musically," he said.

He considered the key events that had occurred in his time on the planet. "I wanted to list all the different icons. I thought, 'Harry Truman, Doris Day, Red China, Johnnie Ray,' and I felt a song coming."

"I'm a history nut. I devour history books. At one time I wanted to be a history teacher."

It happened that he got into a conversation with a young man half his age who started beefing about how Billy's generation had screwed up everything for his generation. Billy, history maven that he is, assured him that every generation feels that way. "Part of the point of that song is, 'Look, you didn't start it, you probably ain't going to end it,'" he explains. "We tried to make the world a better place coming out of the sixties. And I hope people aren't disillusioned to the point where they don't try at all to fight anymore."

"We Didn't Start the Fire" represented another one of the changes on *Storm Front*: It is one of the very few Billy Joel songs in which the lyrics came first. Accompanied by a video that put up images of every point in history Billy mentions in the song, it found its way into many schools. Teachers told him the song was "the greatest teaching tool to come down the pike since *Sesame Street*, which means a lot to me."

"[It] surprised me," he adds, "that it was perceived as a yuppy apology, or that there was so much interest in what I thought was a well-known period of history."

While Billy likes the history and the theme of the song, and it certainly isn't one of his "children" who "grew up to be a bum," nevertheless "We Didn't Start the Fire" is a song about which he has mixed emotions. For one thing, it's a tough tune to sing in concert. "It's a nightmare to perform live, because if I miss one word, it's a train wreck."

For another, he considers it an anomaly. "'Uptown Girl' or . . . some silly novelty song that was a hit like 'We Didn't Start the Fire,'" he laments, "don't really define me as well as the album songs that probably don't get played."

Yet another anomaly on *Storm Front* was using a leftover. Usually, in Billy Joel's musical kitchen, leftovers were discarded rather than refrigerated. "There's no backlog of Billy Joel material," he maintains. "You'll never hear my basement tapes, because there are none."

However, "And So It Goes" is a song that "was written back in 1983 during the time I was writing songs for *An Innocent Man*. I was a newly unmarried man, I was dating beautiful women at the time, it was a great time in my life."

While the single just grazed the pop Top 40 at #37 in *Billboard*, it went to #5 on the *Billboard* Adult Contemporary chart. The next *Storm Front* single fared somewhat better. "I Go to Extremes" became a cross-genre hit, breaking the Top 10 on the Hot 100, Adult Contemporary, and Mainstream Rock Tracks charts. "It's kind of an ode to manic depression," Billy said. "'Summer, Highland Falls' is kind of like that. I think all artists, to one degree or another, are manic-depressive."

Just before beginning *Storm Front*, Billy, Christie, and Alexa moved to East Hampton, at the far-eastern end of Long Island. The Hamptons, as Billy noted earlier, is an interesting study in social dichotomy. On the one hand, it is a playground of the privileged, where summer houses are major status symbols, growing in grade as they get closer to the beach. Such a vacation getaway can cost millions of dollars. Then there are the "working Hamptons," where the people who provide services for the privileged live, along with people who ply professions older than even the area's status as a summer resort. Those jobs—in the fishing industry in the East Bay—date back to when the far end of the Island, more than 100 miles from the new Madison Avenue building that housed Columbia Records, would have taken days rather than hours of travel to reach from the city. These fishermen, called baymen, were experiencing the kind of problems that modern life can impose on people who choose to do things the traditional way.

"The baymen are being put out of business by politicians, developers, industrial pollution, agricultural insecticide runoff and the sport-fishing lobby," Billy said.

They inspired *Storm Front*'s next single, "The Downeaster 'Alexa.'" While a nor'easter is a kind of storm, a downeaster is the type of boat that the commercial fishermen on the East Bay use. Arnold Leo of the East Hampton Baymen's Association said, "The Baymen love this song because it really does catch the feeling of their plight."

"If these guys disappear," Billy added, "we've lost a lot of the identity of what Long Island is . . . Melville wrote about them . . . If they go, we're just a suburb. We're no longer an island. People forget that—we're an island."

While the song made the point, the single didn't reach as many ears as it might have via radio. It hit #18 on the *Billboard* Adult Contemporary chart and #33 on the *Billboard* Mainstream Rock Tracks chart, and it topped out at #57 on the *Billboard* Hot 100 pop chart. But it was a cause about which Billy felt deeply. He played a benefit concert for the baymen at Jones Beach, August 29, 1990.

One of the songs that didn't make it as a single in Billy's hands would still play an important role in his still-emerging career.

"Shameless" was a paean to Christie. "It's a man's ultimate expression of complete love. I'll do anything you please. That's how much I love you," says Billy.

"I actually wrote that [musically] thinking about Jimi Hendrix. I always loved Jimi Hendrix's voice and his pronunciation of words and the way his guitar sounds."

On the strength of the five singles, *Storm Front* once again brought Billy to the top of the *Billboard* 200 Albums chart. It also earned him four Grammy nominations, and the album was cited for Best Pop Vocal Performance, Male, and Producer of the Year by his peers in the National Academy of Recording Arts and Sciences, while "We Didn't Start the Fire" earned nominations as Song of the Year and Record of the Year. When the awards were handed out, however, Billy didn't come home with any. One of Billy's main musical influences, Steve Winwood, won for both Record of the Year and Best Pop Vocal Performance, Male, for "Higher Love," and "That's What Friends Are For" won Song of the Year. R&B heavyweights Jimmy Jam and Terry Lewis took home the statuette for Producers of the Year.

While it is an immensely popular album, *Storm Front* is also one with many dark moments, a foreshadowing of the personal storms Billy saw on the horizon. "There's some malevolence in the album," Billy noted. "Something's going to happen, something's coming . . . You should be prepared to deal with turmoil and upheaval all your life . . . Sometimes you have to create a crisis to get things to happen."

❡ ❡ ❡

Billy was indeed about to enter a world of crisis. As *Storm Front* hit the street, the shit that had been building up for nearly a decade in his professional life hit the fan. Billy's lawsuit against his manager, Frank Weber, was initially filed the same day Billy had surgery for kidney stones, September 25, 1989. His history with this physical malady began around the same time he started making bad deals; he had his first attack of kidney stones at age nineteen, around the time he was making the Attila album. Both kidney stones and careless business deals had been problems throughout his adult life, and it seemed oddly appropriate that they would both peak at the same time.

On September 25, he had been on his way to catch a Concorde to England, where he was slated to make the promotional rounds on behalf of the *Storm Front* album. Instead, he wound up diverting the car, telling the driver to take him to New York Hospital. "I've got a pretty good slice in my gut here," he said about the surgery, but he might just as well have been referring to the lawsuit.

Weber's duplicity shook Billy to his core. Weber had seen Billy thorough the divorce with Weber's sister and had been at his wedding to Christie. Weber is the godfather of Billy's daughter, Alexa Ray, and was executor of Billy's will. "I trusted him totally," Billy said, "but he seriously damaged my faith in human nature."

The lawsuit sought to recover $90 million from Weber, which broke down as $30 million compensatory remuneration and $60 million punitive damages. "It's really quite a shocking story of trust. [Weber] has a very close, personal relationship with Billy Joel . . . Billy Joel had total faith he was dealing with someone who was totally honest," said Leonard Marks, who would litigate the suit. Marks added that "an audit and investigation revealed major incidents of fraud and dishonest dealings virtually from the inception" of his management contract.

"All this came to light when we got the results of an investigative audit conducted in July and August . . . Weber's rampant abuse of his position as Billy's fiduciary has taken many forms," Marks added. He called the incidents "the worst I've ever seen."

Billy took over his own management, forming Maritime Music. The only remnant of his longtime management team—of whom many were now or soon to become Weber's co-defendants in the lawsuit—was Jeff Schock. "He was de facto manager," recalls Schock's ex-wife Elaine, who also retained her role as Billy's spokesperson and publicist as part of the new team at Maritime Music. "[Jeff] was paid as a consultant. He never made a percentage, but he finessed a lot of stuff for Billy and took very good care of him.

"Jeff was completely innocent. Jeff, for one thing, never took any of the money from Billy, and for two, Rick [London] was the accountant. And his brother-in-law, according to Billy, has carte blanch with his checkbook."

Instead of a manager working on a percentage, Billy decided that he was better off having people to whom he paid a salary take care of his day-to-day business. He outsourced most of the rest of the work that a manager would have been responsible for but would have outsourced anyway, like accounting, publicity, and legal matters.

"I'm finding I can get a lot of things done by picking up the phone and making a call. I don't need management," he said.

The idea of a manager, considering all of his misadventures with people bearing that title, began to seem like the ultimate con game to Billy. "The assumption that artists need a 'personal manager,'" he said, "is a persistent myth based on misinformation handed down by generations of naïve, exploited musicians."

"Musicians can manage themselves without ripping themselves off," Billy added. "If I screw me, I'm making love with somebody I know."

༄ ༄ ༄

When he recovered from his surgery and in the wake of these legal proceedings, Billy took *Storm Front* on the road, playing his most extensive tour to date. He played 165 shows during the tour, which started in Worchester, Massachusetts, in December 1989 and finished in Japan in January 1991, playing across the United States and Europe. In all he sold 3.5 million tickets.

"The reason for the length of this tour is financial," he railed. "The accounting firm I'm with now said I was looking at a deep, deep, deep financial hole that would take two years to get out of. So I said, 'OK' and put my head down and went to work and I'm getting back in the black.

"Am I angry about it? Bitter is a good word. The worst thing is having to spend so much time away from my kid . . . When I was a kid, my dad was gone a lot and I swore that when I became a father, I'm going to be home. So here I am—on the road and away from my kid . . . The time I spend away from my kid isn't something you can make back."

As part of the tour, on June 22, 1990, he pulled into the land of his birth—the Bronx, New York—to play two shows at Yankee Stadium. These were the first full-blown music concerts ever at the venerable shrine to championship baseball, an oasis of success in the crumbling South Bronx. "I went to Shea to see the Stones," Billy noted of New York City's "other" major league stadium, home of the New York Mets and host to concerts from the Beatles to Bruce Springsteen, "but Yankee Stadium has no tradition of music: It's been boxing, baseball and the Pope."

In the *New York Times*, Stephen Holden latched on to the boxing angle, noting, "The concert reinforced the image of Mr. Joel as a ferociously talented modern day vaudevillian juggling voices, styles and images with the aggressive glee of a determined pugilist."

As with his historic tour of the Soviet Union, Billy also made a chronicle of this historic show. The video for the Yankee Stadium concert was directed by Billy's old Hassles and Attila bandmate Jon Small, who was rapidly becoming one of the top video clip producers in New York; he would later move on to Nashville, where he'd work extensively with Garth Brooks. In February of the next year the long-form video of the event was certified platinum. Twenty years after slaving through the clubs of Long Island and recording three albums to a resounding lack of acclaim, Billy and Jon had finally collaborated on a successful project together.

Billy needed the success, as his lawsuit was not going especially well. The courts had handed down a summary judgment saying that Weber had to pay back some $2 million in loans while it decided on the other issues in the case. However, Billy's hope of collecting anything near the $90 million for which he was suing Weber started to look much dimmer when Weber declared bankruptcy in the summer of 1990.

✿ ✿ ✿

At the 34th Annual Grammy Awards, Billy became one of the recipients of the second annual Grammy Legend Award. His co-honorees that night were Quincy Jones, Aretha Franklin, and Johnny Cash. Billy was in awe of the company he was keeping. "How does a little pup like me get in there?" he wondered. "It's wild!"

Later that year, during the summer of 1991, Billy's old friend and former roommate saw the culmination of a dream in a tribute to his buddy and their shared Long Island roots. After kicking his drug habit (and forming the first Narcotics Anonymous group on the eastern end of Long Island), Bruce Gentile had bailed out of the music business, leaving behind his days as a full-time professional drummer. He had taken the civil service exam and became a sign inspector for the town of Huntington in Nassau County on Long Island. In this role, he developed a wide array of political connections. Gentile pulled a few of these strings to get a small parcel of land right on the water turned into a park. The thing that put it over was the name: Billy Joel Cold Spring Harbor Park, in honor of the album that failed. What Long Island politician could refuse an opportunity to associate himself with one of the Island's biggest stars and boosters? For Billy's part, he was deeply touched.

When Billy arrived at the naming ceremony for the park, the street was lined with shrieking, cheering fans, some holding banners, one holding up a Florida license plate that read "Joel-1." There were presentations by local politicians and homilies by radio personalities, and a choir sang "The Downeaster 'Alexa.'" Roz came up, got a bouquet of flowers from a local politician who noted how big an influence she was on Billy. It became evident that she was influential in more than one way as she took the bouquet and toddled off the rostrum.

"Roz was so drunk," recalls Bruce Gentile, "that Jane Arginteanu, Billy's assistant, said, 'Bruce, is it possible that you can get Roz a ride out of here?' I said, 'Yeah, my brother has a nice car over there.'"

The park is across the street from a building that Billy pointed out as "a famous brothel. It was a whaling town. We should be proud of all our history.

"I didn't have a boat when I was pulling oysters over in Oyster Bay," he added. "Any boat that I did have in those days I sort of 'borrowed.' It kind of surprised me that they're naming a park after me, a notorious boat borrower.

"I used to live by here five years ago and I remember rowing past a house where John Lennon lived . . . He loved it here very much, that's why he chose to live here right up until he was killed. It is a wonderful place. It was the first place that gave me the idea that there was something worth preserving, that it's a beautiful area that should remain beautiful forever."

A couple of months later, as the trees began to turn color in Billy Joel Cold Spring Harbor Park, Garth Brooks took Billy to an even more exotic place, where no one had taken Billy Joel before. Brooks had just taken the country world by storm with his first two albums, and was making inroads with the pop audience as well. On his third album, Brooks covered Billy's "Shameless" and released it as a single. "Shameless" topped the country charts in the fall of 1991.

"Now, thirty-six years later, I finally have a number-one record by another artist doing my song in a completely different genre," Billy laughed. "This is what I was hoping for a long, long time ago . . . This is definitely a career highlight . . . I told Christie the other night, 'There's a number-one country song about you.' She got a kick out of that."

Ironically, Brooks would overtake Billy as the #2 selling male solo artist of all time—after Elvis—several years later.

CHAPTER 20

I TRY TO KEEP FIGHTING

On June 24, 1992, Billy Joel finally graduated from Hicksville High. While his problem had been truancy more than the "one credit" of English the principal (and Billy's former fifth-grade gym teacher) claimed he was missing, his songs and success finally got him his diploma. "He submitted some of his actual works and we said, 'My gosh, this more than satisfies,'" remarked the principal.

Walking with the class of '92—despite being more than twice their age—Billy wore the gown, but ever the individualist, he eschewed the cap. "Well, here I am, mom," he told the parents, students, and media gathered for the event. "I'm actually going to get my high school diploma . . . I can finally pull myself out of this dead-end job I have and start working on a career with a real future."

As things were progressing with his finances and the Weber lawsuit, he might have been only half kidding. In that context, working on a career and getting out of his dead-end job had more than a little tang of irony. Over the two years he had been pursuing it, the complaint had taken on Frankenstein-like features. Marks had amended the complaint five times, nearly doubling its length from 86 to 133 pages. "They're deliberately trying to make this litigation more complicated than it has to be," said Weber's attorney, Frank Conforti. "I get five pounds of paper a week from Billy's lawyers."

By 1992, the suit had many more defendants than just Weber. As Billy's lawyers proceeded in gathering evidence and information, they discovered that Weber was just the most visible part of a very large, very deep pit of legal quicksand that had sucked in Billy's earnings. Among the people added to the suit was Rick London. London had served Billy in a variety of ways. He was Billy's former road manager and his accountant, and ran the video end of Billy's business before the suit. He was also married to Frank and Elizabeth's sister. London was enjoined in the suit for inflating his bills when he ran the video portion of Billy's business. "He sued everyone who's ever had a drink with me," Weber complained.

After declaring bankruptcy, Weber and Conforti acted on the old adage that the best defense was a good offense. They filed a $33 million countersuit against Billy for breach of contract. The suit was filed in Virginia, and a judge threw it out, saying it was unfair to try Billy anywhere outside of New York, where both litigants lived and did business. They also filed a suit against Christie Brinkley, accusing her of derailing Weber and Joel's relationship after Weber advised Joel on their prenuptial agreement. That suit was dismissed in March 1992, the judge saying that all the things of which Weber accused Brinkley were protected under New York's marital privilege.

Meanwhile, Elizabeth also brought suit against Billy, claiming that he owed her more than $3 million from their divorce agreement, including money from a pension fund, royalties, and money Billy claimed went to settle her share of the tax difficulties that had triggered all the legalities in the first place. Billy settled that suit fairly quickly. Then Weber sued his sister, claiming she owed him a portion of pre-1981 income. Billy promised to cover commission shortfalls. With that settled, Elizabeth countersued Frank for $7 million, charging breach of contract and breach of fiduciary duty.

In addition to the heat of these lawsuits, the FBI started to investigate Weber. They turned up suspicious activity and monetary transactions between Weber and Billy's former lawyer, Alan Grubman, and his law firm of Grubman, Indursky, Schindler and Goldstein. "None of this came to light," said Billy's litigator Leonard Marks, "until their admission to the FBI in 1992."

After signing Billy as a client, Grubman & Indursky had become one of the most powerful law firms in the music business. Using Billy as a high-profile springboard, the firm, in addition to parlaying that relationship into representing other high-powered, high-revenue artists, began representing high-ranking music-business executives as well. Tommy Mottola, president of the Sony Music Group, became a Grubman, Indursky, Schindler and Goldstein client, as did many other music companies and corporate executives.

This led to the big legal brouhaha between Billy and Grubman, Indursky, Schindler and Goldstein. Billy and Marks brought a malpractice suit against the firm on September 23, 1992, accusing it of fraud, breach of fiduciary responsibility, breach of contract, conflict of interest, and a wide variety of other charges, to the tune of another $90 million, the same figure in the Weber suit. The suit claimed that "from the outset of their attorney-client relationship, [the law firm] entered into repeated secret and unlawful transactions" with Weber.

The suit further contended that, inspired by an overweening desire to build up a music-industry client list, the firm courted Weber with payoffs and a wide variety of graft:

* The law firm hired Weber for tax planning and consulting, with Weber collecting fees that amounted to $127,000, despite Grubman claiming to the FBI that he could not recall Weber performing any of these tasks—and indeed the suit maintained that Weber never actually performed any of these tasks, that the firm was paying him money for nothing.
* Grubman invested in several of the same shelters and real estate deals that had cost Billy so many millions, under pressure from Weber that if the law firm didn't invest he would advise Billy to find another firm. The attorneys got rebates on the investments.
* That the law firm was aware of Weber's practice of "burning horses" for his racehorse syndicate.
* The 1988 conversation between Yetnikoff and Grubman about Billy's finances was never acted on by the attorney in violation of the "duties of care and undivided loyalty that they owed their client . . ."
* That the law firm knew about loans Weber made—including one to former CBS Records president Al Teller—using Billy's pension fund as a piggybank.
* That the firm opted for big cash advances in favor of higher royalty rates, to the detriment of its client, Billy.
* The firm represented CBS Records, the company Billy recorded for and had to negotiate with, at the same time they represented Billy.
* That the firm had not informed Billy of previous conflict of interest accusations.

* That the firm generally protected Weber's interests ahead of Billy's, keeping the manager happy at any cost.

The law firm had billed Billy more than a million dollars in the nine years that they represented him. "I thought having a manager, accountant, and attorney, I was protected from the wrongdoing that was detailed in these complaints," Billy said. "I'm very disappointed that my faith in my ex-manager, ex-attorney, and my ex-accountant was so completely and thoroughly abused."

As that suit progressed, it began to be tried in the press more than in the courts. Billy's lawyer, Leonard Marks, appeared on talk shows like *The Joan Rivers Show*. Grubman hired PR firm Dan Klores Associates to spin the remarks and present the law firm's case. Klores allegedly leaked filings to the New York City tabloids. It became a cause célèbre in the music business, and every music-business attorney wanted to weigh in on the issue.

Some commented on the inherent conflict of interest when the same law firms and attorneys represented the record company, the record company executives, and the artist, as was the case frequently at Grubman, Indursky, Schindler. "The record companies want to deal with a house lawyer," noted Los Angeles attorney Don Engel, whose clients included Frank Zappa and Kenny Rogers, "someone who won't rock the boat."

A fellow attorney countered: "Allen [Grubman] is tough and not everybody's cup of tea, but I know how hard they worked at representing Billy Joel."

On the other hand, there was a definite conflict of interest at work. "If you're a lawyer getting paid by a label year in and year out," queried Donald Passman, author of the novice's guide to the industry *All You Need to Know About the Music Business* and an attorney for artists ranging from Janet Jackson to REM, "how hard are you going to push for somebody's contract?"

Part of the spin Klores put on the case was that it was a vendetta of a less-successful lawyer against the industry leader. "I had no axe to grind. There are very few people in this business who would go after Allen Grubman. I didn't plan on it," Marks maintained. "Many lawyers in the entertainment business have forgotten what they were taught in law school—that there are substantial limitations in representing both sides of the table. You are supposed to represent one side vigorously. All the people brought in to protect Bill have wound up in bed with Weber and have not been concerned with loyalty to the client."

Billy's attorney of record, John Eastman, agreed, noting that all they wanted was to recover the money Billy had lost. "This isn't a crusade. I have a number on Billy Joel's balance sheet and if Grubman pays it, this is over. My client has been wronged and he's terribly angry about it."

Marks was more confrontational and direct: "They don't know the difference between a balance sheet and a balance beam."

Billy spent much of the year deposing and being deposed, consulting with lawyers and dealing with the ever-widening aspects of his legal situation. In March 1993, he won a summary judgment from the New York State Supreme court on three of the charges in his suit against Frank Weber, dealing with specific transactions. The court awarded Billy $675,670.68 plus interest. The court refused, however, to find summarily against Weber on all counts, and the suit had yet to go to trial. The whole production left Billy bewildered. "I'm a piano man, not a businessman," he said.

§ § §

All the legal wrangling didn't leave much time for music, but Billy did find time to relive a fourth-grade triumph. In 1992 the Nicholas Cage, Sarah Jessica Parker, James Caan film *Honeymoon in Vegas* featured the gimmick of having contemporary stars such as Bono from U2, John Mellencamp, country stalwart Willie Nelson, and a host of others record tunes that Elvis had made hits. Where most artists did only one, Billy recorded two, "All Shook Up" and "Heartbreak Hotel." His take on "All Shook Up" came out as a single, and while it topped out on the *Billboard* Hot 100 Singles chart at #92, it reached #6 on the *Billboard* Adult Contemporary chart. During the summer, he also ran away to Europe for a week or so, delivering master classes in London and Germany.

By 1993, it had been four tumultuous years since the release of *Storm Front*, and high time for Billy to start recording again. He certainly had a tremendous amount to write about. Not just the lawsuit, though it weighed heavily in the lyrics and in the anger of some of the music. The tumult of his professional life and all the legal proceedings was countered by the security of his life as a happy family man with a wife and daughter he loved. "The essence of the album is a loss of faith, a search for and understanding of how to deal with that, and a renewal of faith in substantial things: faith in love, faith in one's self, faith in the things that have always been there," Billy said.

To help him express it musically, he brought in longtime James Taylor associate Danny "Kootch" Kortchmar, fresh off producing Neil Young and Toto. Recorded mostly at Billy's converted boathouse on Shelter Island, he called the album *River of Dreams*, which was also the title of the first single. The tune had a feel somewhere between gospel and the South African choral music mbube, popularized by Ladysmith Black Mambazo (via Paul Simon's *Graceland*). Billy leavened this mix with some remarkable falsetto vocals and funky piano. "It's really a play on the phrase 'stream of consciousness,'" Billy explains. "There are biblical phrases in there, evocations of baptism and resurrection, and a great deal of symbolism in the river and seas. I'm always using water as a metaphor."

The single preceded the album, coming out in July and peaking at #3 on the *Billboard* Hot 100, #2 on the Mainstream Rock Tracks chart, and #1 on the Adult Contemporary chart. It heralded several elements of the new album. It reflected the juxtaposed soul of a forty-four-year-old man still making rock and roll, still coming to grips with the upshot of several youthful indiscretions, from "borrowing boats" to his first marriage.

In some ways *River of Dreams* was Billy's most personal recording, mostly because he dealt with his subjects in a less personal, more subconscious, or stream of consciousness sort of way. "I realized," Billy said, "I just can't write about myself anymore. It's about things that are more abstract. It's just not so simple to explain things anymore. But also, you don't feel the compulsion to have to!"

"I used to be afraid of being in my forties," he also said. "Now I find out my forties are pretty good. Of course, I'm rich and I'm married to Christie Brinkley. That *will* tend to skew one's view of things."

One of the crunchiest albums he ever recorded, *River of Dreams* featured guest artists like Billy's fellow former Long Island '60s club rat Leslie West, chart-topping R&B vocal group Color Me Badd, and vocalist Crystal Taliefero, fresh off her stint with Bruce Springsteen. Christie painted the cover, a primitive Rousseau-like dreamscape of her sleeping husband. She also, as she had so many times previously, made a guest appearance in the video, shot somewhere in the wilds of Connecticut.

Columbia set the album up well. Billy was the first musical guest on the debut episode of David Letterman's new CBS late-night talk show, *The Late Show*, on August 30. He was also VH1's Artist of the Month. He appeared on *The Today Show* and the TV news magazine *Dateline NBC*. Press coverage was widespread, and the reviews were strong.

"He's hardly the writer of empty pop hits that his critical reputation suggests," critic Greg Sandow, who more often dealt with classical music than pop, wrote in his A-minus review of the album in *Entertainment Weekly*. "Even his early albums are full of off-center surprises: bittersweet vignettes of everyday life ('Scenes from an Italian Restaurant'), wry self-appraisals ('Piano Man') and advice to troubled friends ('James'). But now his serious strain, which he himself called 'journalistic,' takes an intensely personal turn . . ."

On the strength of the single, all that setup, and the fact that Billy hadn't had an album out for four years, *River of Dreams* debuted at #1 on the *Billboard* 200 Albums chart, and stayed there for three weeks, ultimately selling more than 5 million copies. "It's sort of like . . . intercourse without foreplay," Billy joked about starting off at the top of the charts. "I don't know whether to feel cheated or elated."

"Rock is a cannibalizing business—It eats its own. I was hip for about a second in the seventies. But here we are. I'm forty-four. It's twenty years since *Piano Man* and I have a number-one album. That's not supposed to happen."

The other singles from the album were almost afterthoughts. "All About Soul," as heartfelt a love song as "Shameless," peaked at #29 on the *Billboard* Hot 100, and reached #6 on the Adult Contemporary chart. "That song started out very fast," Billy recalls about recording it. "Danny Kortchmar, who was producing the album, said 'Why don't you slow it down?' and when I slowed the song down, it revealed itself to be a whole different emotion. There was a throb in the song, and I just had a picture of a woman waiting for a man at night. And it became sexy; it became really deep."

"The basic inner something which I refer to as soul, the inner core [is] what you call on when the shit really comes down. Soul is what each person has within before there is love, or even after there is love."

Even prettier, the third single, "Lullabye (Goodnight, My Angel)" only made it to #77 on the Hot 100. A tribute to his still young daughter, it had an elegiac quality that foreshadowed much of what was going to happen in the next year personally. It also presaged much of what was to come musically from Billy. "I had a classical piano piece and I thought this would be the ideal lyric idea to set to this piece," he recalls. "My daughter had a great deal of anxiety . . . and I wanted to reassure her that I would never leave her."

"I love hearing Alexa's voice. Something about having a little girl is heartbreaking. It's a feeling I never had before. I don't want to miss her growing up—any of it," Billy said. He also said, "She likes a lot of this 'high life.' But we've told her she's going to have to make her own way. She's got jobs, she has an allowance she has to earn . . . I spoil her in ways that all fathers spoil their daughters, but she's not going to grow up in a cocoon."

River of Dreams offered Billy one more legal challenge in the form of defending against yet another high-profile plagiarism suit. Gary Zimmerman, characterized in the press as "a struggling Long Island songwriter," claimed that both "River of Dreams" and "We Didn't Start the Fire" copped parts from his 1986 song "Nowhere Land." He further claimed that he had gotten Billy the song via a mutual friend.

The other lawsuits had firmed up the resolve that Billy had felt with the first suit nearly a decade earlier. Billy was ready, willing, and more than able to go to court. He had lawyers working for him full time anyway. What was one more thing for them to do?

"Billy Joel has said he is going to fight this case tooth and nail," Leonard Marks said, echoing Billy's sentiments about the older case almost verbatim. "He will never settle this case. Billy has never met this fellow, never heard of him, never heard any song of his."

Zimmerman dropped the suit a little over a year after he filed it.

As *River of Dreams* hit, EMI saw that as an ideal moment to reissue the album *The Hassles* on CD, in a very limited run of 7,500 copies. Billy didn't particularly object to this, but he did have Eastman write EMI a letter requesting that they please, please not call it a Billy Joel record. In fact, according to Jeff Daniels, reissues coordinator for EMI at the time, "He actually asked us to put a song on it."

With a new album to promote, Billy hit the road with a vengeance, facing a tour that started in September 1993 and kept chugging with a few short breaks until June 1994. At forty-four, Billy was beginning to feel his age, and for the first time looked at what his agent Dennis Arfa had booked and found it a bit daunting. "I like to play and make music, but I'm so burnt out with traveling and touring and the grind," he lamented. "I used to be a maniac onstage."

Billy continued the tradition of the family-friendly back stage, and Christie and Alexa were frequently with him. But his daughter would turn eight years old while the tour ran, and was in school. As Billy noted when they got married, both he and Christie worked, and while they might have been better remunerated for their labors than some of their neighbors (and considering where they lived, less well remunerated than others), Christie's work took her away sometimes as well. Still, they did find moments on the road to be together. "I love it when he's on the road," Christie told a TV news crew. "I love all the showbiz stuff . . . I guess, deep down, I'm just impressed by all that stuff."

For someone who doesn't aspire to it, however, the rock and roll lifestyle begins to wear thin. Many musicians have said words to the effect that they don't get paid to play the shows while they're on tour. They play the shows for free. What they're being paid for is traveling on buses for hours on end, not being able to sleep in their own beds for weeks at a time, eating hit or miss food, hurrying up and waiting for equipment and load-outs and sound checks, keeping to a very rigorous schedule, and meeting and greeting local radio personnel and newspeople and retailers after the show. Even at the high line of touring, it can, as Billy said, be a grind.

For a happily married rock star, there are other temptations as well. "Sure there are still groupies," Billy admitted. "But even if I was tempted to screw around I couldn't—everyone knows who I am. And I love my wife."

CHAPTER 21

SO FAR SHE HASN'T RUN

Despite how it looked on TV, the Billy/Christie marriage was going through a bad patch. It was the cause of Alexa's anxiety, which Billy addressed in the lyrics to "Lullabye (Goodnight, My Angel)." Apparently, the union really hit the skids during that tour.

"I'm married to Christie Brinkley," Billy mused at the time, "[and] the comment I get is, 'Man, you've got it made . . .' But you know what? Nobody really knows the inside of somebody's life."

In divorce, as in marriage, it takes two to make it happen. In the case of Billy and Christie, part of the reason for the divorce might have had to do with Billy's devotion to the trinity of sex and drugs and rock and roll. Christie didn't mind the rock and roll, but she was not big on the drugs.

"Outside of Rocky's Sports Arena, during Brian Ruggles's fortieth birthday party, I caught Christie bawling out Billy," recalls Gentile, who, in addition to attending the party, also provided the entertainment, a band that featured Jon Small and platinum producer Ken Wallace. "He had gone out to have a Marlboro. She was saying, 'I'm sick and tired of you and your friends passing drugs around me. They're all drunk and they think I'm stupid enough not to know what's going on.'"

Billy and Christie separated around Thanksgiving 1993, during a two-week break in the tour. When the tour began a short West Coast leg during the first week of December, Christie and Alexa weren't there.

One "divorced dad" thing Billy did was to arrange a coming-out party for Alexa, a very elaborate affair at a legendary Suffolk County landmark, the Castle. It was planned for the spring of 1994.

For her part, Christie decided to honor one of her New Year's resolutions and go skiing. She chose Telluride as her destination, and was invited to join a friend at the home of reputed millionaire Rick Taubman. Taubman invited her to return a couple of weeks later to try out heli-skiing—in which a helicopter drops skiers on an otherwise inaccessible, previously unskied slope in the Rockies. Christie took Taubman up on his offer and returned several weeks later, in early April 1994. As they were finding their destination, the helicopter got caught in a crosswind and crashed into the side of the mountain.

"We just dropped," she said. "All of a sudden it was like someone cut the cords to the elevator, like the mountain was sucking us in, zooming into us."

The copter landed, and then it started to roll 200 feet down a 40-degree slope. "I would look out the window," Brinkley says of the fall, "and see sky-mountain-snow, sky-mountain-snow."

Considering how bad the crash was—the tail snapped off of the helicopter during impact—most of the injuries were relatively minor. Taubman, the first thrown from the helicopter, was the worst injured, breaking several ribs, his scapula, and his collarbone, and suffering a collapsed lung. He spent some time in intensive care. Brinkley was badly shaken up and banged around but was ambulatory at the scene. A week later, the only evidence that she had been in the crash was a splint on her wrist.

Billy canceled several dates on the tour, rushed to her side, and brought her back to Long Island. "We have been there to support each other during critical times, and expect to be there for each other in the future," Brinkley said. "When Billy was stricken with kidney stones in February, [I] helped nurse him back to health. And when [I] was involved in [my] hellish skiing accident, Billy came to [my] rescue."

Despite Billy's ministrations, after Christie recovered, she rushed back to Colorado to be by Taubman's side. Because of the accident, Billy canceled Alexa's party.

Billy was still on the road the day he and Christie made their separation public. During the previous few days, on a short break in the tour schedule, Billy had done a session in Nashville, recording "Light as the Breeze" for *Tower of Song*, a tribute to Leonard Cohen that would also feature Billy's buddy Sting and his soon-to-be-frequent touring partner Elton John, among many others. He did the session with noted country producer Tony Brown. It seemed like a good possible direction for Billy to explore.

"'Shameless' had already become a big hit [for Garth Brooks]," noted Elaine Schock, "so I thought it would be a really good idea for him to become involved in country music."

Billy and Christie announced the separation before the report of Christie's helicopter crash appeared in a *People* cover story. The story still called Billy her husband, which would be technically true until August, when the divorce became final.

"Although we have been separated since Thanksgiving," Schock quoted Billy as saying in a press release, "we felt it was best to keep the situation private while we were resolving the details. This was out of our enormous love and concern for our daughter and our desire to protect our friendship, which is one of great affection and respect."

"Some believe Joel's roving eye destroyed the marriage," Mike Knapp wrote in the English *Daily Mail*, "that the short, plain man whose low self-esteem was boosted by the love of a beautiful woman found he had to go on discovering new young beauties to repeat that ego boost."

Other rumors circulated that Billy wasn't the only one with a roving eye (and other anatomical areas). Those reports had Christie already carrying Taubman's child when the helicopter went down, though she didn't give birth to their son, Jack, until a year after the crash.

All Christie would say was, "My divorce was a long time coming."

"We had so many laughs and adventures," she considered. "It was great for years, and then it turned . . . One thing I do for our daughter, Alexa, is that I don't talk about it in the media, because I don't think she needs to hear it. Whatever he did is in the past."

The day the announcement was sent to the papers, Billy was playing the first of two nights at the Miami Arena in Florida. "I was on tour with Billy and I knew he was very distressed because of the breakup of his marriage to Christie . . . Suddenly, he cut 'Movin' Out' from his set because a local writer had wrongly said it was a slap at Christie," said old friend Bill Zampino, who was Billy's road manager at the time. "Samuel Barber's 'Adagio for Strings,' one of the most emotional pieces in classical music—it was the music played across America when President Franklin Roosevelt died . . .—[was] probably Billy's favorite piece of music in the world . . . he substituted 'Shades of Gray' from *River of Dreams*, but as a prelude, he went into 'Adagio for Strings,' playing it on his synthesizer's string setting. I looked at the pain on his face, and it was a heart-rending moment. But, that's one of Billy's great talents: He finds ways to preserve and keep alive the things he loves."

The divorce might have improved his relationship with his daughter. "When you have scheduled time, you make the time," Christie said. "And he dove right in and became a really good dad. Now he's like our built-in babysitter."

"I enjoy my daughter's company and that's the most important thing in my life for me right now," Billy concurred.

"I owed it to her," Christie said, "to not have her feel like she had to choose camps."

Billy tried to put a cavalier spin on the whole matter. "Now that she's gone," he said, "I park my motorcycle in the living room."

Very shortly after her divorce with Billy was finalized, Christie married Taubman. Months later, they were divorced, and Christie had both Alexa and Jack, her six-week-old son with Taubman, in tow when she moved back to New York. She credits the whirlwind courtship, marriage, and divorce to post-traumatic stress syndrome, and refers to the marriage to Taubman as "the Colorado disaster."

About three weeks after the *River of Dreams* tour pulled off the road after a European leg that saw the band play throughout England, the Netherlands, Belgium, Italy, Austria, Germany, France, and Switzerland, Billy was back on the road again, this time with Elton John for the first leg of their "Face to Face" tour. It was something the two of them had been considering for some time.

The two had a great deal in common, beyond being a pair of singer/songwriter/pianists. They were contemporaries, whose first U.S. albums came out not only at just about the same time, but also through the same distributor. Elton was often the artist whom record company people had told Irwin Mazur that Billy was too similar to when they turned down Billy's early solo demos. They were both big fans of soul and show music, and both used the piano in rock music as few artists since Little Richard and Jerry Lee Lewis had been able to do.

"We first met in a hotel in Amsterdam in the seventies and both expressed professional admiration," Billy says. "It was my idea to tour."

Billy says he floated the idea again, "just prior to the *Storm Front* tour, which began in 1989. Unfortunately, the timing wasn't right for Elton."

In 1994, the time was right for both artists. John was already on a duets kick anyway, having just recorded *Duets*, an album that paired him with artists ranging from Little Richard to RuPaul to Tammy Wynette. The tour with Billy, while not nearly so wildly eclectic, worked in a similar manner. Both artists brought their bands, book-ending their separate sets with duets—Elton and Billy on a pair of pianos that rose from under the stage, both bands working together. "The funny thing is," notes Billy's drummer Liberty DeVitto, "way back when, when I got the phone call for the Billy audition, I asked, 'What is Billy into?' They said, 'Go buy [John's] *Captain Fantastic*.' So I learned all of Nigel's licks."

"When I get together with Elton, I get to sing his songs, he sings my songs, we sing both of our songs together," Billy said. "It's something different. I like him. He's a good guy."

"He had a nine-foot piano and I had a nine-foot piano, facing each other and looking across eighteen feet of gleaming ebony, and there was Elton John and we were in a stadium with seventy or eighty thousand people screaming . . . I was struck every night by how amazing this was."

Not only was the show selling out stadiums, it was selling them out for three and six nights at a clip—two nights at Foxboro Stadium outside Boston, three at Veterans Stadium in Philadelphia, six at Giants Stadium in New Jersey. The tour went through the better part of July and August of 1994, around the time Billy's divorce was being finalized.

"He's a very caring man," Billy says of John. "Around the time I was getting divorced, I thought one of our shows at the Meadowlands was canceled. There was a big storm. I was home in East Hampton and had a couple of bottles of wine. Then last minute, the gig was on . . . Elton took me out to lunch the next day. He goes, 'Are you OK?' I said, 'Yeah.' He said, 'No you're not! You were blitzed last night . . . Is there anything I can do? I care about you.' . . . Elton John, he's got a big heart.

"When we're on stage together, part of me is wishing I could see this because it must be a lot of fun to see 'cause it really feels good," Billy said.

Touring with Elton also offered him something that he really hadn't had for a while, especially on stage: competition. Until the "Face to Face" tour, the only person Billy had to live up to on stage was . . . Billy.

"It definitely lights a fire under you," Billy said. "I mean, he's knocking out hit after hit after hit, and you're sitting backstage going, 'Oh, my god, how am I ever going to follow that?' and we have to."

"He's a better piano player than I thought he was, which has motivated me to play better than I normally would have."

A little over a month after getting off the road with Elton, the *River of Dreams* caravan pulled out again, playing the Midwest through October before moving on to spend much of November and December in Australia and the early part of 1995 in Japan.

For the Japanese tour, part of Billy's entourage was his new steady girlfriend, artist Carolyn Beegan. He had already helped her get a show of her paintings, set her up in a new beachside condo, and bought her a new Mercedes. On January 17, Billy and Carolyn were in bed on the twenty-second floor of an Osaka hotel. At a bit after 5 A.M., an earthquake with its epicenter in Kobe, 20 miles away, woke them up.

"I still don't know how that room held together," he said. "What we did immediately after the shaking stopped was to throw our clothes on, run downstairs and try to get clear of the building."

It was not Billy's first major earthquake. He had become as used to them as anyone can be while he was living in Los Angeles. However, it was probably the worst quake that Billy had ever been through, and it was Carolyn's first.

"Carolyn hadn't done a lot of things before she met Billy," said Elaine Schock.

Billy and Carolyn made it to the lobby, where they hooked up with the rest of Billy's entourage, who were in the same hotel. They had all made it down the pitch-dark stairs, and they all left the building together. They were quite lucky. The quake devastated that part of Japan, killing around 5,000 people.

The first thought on Billy's mind was that this scene of devastation would be all over the morning news, and he needed to get word to Alexa that he hadn't been hurt in the disaster. As soon as he could locate a working telephone, he called his daughter to let her know he was okay. "We understood the news reports made it look pretty bad," he said.

"It was a tough tour," recalls Elaine Schock. "Billy was brokenhearted half the time, desperate to see Alexa . . . I don't think Christie made it easy for him to see his daughter, and she was his world. She probably still is."

In March, Elton and Billy took the "Face to Face" tour on a West Coast swing, playing through San Diego and Las Vegas before moving through Texas and the Midwest, finally ending up in Miami about three weeks later. The tour was a phenomenon, breaking house records wherever it went. "I can make a lot of money with Elton John," Billy noted. And he would.

CHAPTER 22

I GIVE MY TIME TO
TOTAL STRANGERS

By 1995, the lawsuits were over. Everyone had settled with Billy—Weber, the former accountants, Weber's attorney, and a variety of others. Billy settled the Grubman suit, taking home about $3 million, late in 1993. The money was paid by one of Grubman, Indursky and Schindler's major clients, Sony Music. Rick London was the last to settle, holding out for a document that would prevent Billy from pursuing the suit in the future. That effort got thrown out of court when a judge granted Billy's motion to discontinue the London suit but preserving his right to pursue the claims sometime down the road, if need be.

"It's done," Leonard Marks said of the legal proceedings. "Full-stop. No one is going into any detail. Everyone believes [the suit] should remain dead-ass neutral."

In the wake of the case, despite no high-profile trial (save the one in the press), attorneys in the entertainment business began to mind their ethical p's and q's a little more closely. "Everybody's being a lot more cautious about conflicts of interest," noted one Los Angeles entertainment lawyer.

After the dust cleared, the kind of money Joel could have been making for years became evident. During 1993 and 1994, according to an estimate by *Forbes*, Joel's gross income was $33 million. Between the settlements (perhaps 10 percent of the $90 million dollars he had originally sought actually landed in his pocket), the chart-topping, multi-platinum success of *River of Dreams*, and the incessant touring over the course of the previous year, Billy was finally sitting pretty financially.

He threw his new paramour, Carolyn Beegan, a birthday party in 1995. One of the people who attended was Sting, who found himself in a similar position to the one Billy had been in when Billy sold Sting his New York City digs: Sting's accountant had just been jailed in London for stealing nearly $10 million from Sting. Now Billy could provide tips on coping. They spoke about it during Caroline's party.

"She's very lovely," said Elaine Schock, who, as Billy's publicist found herself publicizing events for Caroline as well, "and I really liked her."

Beegan was also with him when Christie Brinkley got married for the fourth time, to Peter Cook in a late-summer 1995 ceremony in the Hamptons. Cook, a former cover boy (he had been on the cover of *GQ* as a model), was now an architect. He and Brinkley had been dating since that winter. It was one of two major celebrity weddings that weekend, the other being the union of John F. Kennedy Jr. and Carolyn Bessette. Perhaps Kennedy's lineage made it easier for his secrets to be kept, as no one found out where his wedding was—except for the invited guests—until long after it was over. The Brinkley–Cook wedding, on the other hand, was punctuated by the sound of helicopters, full of eager paparazzi, hovering above.

"If the press had gotten wind of the Kennedy wedding," said one of Brinkley's friends, "that's where all the helicopters . . . would have been."

The ceremony, at twilight, found the bride wearing another long white gown. "I'm happy for her," Billy remarked.

Rather than tour or even think about a new album in 1996, Billy took the concept of the master classes he had done occasionally over the course of the previous decade on tour. "I wanted to concentrate on students," he said. "Hopefully it will be a core audience of people who are interested in a career in some kind of industry related to music, whether it be as a composer or recording artist or someone who might want to work as a journalist or at a record company."

"What I have on this mission, doing these colleges, is all of this information going around in my head about the type of work that I do, that I don't get asked by journalists," he added.

Like so many of his tours, this one kept him on the road from the middle of January through early May, primarily on the East Coast, though veering as far west as Akron, Ohio, and Memphis, Tennessee. Only this time he wasn't hauling a band and entourage with him. When he got on stage, for the most part, it was just him and a piano.

"I think it's such a good thing for people to be able to listen to a professional when it comes to the creative aspect of this gig," he said of the tour. "Because when I was starting out, there was nobody to ask."

❀ ❀ ❀

Billy was involved in another ceremony in March 1997, this one honoring him. The American Society of Composers, Authors and Publishers (ASCAP) invited him to Washington, D.C., to present him with their annual Founder's Award. The reception, dinner, and ceremony were held in the House Ways and Means Committee hearing room. It was understood that in addition to bringing him to Washington to honor him, they wanted to use his star power to lobby for the songwriters' agenda, including the Digital Millennium Copyright Act, the Sonny Bono Law, and especially the Fairness in Music Licensing Bill, which brought the life of a copyright in America into parity with the life of a copyright throughout most of the world. One of those meetings would be with Senate majority leader Trent Lott. The task of briefing Billy on all this pending legislation fell to ASCAP's chief of staff, Bill Thomas.

"I was kind of nervous about meeting the guy," Thomas said. "Billy had a reputation as being uncooperative and a bit of an SOB. I found him very gracious.

"I was supposed to meet him in the bar at three. We knew there was a lot riding on the meeting with Lott. We used the Billy Joel card to open the door. When you really want to get their attention, bring a star.

"Billy had a beer and I had an iced tea. He was incredibly focused, really, really smart. He asked great, direct questions, no pop star attitude at all. He asked me to repeat certain phrases. He acted as if he was in training, as if he was given this assignment and he was going to wow them. He totally got it, was willing to do whatever we asked him to do.

"He never mentioned his personal politics. He fired questions at me for an hour and a half. He totally understood why we took the opportunity to give him the award in DC. He was very proactive about it.

"This guy is tough and pugnacious, but I didn't get any of the negatives. He went through the congressional rigamarole, was ushered into Lott's office. Everyone's staff was flipping out. He was incredibly gracious. He went in with Marilyn (Bergman, ASCAP's chairperson) and Lott for forty-five minutes. The message was the same as the lobbyists would give—he just gave us access.

"At the [awards] event he was also incredibly gracious, did lots of 'grip and grin' shots and autographed them later, but he really lit up when he played, so full of joy when he had the opportunity to play."

❀ ❀ ❀

On August 7, 1997, Garth Brooks played to a huge crowd at a free show in New York City's Central Park. The show was cablecast live on HBO, produced by Jon Small. During the show, one of Brooks's special guests was the guy who wrote "Shameless."

The one thing Billy wasn't doing during this period was writing songs. He had started once again dabbling in composing more "serious" or classical music—as he had inadvertently been doing when he was faking his way through Ms. Francis's lessons forty years earlier.

It had started when he wrote the music for "Lullabye." He had this wonderful composition, and then he realized that he needed, for his purposes on *River of Dreams*, to write lyrics for it, to turn it into a song.

Some, even among his inner circle, attributed his lack of new songs to a near crippling case of writer's block. For whatever reason, four years came and went without a new Billy Joel album, and Columbia Records wanted one. As is so often the case when artists can't or won't create, Columbia decided it was time for another "greatest hits" collection.

"This was actually suggested by Columbia Records," Billy noted about the album. "They came to me and said, 'You know, you have enough material for a third greatest hits album.' And I said, 'No, it's impossible.' And then I realized that the last greatest hits, which was a double greatest hits album, came out in '85. Here we are in '97. So twelve years, that's a while, you know, in the music business."

Where most greatest hits collections included some new material as an incentive for fans with all of the other records, and other anal-retentive completists, to actually shell out money for it—the record company phrase for this is "filling out the package"—Billy wasn't writing songs. That was what made the record necessary in the first place. Billy had no new songs to offer. Nor was he about to include one of his classical compositions on a pop album—not that that idea would have thrilled Columbia particularly, either. So instead of new Billy Joel songs, *Greatest Hits, Volume III* had something Billy had never done before on one of his studio albums: covers.

"I've been writing classical music for the last three years now," he explained. "It's not like I can turn on a dime and crank out a pop tune. My heart just wasn't in it."

It wasn't that Billy was averse to covers. He actually had a minor hit with his version of the Beatles' "Back in the USSR" from the *Kohuept* album, and had recorded the Elvis tunes for the *Honeymoon in Vegas* soundtrack. His self-image, however, was caught up in being a composer. He became a recording artist to show off his songwriting rather than his performing. Cover tunes, on the other hand, were the domain of the performer. Yet during sound checks before their live concerts, the Billy Joel Band never played songs they were going to do during the show.

"We do Traffic and Hendrix and the Beatles and Stones," Billy says. "We know them because we were all in bar bands at one time or another."

"He has a stable of songs that I've come to know over the years," adds David Rosenthal, the other keyboard player with the band, "but sometimes he surprises everybody. The guy knows thousands of songs! Just about any song he's ever heard in his life, he can sit down and fig-ure out in real time. He never practices it."

One of the covers on the album was Billy's version of Leonard Cohen's "Light as the Breeze," which came from the session he'd done in Nashville and had already appeared on *Tower of Song* two years earlier. "I just thought that song was so great as soon as I heard it," Billy said.

The second cover was Jerry Goffin and Carole King's "Hey Girl," a song he had done live with the Lost Souls. It had already been a hit three times—in 1963, it became the first major chart record for soul singer Freddie Scott. Pop star disguised as rocker Bobby Vee recorded it as part of a medley in 1968, and teen-pop idol Donny Osmond took it into the Top 10 in 1972—an interesting, if spotty, pedigree.

"I recorded that song a few years ago," Billy said. "I had just split up with Christie and my daughter was going to live far away, and I was very sad. When I was singing that song, that's who I was singing it to, my little girl."

Columbia released the third cover, "To Make You Feel My Love," as a single. The song was a previously unreleased Bob Dylan tune. "[Dylan] sent a guy to my house with this demo tape of Bob singing 'To Make You Feel My Love,'" Billy recalls. "They wouldn't send the tape by mail . . . I guess he's paranoid about tapes getting out . . . Anyway, as soon as I heard the song, I said, 'This song is fantastic. I want to do this song.' And Bob actually wanted me to do it. So, who am I to disagree with Bob Dylan?"

"A Bob Dylan song is not supposed to be all sweet and sugary . . . It couldn't be too polished, it couldn't be too smooth, it couldn't be too rich. It has to be a little lean and salty . . ."

Billy's lean and salty version of the Dylan song, performed starkly with piano and drums, and in a somewhat unconsciously nasal tribute to the original, hit #50 on the *Billboard* Hot 100.

Another one of the songs on the album was "Allentown." To celebrate the fifteenth anniversary of the song, a group of Lehigh Valley industrialists wanted to revisit the song, to use it to highlight the changes in the area over the previous decade and a half. "People still have certain beliefs about Allentown and the rest of the Lehigh Valley based on that song," noted Sara Anderson Greer, director of marketing for the Lehigh Valley Economic Development Corp. They made an upbeat video of the growth the area had achieved in the previous fifteen years. They also held a Billy Joel look-alike contest.

The album probably didn't do as well as Columbia would have hoped, reaching #9 on the *Billboard* 200 Albums chart and selling "only" platinum.

❄ ❄ ❄

Billy has always like the sea, from the winter he spent on the oyster boats to the boats he would "borrow" out of the harbor, to the rowboat he would sand and finish while Jon and Elizabeth worked out their post-marital problems, to the boats he owned during his years of stardom. He enjoyed fishing, enjoyed just going out on Long Island Sound or the ocean. He also very much enjoyed the idea that he lived on an island, and that much of it was approachable by water. With that in mind, he helped design the Shelter Island Runabout, a high-end ($300,000) luxury speedboat that can hit 55 miles per hour. He even owns the patent on the hull design and collects a royalty on that piece of intellectual property for each of the seven crafts his company turns out each year.

"We came up with an idea that I though was a pretty good idea. A boat that goes fast but looks like a traditional commuter boat," he says with no small amount of pride. "It's a limited production. It's a very small boat building yard out here in the east end of Long Island."

The company continues to employ fourteen carpenters and electricians to turn out the crafts. They have more orders than they have boats but seem determined to maintain a level of handcrafted quality. One of the first of these boats went to a very high echelon person at Microsoft. "Even sailboaters who look down their noses at powerboats wave to this one," Billy notes.

"I'm not going to become wealthy from it," he adds. "I wanted to help revive a traditional old boat building industry."

While Billy was spending a great deal of his time around Shelter Island, the Hamptons had gone from a bohemian retreat to the summer playground of the rich and famous. The property values went through the roof, and beach houses became a premium item, one of the last words in New York status symbols. In this environment, comedian Jerry Seinfeld, the star and co-producer of the most successful situation comedy on television, decided he wanted a place in the Hamptons, and asked Billy how much he wanted for his. Billy offhandedly came up with $34 million.

"I threw out a number," Billy notes, "and he said OK. So I asked my daughter, 'Should I sell this house?' And she said, 'Daddy, change is good.'"

He had bought out his ex-wife Christie Brinkley's share of the house only a couple of years earlier, when Christie was suffering some business reversals and needed the cash. She got $3 million for her half of the house as part of their divorce, and Billy stayed in the Hamptons. However, the sale of his home now left Billy, effectively, homeless, and for a while he had problems committing to a new house, backing out on a deal for one in Southampton, before finally settling on palacial digs on Shelter Island.

With all this going on, there was one thing that wasn't evident in Billy's life: new music, and this was taking a toll on his band. Liberty DeVitto, to supplement his income, had taken a job as one of the "pros" at Rock and Roll Fantasy Camp, where, for $5,000, people could spend a week playing with people like DeVitto, Leslie West, and even Who lead singer Roger Daltry. DeVitto also volunteered with an organization called "Little Kids Rock" that brought music and musicians into public schools.

It beat doing nothing while waiting to hit the road with Billy.

CHAPTER 23

COULD I HAVE MISSED
THE OVERTURE

The reason for this dearth of new Billy Joel songs was simple. There were none. When Billy finished the *River of Dreams* record with the song "Famous Last Words"—"These are the last words I have to say"—it turned out that it wasn't just a song, it was a manifesto. Billy decided to go back to his earliest training, go back to where his father and half brother lived (in the musical sense). Billy stepped out of rock and back into the classical music he had abandoned when he became an Echo more than thirty years earlier.

He wouldn't be the first, and he certainly wouldn't be the last rocker to give up the raw electric power of the Marshall amp for the subtler dynamic power of the orchestra. Paul McCartney had already debuted his *Liverpool Oratorio* at Carnegie Hall. Frank Zappa had put out several albums of Pierre Boulez's avant-garde compositions as well as his own in an orchestral setting. Peter Townshend of the Who described the popular perception of this type of shift beautifully when he debuted an orchestral version of his material from his never-completed movie *Lifehouse*. "Oh, you know, what Sting does, or Paul McCartney does, or Paul Simon, or Pete Townshend does when they're a bit bored with their old rockers is they hire an orchestrator and an orchestra and masturbate in front of it."

This was not Billy's brief, however. His "classical training" had become a negative thing when people started slagging him in the press about *The Stranger*. But it was so ingrained in him, he felt he had no choice but to explore it. The idea had been bubbling in the back of his brain for years. Even as far back as 1989, he noted, "Writing orchestral work is something I've always wanted to do . . . If I'm going to live to Shostakovich's age, I've got a lot of stuff to write. And if it's not all rock and roll, so be it."

Like so many listeners, Billy had a catholic taste in music. He was very fond of Garth Brooks and Elton John but had been brought up in a classically oriented household. If rock and roll was rebellion against that, as he moved grudgingly into adulthood he came to appreciate "more mature" music. And like his influences and inspiration in rock— Paul McCartney et al.—he selected similarly lofty inspirations for this musical transition.

"I love other kinds of music just as much [as I like rock-and-roll]. George Gershwin was the greatest American composer because he worked in all different mediums and brought the street into the opera house," he said.

"I've been listening almost exclusively to classical music for the last half a dozen years," he added, "and now that's what I'm writing: classical music, piano pieces and sonatas and concertos and I'm even working on something that may turn into a symphony."

He was even using classical music as the introductory matter to his on-going, albeit sporadic, series of master classes. "This is magnificent music which reaches out and touches us two hundred years later, and here *I* am writing, 'I'm So Tired.'"

"I let these symphonies pound over me. Last time I felt like this was the first time I listened to Led Zeppelin. I felt puny. I am nothing. I am insignificant . . . I'm in my forties. I want to get out of this box I've been working in."

But, finally, he attributed his exodus from pop music mostly to ennui: "It was a real sense of 'I have done this and done this and done this and done this and now I want to do something else.'"

Any pop fan with some background in classical music realized that a great deal of Billy Joel's pop work had classical frames of reference. The orchestration in "Ballad of Billy the Kid" has touches of Copeland and Morricone. "Miami 2017" has elements of Bernstein. "Pressure" has a synth break that wouldn't sound out of place being played by a baroque string quartet.

"'The Longest Time,' could be a Haydn piece," Billy says. He also notes, "I was always writing classical music, even the popular songs I wrote. I recognize a lot of them as being classical piano pieces, and that's how I started composing when I was a kid."

He even began to recognize long-sublimated riffs from his youth that had innocently cropped up in his songs. "I was listening to a classical station and I heard a Mozart piece and it was 'Uptown Girl'—not the whole song, but the first few notes, and then it went away. I said, 'Holy shit! Mozart wrote that, too?'"

There could be little doubt at that time that Billy Joel had had his fill of creating pop. As for the reasons, that was open to question, and he really didn't deal with it in a very direct way except to say that it was what he wanted to do. Could it have anything to do with his younger half brother's success in that venue? Alexander Joel was twenty-five and a rising conductor and concert pianist when Billy made this leap of musical faith. Could it have been having the comfort and ability to choose a road his father had chosen not to travel in favor of the relative safety of engineering? Billy did spend time during the '90s with his father and Alexander.

All Billy would say was, "I have a drive to create another kind of music, classical music, which is my first love . . . I started out as a writer and composer and I got sidetracked being a rock star."

"Classical music was like the girl next door. Very sweet, very nice, but she didn't turn me on. I was a young stupid guy and I didn't appreciate her."

"I was kind of seduced by this, rock 'n' roll, what I call the flaming redhead with torn fishnet stockings."

"After thirty-five years of the affair, she didn't look so good anymore . . . And the girl next door was now a hot babe."

Of course, every hot babe has to be wooed. Billy went into creating composed "classical" music with a certain amount of trepidation. Could he bring anything to the party? What would the people at the party have to say about him? In a way, it was like the nouveaux riches in the Hamptons trying out their newly acquired manners in the old-money manors. Could he write this music and remain true to himself?

Could he write music that would be accepted by and speak to a classical audience? This was an audience, after all, that was way more critical and far less egalitarian than the rock audience for whom he had been writing during the previous four decades of his life.

"My greatest fear is that it's been done before. I assume that one way or another it probably has, but maybe with a different intent," he said.

He also realized that the classical audience could be way nastier than the rock audience. "In the classical world, they're real finicky," he said "They're going to be waiting for me with a knife and fork . . . But if I let that stop me, I'd never have done anything."

Nor did he let current trends influence what he did. Much of the composed music of the twentieth century took on a musical mantle that was perhaps more about academics than it was about aesthetics—twelve-tone music like that of Schoenberg and Berg, serialism like Phillip Glass and Steve Reich, atonal music like Boulez and Webern, aleatoric music like John Cage and Henry Cowell, third-stream music like Anthony Braxton and Gunther Schuller. These were the contemporary, modern threads in composed music during the later half of the twentieth century and into the twenty-first. Even in classical "composed" music, Billy Joel was a romantic at heart. However, he felt that his becoming a "throwback" of this nature could only be good for classical music.

Rather than introduce the world to Billy Joel, classical composer, with the piano pieces on which he'd been working, he did it with a London Symphony recording of "Elegy: The Great Peconic" for the *Music of Hope* CD. A compilation of world-premier classical recordings either composed or performed by Paul McCartney, Ray Charles, Billy, and others, the album came out in the winter of 2000. Billy's contribution was part of a larger, 40-minute orchestral suite called "The Scrimshaw Pieces," a musical evocation of the history of Long Island. "I wanted to write music about where I came from," he said.

"I've got to get this stuff orchestrated," he added, "and I've got to have it performed. And that's a big, expensive project. There's already been some interest from different orchestras—the Boston organization, the Pittsburgh organization, the Long Island Sympony . . . I think I'm capable of composing a good, substantive piece of classical music . . ."

While he wasn't sure what the classical hierarchy (if indeed there was such a thing) would think of this Johnny-come-lately pop star encroaching into their world, and with *romantic* music, no less, he felt that he could be good for a classical music business that had alienated younger listeners.

"The classical world is pretty much running out of audience now," he said. "They're dying off. They didn't reach out to enough boomers. The powers that be were pretty much promoting late-twentieth-century dissonant, atonal, modern twelve-tone compositions. They were scoffing at melodic composition."

His effort to embrace melodic composition, a cycle of piano compositions called *Fantasies & Delusions*, came out via Sony Classics, a sister label to his longtime "home" at Columbia Records, in 2001. As soon as he began writing the pieces that became *Fantasies & Delusions*, he knew he couldn't play them. He had never had the desire to make his mark in the competitive field of the classical concert pianist. More than three decades playing rock had both lessened that desire and atrophied the mental and physical muscles it takes to be a classical pianist. The pieces he was writing tended to be more complex than he could handle at the piano.

"When I got into rock, I lost the classical technique. I don't know if that's necessarily good or bad," he conceded.

For rock it might not have been a problem, but unlike Gershwin, he would not likely play his own classical compositions in concert. "The stuff that I'm writing is not music that I can actually play," he said. "The composition is beyond my capacities as a piano player. I would need a virtuoso, classically trained pianist to play a lot of this stuff because I'm not that good."

"My left hand was always a piece of ham; it just flopped on the piano . . . I wasn't going to be Vladimir Horowitz. I thought, 'I'll be a writer or an organist who just plays chords.'"

So Billy was no longer a composer who wrote for himself. While billed as a Billy Joel album, *Fantasies & Delusions* features Richard Joo, a classical pianist Billy's half brother, Alexander, had made known to him. "My brother is a classical conductor who lives in Vienna," Billy explained. "Richard is one of the guys my brother knows . . . I met him about seven years ago after we had done a concert and my brother introduced us."

The album did well—perhaps it was not up to the gold and platinum status of a Billy Joel album, but it certainly parlayed Billy's name recognition into extraordinary classical sales. The album reached #83 on the *Billboard* 200 Albums chart and #12 on the *Billboard* Top Internet Album Sales chart, and it headed the *Billboard* Top Classical Albums chart for more than a month. "Even with my pop albums, I've never been #1 for a month," Billy said. "Do you know who #2 is? Yo-Yo fucking Ma. This is a legitimate classical artist. I want to write him a letter and, you know, 'I'm sorry.' This guy is a *shtarker* [the Yiddish title of the Billy Joel song "Big Shot"] . . . a big heavy hitter. This is the Babe Ruth of the cello, and we're keeping him out of #1."

As of this writing, the album has sold close to 200,000 copies in the United States, a remarkable feat for a classical recording.

In many ways, when talking about the differences between pop music and classical music, Billy sounded as if he'd outgrown pop; whereas the babe in the high heels had been a turn-on, now she seemed tawdry. "One of the things you like about this kind of music is its variation, its shadings, nuance, subtlety," he said. "Rock and roll, on the other hand, obliterates. That's the essence of rock: to shatter, to shock. But the things we like about rock—it's sexual energy, passion, angst, rage—are in classical music, too."

If he found composing "classical" piano pieces melodically challenging, he found them structurally similar to his work in rock. "It's not all that different from well-written popular songs," Billy said. "There are themes, there are melodies, counterpoint. There are bridges, choruses. It's just a different way of doing them."

"The last song I wrote was on the last album of original material that I wrote, called *River of Dreams*. And the last song was 'Famous Last Words.' I was tired of writing songs. And I said, I'm just tired of talking about me, me, me . . . I wanted to write a different kind of music."

While "Famous Last Words" might have been the manifesto of not writing any more pop music for the foreseeable future, the piece that got him started was "Lullabye." He had written a lovely piece for piano and then that old feeling came over him. "A lot of times I feel like I've written a complete piece of music and then say, 'Oh, right, right—I'm writing a song,' so I'll put lyrics to it," he says. "If . . . there's some sort of emotional code inside of the music, to me, I feel like it's complete. I almost resent having to write words . . . I hate the tyranny of rhyme, too."

He decided that, after more than thirty-five years of setting lyrics to his music, his music was strong enough to stand on its own. Besides that, he just didn't feel like writing lyrics. "I suspect I wouldn't be very good at it now . . . you have to have the insane drive to need to do it, and I don't have that," he said.

Billy also hinted that his lyrics needed a level of inspiration that he just wasn't receiving at that time. "I write my best stuff to a particular person, but right now I'm between relationships."

When he mentioned this to one writer, that writer suggested maybe Columbia Records should set him up on blind dates. "Don't think they haven't tried," Billy retorted.

Another reason for his retirement from writing pop music harked back to his reason for making his solo album *Cold Spring Harbor* in the first place. He had wanted to be a songwriter whose work other people performed. Instead, with the success of *Piano Man* Billy wound up being the personal writer for one performer—himself. Just as he felt the need to stop writing to his limitations as a vocalist, he didn't want to write to his limitations as a musician anymore either. "The recording artist who has been doing my songs is this guy named Billy Joel and . . . I'm bored to death with him because he only has a . . . particular range and vision as a performing artist," he said.

Another aspect of this change in his career was a growing maturity. Rock and roll was a young man's game in most people's eyes (the Rolling Stones notwithstanding). Billy had always had this love-hate relationship with being a rock and roll personality, and now he had the opportunity to shuck it.

"I've had it," he said. "I don't want to be Willy Loman. I don't want to be a rock star. I want to be an artist . . . Now you got Elton doing Disney musicals. Paul Simon is working on a musical. Bruce is being John Steinbeck with a guitar. We're all trying to do something different."

Part of the conundrum of Billy Joel is that, while the world put the cape and cowl of "rock star" on his head, he never really accepted it. Beyond that, he never really felt that it fit right. "I don't feel like a rock star today," he mused. "Rock stars to me are still Paul McCartney and Mick Jagger. I'm supposed to be a rock star, but I just feel like a guy from Hicksville."

Despite not writing a new song in seven years, Billy didn't fall off the pop music radar. In the spring of 1999, Ray Charles inducted Billy into the Rock and Roll Hall of Fame. Even as he was recording demos of his classical pieces he went on tour as Billy Joel, the performer with the limited range. The last show of his 1999 tour fell on New Year's Eve at Madison Square Garden, and it was decided that Billy should record it.

"The New Year's Eve concert was a very different concert even without planning to record because of the date, venue, and situation. It was the last concert I had planned on my last tour and it just happened to be in New York, my hometown, and at Madison Square Garden, so we had a longer show and played songs we hadn't done . . . for many years. It was geared toward the change of the Millennium," he said.

"Remarkably enough, there were no screw-ups. Considering the fact that we were doing so many songs that we weren't used to doing, it was a very smooth evening."

❦ ❦ ❦

During the summer of 2000, Billy appeared on *The Today Show* with one of the world's most renowned sax players, President Bill Clinton. Together they tried to help promote music education. Ironically, Billy would get Bill's wife in trouble several months later when "Captain Jack" reared his ugly head in the hard-fought New York senatorial race. Someone doing sound at the rally where Hillary Clinton announced her candidacy put on a CD of *Billy Joel's Greatest Hits, Volume I & Volume II*. Of course, one of the songs on it was "Captain Jack." Her opponent, Rudolph Giuliani, the mayor of New York, used the song's lyrics to make political hay, claiming that "the song glorifies drug use and masturbation."

Even as a classical composer, Billy remained one of pop music's most popular live attractions, especially in his continued pairing with Elton John. The two revisited the "Face to Face" tour in 2001 and 2002. In 2001, they did thirty-one shows, grossing nearly $2 million a show. The tour broke records all across the country. "This is a hell of a show," said promoter Larry Magid. "It's three hours and twenty minutes of hits, but beyond that, it's the way the show is presented and the repartee between the artists on stage."

In November 2002, *Billboard* proclaimed it the most successful touring package of all time.

Despite the fact that no new Billy Joel songs were forthcoming, his old ones were a staple on classic-rock and soft-rock radio, and the videos continued to be presented on VH1. One of the most popular shows on the adult-oriented video music channel was a program called *Pop-Up Videos*. On this show, little factual nuggets would appear in text balloons throughout favorite videos. "Keeping the Faith" got the pop-up video treatment, and the show made snide comments about the white shoes Joel wears and his dancing. It also included a swipe at Christie: "It's rumored Christie didn't keep the faith with Billy."

Billy called VH1 to complain—he claimed kids would tease Alexa about it in school. VH1 pulled the *Pop-Up* version of the video.

By the turn of the millennium, the pop artist Billy Joel had sold 60 million albums in the United States alone. "I couldn't have been born at a better time," he remarked. "I was born at the height of the baby boom, fell in love with popular music, learned how to play an instrument . . . and, for some reason or another, communicated with a great many of my peers . . . I was in the right place at the right time."

❀ ❀ ❀

One thing that no one could have anticipated at the turn of the millennium was terrorism hitting New York City, but that's what happened on September 11, 2001, as followers of Saudi Arabian terrorist Osama bin Ladin audaciously hijacked four passenger jetliners and aimed them at the two towers of New York City's World Trade Center (for a long time the tallest buildings in the world), the Pentagon in Washington, D.C., and the White House. The passengers on the plane bound for the White House brought it down in a field in Pennsylvania, but the other three hit and devastated their targets. The planes aimed at the World Trade Center ultimately caused the buildings to collapse, and close to 3,000 lives of office workers, firemen, and police were lost in the cataclysm.

Rockers entered the fray, in part to feel somewhat less powerless in the wake of such a calamity, in part to raise money for the people the dead left behind. One key component of this effort was the Concert for New York City. Held at Madison Square Garden, the show featured occasional New Yorkers, like U2 and Eric Clapton; people who do some of their best performing in New York, like the Who and Elton John; and of course area locals like Jon Bon Jovi (who could see the Towers from the beach near his home in Rumson, New Jersey) and Billy Joel. Billy looked especially anguished as he donned a New York Police Department hat and performed a somber version of "New York State of Mind" before launching into an apocalypticly rocking rendition of "Miami 2017 (Seen the Lights Go Out on Broadway)," a strangely appropriate juxtaposition of songs.

Another project Billy was involved with that year centered on a different holocaust. Billy participated in the making of *Die Akte Joel*.

❂ ❂ ❂

Die Akte Joel (*The Joel Files*) is a German documentary about Billy's grandfather's factory and what happened to it during the Nazi regime. As part of the documentary, filmmaker Beate Thalberg set up a meeting with Carl Joel's grandchildren Billy and Alexander, and the grandchildren of the 1936 Olympic equestrian medalist Josef Neckermann, whose family took over the Joel's mail-order fabric company when the German government decreed the "aryanization" of all German businesses.

The film came about because the filmmaker had already done a documentary on Billy's brother, Alexander. In the course of creating that film, he came across a picture of the Joel factory in the 1930s. The Joel mystique helped the film get funded and interested the other family, the Neckermanns, in having the meeting. One of the Neckermann children had hosted a Billy Joel radio show on his college station.

"My first reaction," said Billy, "was, 'so that's what happened.' Because I didn't really know my father well when I was growing up, and by the time I met him again, he really didn't want to talk about it . . . It did give me some understanding of the mystery of the man who is my father. I know my father has a dark area in his life that he doesn't discuss."

Billy acquited himself well and both brothers displayed a great deal of class during the course of the meeting. The Neckermanns might have stolen the Joel family's birthright, but as Billy pointed out, because they bought the factory, even at a fraction of its worth, "I might owe Neckermann my existence."

"I talked with my brother before the meeting," he also said. "We weren't going to respond. I didn't want my family's history to be played out like a Jerry Springer show."

Billy found the Neckermanns' reaction to the meeting disappointing. "I came away with the sense that they didn't really try in any way," he said. "I sensed that a lot of this was new to them and they didn't know how to deal with it."

The film first aired in Germany and France in December 2001. It finally made its way to America, when it played at the 2003 New York Jewish Film Festival. The narrator for the English version was actor John Hurt.

CHAPTER 24

EVERY DRUNK MUST HAVE HIS DRINK

On June 12, 2002, Billy lost control of his 1999 Mercedes and wrapped it around a telephone pole. He claimed that he realized he was going to miss his turn, and when he tried to correct that, his car started skidding, running sidelong into the pole. Fortunately, he was alone in the car, as the passenger side of the vehicle was crushed.

While he walked away from the crash, it blackened his eyes and left him generally sore. He had to blow off an appearance at the annual Songwriters Hall of Fame dinner. There was no mention of whether drugs or alcohol was involved in the crash.

A little over six months later, on January 25, 2003, at around 10:30 P.M., Billy was traveling southbound in his new, $120,000, 2002 Mercedes on Route 114 when he "drifted off the side of the roadway and struck a tree, and then came to a stop in the middle of the road." Once again, the car was totaled. This time Billy had to be medevaced to the University of Stony Brook Hospital.

From his hospital bed, Billy told detective Paul Fabiano that a week before the accident he had had "an operation on his nose and face which caused a great deal of swelling," adding that, since the operation he had "been on medication." Billy contended that the medication and the swelling had hindered his night vision.

Subsequently, one witness came forward and told the police that Billy had "gone by him at a high rate of speed and then struck the tree." Another witness said that, before the accident, Billy was having dinner with friends at the American Hotel Restaurant and that he and his dinner party had wine with dinner. Billy admitted to having "a glass of champagne." For some reason, his blood alcohol level was not on the accident report, and he was not given a Breathalyzer test. The report was submitted as "changed" on January 31.

People began to fear not only for Billy's safety, but for the safety of the people who might ride with Billy. "The seat Alexa was sitting in only hours before the latest crash was completely decimated," said Christie Brinkley. "I'm worried about Billy, but like any mother would be, I'm alarmed and concerned about my child's safety by this frightening pattern of events . . . I hope Billy will honor his promise to use a professional driver when he's with Alexa. It eases my concern for the safety and well being of both of them."

"In my whole life, I've only had two car accidents," Billy said. "They happened to happen within the space of one year. Neither was related to the other. There was no illegal reason for those accidents. People have car accidents. Unfortunately, when they took me out of the car on the last accident, the car had been squinched up against a tree. I had sinus surgery the week before so my eyes were all black and blue . . . I had a little cut on my scalp. When you cut your scalp, it bleeds like Niagara Falls. So, they looked in the window and they saw this guy with a big black and blue face and blood running down and said, 'Oh, we have to peel the car open.' So they use the Jaws of Life . . . and they literally peeled the car open like a can of anchovies. That's the photo they showed in the paper. 'This was Billy Joel's car accident.'"

On a rainy Sunday, April 25, 2004, at around 4:00 in the afternoon, Billy went out to buy a pizza in his classic 1967 burgundy and black Citroen. Once again, he lost control of his car on the wet roads and went through the bushes, across the front lawn, and crashed into the home of ninety-year-old Maria Dono of Bayville with enough force to crack the foundation. Sometime later, she came back home from a shopping trip to find the little French vehicle still lodged in the side of her house, and the little New York driver with a fresh cut on his hand standing beside it talking to police. "He hit my bushes and the wall," Dono said. "He'd better come fix it. I'm sure he has the money."

A Long Island radio station managed to rescue the Citroen's grill from the crash scene. They put it up on the Web auction site eBay. The proceeds went to charity.

Once again, the police said that there was no evidence of drugs or alcohol, and once again, Billy didn't get so much as a traffic summons.

Still, this behavior was beginning to attract attention. An insurance agent on Long Island postulated, "It looks like his insurance premiums would at least double. I would say he definitely fits into the high-risk category. People do get into accidents. Some are more prone than others . . . he's a pretty reckless guy. He has a lot of money, and I think he has a disregard for the privilege of driving."

"I think that he can be irresponsible," agreed Artie Ripp. "Is he drinking? Is he high? Is he then getting behind the wheel? I don't know that that is what he's doing, but I do know other people, if they're going to fuck themselves up, they have a personal driver, a personal bodyguard. They don't dare get behind the wheel, because they know they're incapable of acting in a responsible way . . . Who knows what's going on? Van Gogh cut off his ear, Billy crashes into trees."

❂ ❂ ❂

Billy's history with alcohol goes way back. Even with the Parkway Green Gang, when he was barely in his teens, by his own admission he would "use phony draft cards to buy beer [and] . . . drink Tango wine and screw around with the gang." During the '70s, Bruce Gentile recalls Billy as being a "blackout drinker. The cat can't remember what he did the night before, he gets that drunk." In 1980, Timothy White recalled that Billy "cajoled me into helping him empty two bottles of Dewar's Scotch."

He even used alcohol references frequently as metaphors, like, "I've become more of a baritone than I am a tenor, and I like that. It's thickened out. It's like a wine. The top end isn't as bright, but the bottom end is nice and robust."

As the new millennium put on a few years, however, Billy's alcohol use became more and more evident and public. Billy claims it started with his January 2000 breakup with Carolyn Beegan, but people could recall seeing him walk Beegan's pug Lola in New York's Chelsea neighborhood, sit down at a sidewalk café, and polish off a bottle of brandy. At an April 2002 date at Madison Square Garden, Joel spent a good part of the show chewing out the promoters and the Garden management for the high ticket prices. He went on about war, and then nearly fell out onstage. One wag observed that while the audience had been warned that Billy had a cold, he "seemed to have ingested something quite a bit stronger than cough syrup."

He was also known to commandeer the piano at piano bars. "You know, sometimes I'm in a bar, I get a little lit, okay, I'll sit down [at the piano] just because the mood strikes me."

In October 2003, he hurt his wrist in a fall, claiming to have been unable to find a light switch in his new home. "I mean, he fell down the stairs?" said old friend Sandy Gibson. "How drunk were you?"

Billy chalked his drinking at this time up to woman trouble. After Beegan and he split, he dated TV anchor Trish Bergin for two years, allegedly asking her to marry him and being rejected. She later married a Long Island lawyer and, at the time of his binge, was pregnant.

"[She was why I] started drinking all that wine," Billy said. "The more I think about it, the more I think it was all four of those relationships. I never really stop thinking of any of them."

"His ex-girlfriend just got married," a friend expanded, "and he's a little down about that. It's not one thing. It's a bunch of stuff."

"I can abuse alcohol," Billy admitted. "If the demons get me, I'll go on a bender. It's happened before."

Benders were not unknown to Joel. His mother, Rosalind, has been known to have a drink or two. Or three or four. "I was the guy who got the phone call when Roz was binging in Huntington," said Bruce Gentile. "All of a sudden I would get a crackle over my radio. One of my fellow inspectors who was on the complaint desk called me in the field on a secured radio channel, and said to me, 'There's this lady Jane [Arginteanu, Billy's assistant] that called up from Maritime Music, you've got to call her immediately.' I knew Roz was fucked up. When I took lunch, I would check her out. I became like the buffer zone, made sure she got off the street before she got in trouble. And I did, too. I kept her out of the papers.

"Roz was crowing at the bar before Billy got there," Gentile adds about the day of the dedication of Billy Joel Cold Spring Harbor Park. "Then, as soon as Jane got there, I never heard so many curse words come out of an old lady's mouth. She was going, 'Where is that cunt bitch parasite that lives off my fucking son?' She's talking about Jane. So me and Jane are walking her to the car. Billy leaves without Roz, even though we all had lunch at Coco's Water Cafe. Jane was squeezing my hand so hard I thought it was going to fall off. I had to say, 'Roz, knock it off already. You know Jane does a real good job for your son. If not for Jane, your son's shit would be in turmoil. Now get it together and go! Here's my brother. He'll take you wherever you want to go.'"

What ultimately got Billy out of the bottle was the love of his daughter. A friend of Billy's noted that Billy drinks when he's out with his buddies or on the party circuit, but never when he is with Alexa, adding, "He's a great father."

Another friend added, "He may have felt that he was drinking too much, but I don't think it was evident to anyone else. It's not like there was an intervention."

While it might not have been an intervention, exactly, a lot of people were putting it to Billy that he had a problem. Elton John suggested it. Christie Brinkley required that he get a driver and get sober if he was going to have custody of his daughter again.

"I told my daughter that I recognized I was having a problem," Billy conceded at last. "And my gift to her for Father's Day was going to be cleaning up my act."

"He would do anything for his daughter," said Elaine Schock.

On June 14, 2002, Billy checked into Silver Hill Hospital, in Connecticuit, noted for treating substance abusers. Fellow Sony recording artists Mariah Carey and Liza Minnelli had both been through the program. Billy spent ten days at the $1,000-a-day facility.

"Billy has felt his drinking has really been controlling him in ways he did not like," said a friend of his, "and he is hoping to get it behind him."

"I was on a binge, I was on a bender," he said. "I've learned to recognize what those signs are. Everybody can abuse alcohol, anybody can drink too much, but I've cooled that out."

When he took the road with Elton John again, he also had a dry backstage dressing room. Where the rider on the concert contract for Elton's dressing room required the promoter to have a dozen bottles of beer, a bottle of "excellent quality" white wine, and two bottles of Bordeaux, as well as, in the band room, a six-pack each of Amstel Light and Corona beer, two bottles of white wine, two bottles of red wine, and a half-liter bottle of Stolinchnaya vodka, the most stimulating beverage in both Billy's dressing room and Billy's band's dressing room was coffee.

Just after he got out of rehab, Billy called the legendary Chicago Italian restaurant Spiaggia's and asked them to keep the restaurant open for him and his party. Billy picked up a $2,000 tab so that his friends and he could feast on wine and cheese. According to the restaurant, he didn't drink.

However, Billy continues to deny that he is an alcoholic. "I'm an alcohol abuser," he concedes. "I mean, alcoholic is you can't live without the stuff and it's toxic to you. If you drink too much, no matter who you are, whether you're an alcoholic or not, you're going to do harm to yourself."

CHAPTER 25

YOU KNOW THOSE LIGHTS WERE BRIGHT ON BROADWAY

Billy had not gone to Chicago simply to try the cuisine. He scheduled his rehab so that he could be in the Windy City for the June 25, 2002, opening of the Broadway-bound show based on his music, the Twyla Tharp directed and choreographed *Movin' Out*.

For years, people had been telling Billy that he should be writing musicals for Broadway, citing the theatrical nature of his performances and the drama inherent in his songs. Even as early as 1974, *New York Times* music critic and longtime Billy Joel advocate John Rockwell noted, "There is an overt theatricality in his work." As far back as 1989, Joel was saying, "Writing a Broadway musical? Certainly."

Former rhythm guitarist Russell Javors saw it, too. "Billy could turn Broadway upside down," he said. "He could be the kingpin. He can wipe the floor with guys like Andrew Lloyd Webber."

Broadway was being dragged kicking and screaming into rock and roll, and to many in rock and roll, the feeling was mutual. While rock had made nominal appearances since the '60s with the advent of *Hair* and *Godspell* and even *Grease*, the powers that be in the theatrical community were still hung up in the "golden era" of "the great American songbook" and "Tin Pan Alley." They felt that the people who went to the theater didn't really care for rock, and that the people who liked rock didn't particularly care about the theater. This type of thinking led to the graying of the Great White Way, and to the same kind of audience problems that Billy cited for the classical constituency—they had alienated an entire generation, the biggest generation in history, the baby boomers, and had not refreshed the potential pool of ticket buyers. Drastic measures needed to be taken to get this generation, now the moneyed generation that would go to the ever-more-expensive Broadway shows, into the theater.

Off Broadway in the '80s, shows like *Little Shop of Horrors* and others merged theatrical and rock sensibilities. Andrew Lloyd Webber tried to inculcate a rock sensibility into theater pieces like *Joseph and the Amazing Technicolor Dream Coat*, and *Jesus Christ Superstar*, but as his shows progressed, they became more and more mainstream and less and less rock. Webber shows like *Cats* and *Phantom of the Opera*, while wildly popular, couldn't lay claim to even have the whiff of rock that the earlier shows pretended to have.

Late in the '90s, the rock musical *Rent* started its long run on Broadway to renown and a Pulitzer Prize. Peter Townshend brought a theatrical version of his original rock opera *Tommy* to Broadway. At the opening of the Rock and Roll Hall of Fame in Cleveland, Townshend encountered Billy. Deep into the plans for the theatrical production of *Tommy*, the godfather of rock adamantly told Billy that he *had* to write a Broadway musical. "He was insisting that I do this," Billy said in 1993. "'You're probably the guy best suited to do this in this day and age, to bring pop and the rock and roll sensibility into the musical theater.' I had been approached by other people about doing a Broadway musical, but when Pete Townshend told me that, it was the first time I really seriously have considered that I am going to do that. I intend to do it."

A year later, at one of the stops on his "Evening of Questions, Answers and a Little Music" lecture tour at Princeton, Billy expressed his reservations about doing a show. Writing for the theater would take a year or two out of his life; he'd have to write twice as many songs as usual, and then leave them at the mercy of actors and directors. He also didn't like the fact that Broadway cost so much. He didn't want to price people out of seeing a show of his. "A project of that nature is at least a two year process, so I would have to have my decks cleared."

By the turn of the millennium, Billy's frequent tour partner, Elton John, had shows on Broadway. One of them, an updating of the classic tale *Aida*, was written with Webber's former partner Tim Rice. Others incorporated the music he'd done for Disney films that had been translated to the stage.

Even some of Billy's frames of reference are theatrical. At the Billy Joel Cold Spring Harbor Park dedication, he commented that driving up to the ceremony and seeing all those people there made him feel like Conrad Birdie, protagonist of the musical *Bye Bye Birdie.*

As with so many advances in his career, Billy had to be prodded to make this one. It happened that, nearly a decade after Townshend insisted that Billy needed to be on Broadway, choreographer Twyla Tharp thought the same thing. A legendary revolutionary in the field of modern and classical dance, she had taken the modern art of movement out of the lofts in Soho and brought it uptown to the New York City Ballet, setting her choreography to such music as that of early jazz great Jellyroll Morton, pioneering New Waver and Talking Heads founder David Byrne, pop stalwarts the Beach Boys, and classical giant Ludwig van Beethoven. She had choreographed the films *Hair* and *Amadeus*, and the Broadway show *Singin' in the Rain.*

Tharp's initial inclination was to do a piece as a way of thanking the veterans of the Vietnam War. While against the conflict itself, she thought the way the returning soldiers were treated was shameful. "In all of history," she said, "whether it's Huns or Goths or Romans or whomever, no man has ever been drafted, brought back and treated like he was a hired gun. What is this insanity?"

She approached Billy with the idea of using his songs in a theatrical piece to this effect, with "Goodnight Saigon" obviously in the forefront of her mind.

"I want to do a narrative," she told Billy, describing the basis of her plans.

He said, "What story?"

"Well, I don't know," she admitted, "but to begin with, did Brenda and Eddie talk to each other twenty years later?"

He said, "I don't know."

"Well, let's find out," she responded.

Billy liked the idea for *Movin' Out*: "Just the fact that it was unorthodox, it was untried, it was different, it was risky, it was daring, it was crazy, it was ludicrous. I said, 'This is fantastic. What a great idea,'" he said.

He added at a later point, "This was really Twyla Tharp's vision.

She liked this music well enough to choreograph it and work with her own dance ensemble."

Using twenty-four of Billy's songs, Tharp was able to tell her story in dance. Beyond that, the incredibly popular music of Billy Joel acted as a selling point for the show.

"It's a full-length ballet, but we can't call it that . . . Billy's suggestion [was] just use the title and let everybody else call it whatever they want," Tharp asserted. "You show me . . . a better *pas de deux* than 'Shameless.' Anywhere, on any stage in the world. You show me a better operatic sequence in dance than 'Goodnight Saigon.'"

While the show was billing Billy prominently (as it did Tharp), she resisted the idea that the point of the show was to capitalize on his fame. "[This] is not about exploiting Billy Joel, it's about investigating his music and looking at it from a different perspective. It wouldn't work with a songwriter whose music wasn't as visceral as Billy Joel's."

"Billy Joel is an amazing storyteller," says Keith Roberts, who plays Billy's alter ego in the show, "and people have an attachment to his music. That's why *Movin' Out* is a success."

For Billy, it was like watching his children grow up and star on Broadway. More than that, it was like his children revealing things to him that he had never known about them. "I've always referred to my songs, or the music that I've written, as my children. I feel like these songs grew up and they've gone to live in a theater on Broadway, these kids. I'm very proud of them," he said.

"I went, not knowing what I was going to see. I mean, it could have been a cringe fest . . . I looked at this and I thought, 'This is really good.' The dancing was unbelievable. I was actually very moved by it . . . I like it. Then again, what do I know? I'm a piano player."

Billy finally landing on Broadway did not surprise Artie Ripp, who thirty years earlier knew it was just a matter of time. "I always thought his music could be on Broadway. At one time, I said, 'Billy is, in a way, a new George M. Cohan. It's just a question of him directing his talent.' He always wrote songs that had great production value, but there's a whole lot more drama to those songs. 'Piano Man' is like a little movie. I suppose you could take other of his songs and rather than them being dance numbers, they're dramas, they're comedies."

The critics thought so, too. *Movin' Out* opened to terrific reviews. The ever-rough *New York Times* critic Ben Brantley called it a "shimmering portrait of an American generation set to Mr. Joel's music." Other reviewers had similar things to say. They found the combination of Joel's songs with Tharp's choreography to have a dynamic tension that Charles Atlas would envy. As of this writing, the show continues to run strong on Broadway and in traveling companies on the road.

Yet even a success like *Movin' Out* seemed to fall into tragedy. In one of the more cruelly ironic twists, considering the writer, one of the cast members died in a motorcycle accident. Another fell into a coma due to complications from surgery. That marked one of the play's greatest offstage success stories, actually. The doctors had written this dancer off, but playing music from the show in his room helped bring him back to consciousness.

On the evening of June 8, 2003, Billy sat up on a raised platform in Duffy Square, where Seventh Avenue and Broadway converge between 46th and 47th Streets. The American Theatre Wing and the League of American Theatres and Producers were going to hand out the Antoinette Perry—Tony to her friends—Awards that night. As the show opened, Billy performed "New York State of Mind" out there on the street. "All these people in buses are going by," he describes the scene, "same as every day, very surreal."

The camera had a little trouble with the wind (at one point it drifted off Billy and onto one of the ubiquitous "Going Out of Business" signs on Seventh Avenue), but when Billy was done, the scene switched to the inside of Radio City Music Hall, a couple of blocks away on Sixth Avenue and 50th Street, where the rest of the cast from *Movin' Out* was on stage. They performed a medley of "River of Dreams," "Keeping the Faith," and "Only the Good Die Young."

The show was nominated for ten awards, but at the end of the evening, the actors, the actresses, the lighting director, and the show itself would come up empty. Tharp would not get the Best Director award, but did win the Tony for Best Choreography. Billy was the winner for Best Orchestration.

Backstage that night, he announced that he was working on a new show. "I'm working on a book," he said. "I'm talking to numerous people about writing a book and I have sketches of music. The working title is *Good Career Move*. It's about the music business. I'm going to take it apart. What Mel Brooks did to Broadway in *The Producers*, I'll do to the music business."

The year 2002 was a good one for awards for Billy, especially considering he had not recorded a note of his own for public consumption in more than five years or written a song in nearly a decade. Even before receiving the Tony Award, he was honored with the 2002 Grammy MusicCares Person of the Year. At the awards dinner, given the night before the main event, he was serenaded with his own music by a who's who of popular music: Garth Brooks, Diana Krall, Jon Bon Jovi, Richie Sambora, Tony Bennett, and Rob Thomas from Matchbox Twenty. Richard Joo, the pianist who recorded *Fantasies & Delusions*, also performed.

"Having somebody with such an amazing body of work makes the evening so much better," said Michael Greene, the head of the National Academy of Recording Arts and Sciences, the organization that presents the Grammy Awards, "because the other artists are there on stage singing that person's music back to them."

"It will be a lot of fun to hear my songs I've written over the years performed by a great line-up of artists," Billy concurred.

§ § §

With all the accolades, however, Billy was not a happy camper. In fact, to those around him, now without the rosy glow of rosé, he could get positively testy. He was horribly forlorn at the state of his personal relationships. "Whatever subject we touch on," wrote Chuck Klosterman in a revealing portrait in the *New York Times Magazine*, "the conversation inevitably spirals back to the same thing: Women."

Klosterman was not the only writer to have this experience. A journalist from a fairly staid magazine for classical piano players got an audience with Billy when he told Billy's office that he wanted to concentrate on the musical aspects of Billy's work instead of the usual fan-mag/tabloid drivel. Billy greeted the idea with enthusiasm, but when they sat down to talk, he kept bringing up stories about the beautiful women he had been with.

He had come from a "broken home," and now he had created two of his own. His high-profile relationships with Carolyn Beegan and Trish Bergin had washed out. At fifty-three, his hair was thinning and his beard graying. And he despaired of ever finding someone who was interested in William Martin Joel, formerly of Hicksville, as opposed to Billy Joel, semi-retired rock star, Tony winner, and serious composer. "In my whole life, I haven't met the person I can sustain a relationship with yet," he said. "So, I'm discontented about that. I'm angry with myself. I have regrets."

His discontent on this subject had informed his art for years, however. "Scenes from an Italian Restaurant" is about a doomed relationship. "Honesty" says if someone cares about you they'll put you down. In "All for Leyna," she leaves her lovers shattered and alone. "So It Goes" says every woman will eventually leave.

"He talks like a guy who has conquered every goal he dreamed of only to discover that those victories have absolutely nothing to do with satisfaction," wrote Klosterman.

On *The Today Show*, he told a reporter who asked if there was something he'd like to do that he'd never done before, "I'd like to have a successful long-term relationship with a woman. How about that?"

As much as he wanted to be loved for William Martin Joel, human being, rather than Billy Joel, pop music icon, more than thirty years in the role had left the two entwined in a double helix. "I was recently on a date with a woman," he said, "and she told me, 'You're one of those guys who comes with all this stuff. You're always being written about and photographed and all that star stuff.' And it dawned on me that she was probably right."

A friend put it sadly and succinctly: "He's looking for a real relationship."

In the winter of 2004, that changed. He found a relationship, and in February he announced his engagement to twenty-two-year-old news correspondent Katie Lee, a very recent college graduate who worked covering restaurants on the PBS show *George Hirsch: Living It Up.*

Creatively, he continued to explore new horizons. In the summer of 2004, he announced that he had made a deal with Scholastic Books to create books for children. The first release as part of this venture repurposed his song to Alexa, "Lullabye (Goodnight, My Angel)" as a book with illustrations. Suddenly, the afterthought lyrics were pushed front and center and the music they served was totally absent. "Reassuring a child that they are not alone or could be abandoned is very important for their well-being," he said.

Katie Lee was with Billy in September when he went to Hollywood for the unveiling of his star on the Walk of Fame, right in front of the Pantages Theater, where the road company of *Movin' Out* was ensconced through October. Earlier that week, the pair had run into Barbara Walters at lunch at the New York restaurant Michael's. Billy chatted with Walters and mentioned her retirement from *20/20*, which she had recently announced. She corrected him, saying that she wasn't retiring, she was just leaving the show. Billy retorted, "There's nothing wrong with leaving. I left rock and roll."

Alexa was the maid of honor when her dad married Katie Lee at Billy's Center Island estate on October 2, 2004. It would seem on the surface that Alexa had more in common with the bride than the groom did (ain't it always the case?). They certainly were closer in age, with Alexa a scant five years younger than Katie, about the same number of years Billy was older than the bride's father.

In addition to the $23 million Center Island estate, Joel bought a pied à terre for his new bride—a $4 million, 2,681-square-foot apartment in TriBeCa.

They married as the sun set over the harbor.

CHAPTER 26

I CAN'T TELL YOU MORE THAN I'VE TOLD YOU ALREADY

"Billy can be an intense guy," says Jerry Schilling, Joel's former road manager, "but he has a great sense of humor. I don't think—not that I'm a hugely successful businessman—but without the time I spent with Billy, and I give Elizabeth some credit, too, that I would be able to accomplish whatever I have accomplished. It was a real great learning experience."

While Schilling went on to manage the Beach Boys and took on the mantle of head of the Memphis and Shelby County (Tennessee) Music Commission, his most important and famous link would remain as a member of the Memphis Mafia. He has produced several films using performance footage of Elvis. He lives in Elvis's old home in the Los Angeles area.

"Billy was probably the most significant and long-lasting artist I worked with," says Artie Ripp. "The Spoonful didn't last this long. The Shangri-Las didn't last this long. Bubblegum music didn't last as long. The fact of the matter is, Billy is one of those unique artists who has lasted. I signed him in 1970. It is now 2004. That's a pretty good run. John Sebastian still tours, but the Lovin' Spoonful really doesn't exist. But Billy does, thirty-four years later. And the music goes on."

Ripp pretty well lays out what he'd done in the music business, but he bailed out of it many years ago, opting to go for the big money in movies. He's produced some moderately successful films, including the comedy *Meet the Deedles*, and currently can schmooze with the best of them and still loves Billy from the bottom of his wallet.

"When Billy played LA a few years ago," recalls Sandy Gibson, "he asked Elizabeth to be with him. You know, Elizabeth stayed in great shape. Elizabeth is healthy, she's the same size she was, she hikes, she goes to a trainer. Billy looks like her father now."

Elizabeth Weber Joel lives fairly quietly and well out of the limelight now, but as you can see from the picture of her in this book, she looks marvelous. Sandy Gibson runs a program that teaches incarcerated teens how to read and write creatively. Michael Lang went on to produce two more "Woodstock" festivals centered on the twenty-fifth and thirtieth anniversaries of the original. He also has a variety of interests in the entertainment biz, including artist management.

Bruce Gentile came off the road, after having played with no less than fifty inductees in the Rock and Roll Hall of Fame. He dealt with his chemical dependencies (forming the first Suffolk County branch of "the organization that dares not speak its name" for drug abusers), took the civil service exams, and became a code enforcement officer for the Town of Huntington. Now retired from civil service, he is raising a family on Long Island while he continues to perform as the Plain White Rapper, play the drums locally, and develop a music therapy technique.

"What's the difference between a pop artist and a rock artist?" asks Howard Bloom. "Rock [is] a religion. Rock is a religion that says you have the right to rebel and you have the right to an identity of your own . . . Billy, with his rage and anger, especially with the rage and anger against Elizabeth, his first wife, that filled his records, was a rock artist."

Howard continued to run the Howard Bloom Organization, one of the most successful independent publicity companies the music business has ever seen, until he fell very ill in the late 1980s. When he recovered sufficiently, he went back to his first love, academics. He currently teaches at New York University and is the author of *The Lucifer Principle* and *The Global Brain*. Elaine Schock continues to run Schock Ink out of Los Angeles, with a bevy of top-line music-business clients.

Jon Small is one of the most successful video producers in Nashville, working with a who's who of country music, having earned special kudos for his work with Garth Brooks. Sean Small followed in his biological father's footsteps and also is a video producer, in California.

From CBS, Irwin Mazur went back into management, working with artists including Patti LaBelle. He then became a music supervisor for films, including *Ghostbusters*. In that capacity, he was the first to use Madonna's music in a film. Tiring of the huge risks and moderate returns of the music business, he went into investing. He currently is a senior VP at Morgan Stanley: "It's easier to manage money," he says, "than to manage crazy people."

❧ ❧ ❧

Billy Joel never wanted to be a rock star, at least not after he turned twenty. Once he was one, however, he developed a real love/hate relationship with the idea. He loved the effect his music had on people, especially women. "You get up on stage and the crowd roars," he said. "The girls scream and the guys shout, the hair goes up on my neck and I get a tingling on my spine. For a minute I feel we can invade another country!"

He loved the respect it got him, even more than when he boxed. It almost filled the voids in his life but never quite made it. "I'm glad that people like my music enough to buy it, but it's an embarrassment to me that I get compliments on top of it.

"We carry two acoustic pianos, both Baldwins: a five-foot eight-inch and a seven-foot," he has also said. "You can't carry a piano around like a guitar, you can't make moves, so I said, 'Why don't we put a smaller piano stage left and higher up so I can run up to it and face the other side of the room . . . That makes me feel better, because you want the audience to get its money's worth when they come to see you. That still amazes me. I mean, they want to see this face!"

On the other hand, the whole rock star trip puzzled and disgusted him. He never seemed to get past the idea that, if he was going to be a rock star, earn money from selling out arenas and stadiums, and sell millions of records, there was a trade-off involved. A star, by the very nature of becoming one, gives up a certain amount of privacy, and pretty much has to buy the rest of it. "A star," he said, "is a big ball of gas, and basically that's what a lot of stardom is."

"I look in the mirror every morning and go, 'You're a rock star. Ha, ha, ha, pretty funny.'"

Nor did he ever get really comforatable with the trappings of that stardom. "That's what makes it fun to be in a limousine—I don't belong there. That's what makes it fun to live in this big house out in the Hamptons—I don't belong there. I'm from Levittown. I was a greaser. I was a beatnik."

"I think success is . . . superficial. Okay, you're famous and you've got a lot of money. That doesn't necessarily resolve any emotional trauma you've had, and sometimes it can add to your discontent. Especially if you have a modicum of intellect, you'll say, 'This is such a pile of crap, what does this really have to do with what's important to me?'"

But when Billy became a rock star, he fought hard to earn and maintain his credibility. When he was described on the underground hit TV show *Queer Eye for the Straight Guy* as "the iceberg lettuce of rock and roll," it must have stung. "You don't necessarily have to be on the cutting edge or a celebrity or a rock star to be a musician," he said. "I don't intend to stop making music just because I'm not a commercial recording artist."

One aspect of his switch to composing classical music and his incipient invasion of Broadway was his recognition that he had probably outgrown rock. "I'm not cutting edge and I haven't been for a long time. And I kind of resent being deemed irrelevant as a musician," he also stated.

Of course, his fans *want* him to make the same music he's been making for the last twenty years. While they would have loved some new Billy Joel music, they proved to be perfectly content to shell out hundreds of dollars to see Billy perform, by himself or with Elton John, a decade after he had written "the last words he had to say."

"I don't want to be an oldies act," he added. "Then where do you end up? Las Vegas . . . the elephant's graveyard of rock stars."

Of course, Billy and Elton played the casinos. They were a hot ticket at the MGM Grand with the "Face to Face" tour. It wasn't the first time Billy had played the Elephant's Graveyard, either, having performed there first during the *River of Dreams* tour.

One of the things Billy did want was to be a songwriter, yet while he describes his songs as his children, he describes the songwriting process as something near as painful as giving birth. "I don't like writing," he has often said. "When I have to do it, I go around and kick things. I don't shave. I get up in the morning, have coffee and sit down at the piano. You have to have discipline, but I always find the best songs are the ones you write quickly."

This could account for his not having recorded an original Billy Joel song since *River of Dreams*. As he said at the time, "You have to have the desire to do it, the compulsion to do it and you have to have the insane drive to need to do it, and I don't have that."

However, many people who are close to Billy or who have longtime attachments to Billy recognize this kind of drought and the seclusion that goes along with it. People who were unable to talk on the record described the way Billy remained in hiding, especially between his 2003 car accident and his 2004 wedding. Many of them spoke of writer's block.

"Is that merely a cover for him not writing great new tunes anymore?" Artie Ripp asked rhetorically. "I don't know. To me, the great songs, there's only so long you can squash 'em, even if you give the songs to another artist because you won't record them personally. Maybe all of a sudden the well is creatively dry. He's too rich, too fat, too accepted, too scrambled, whatever it is, to be as magical as he could be as a composer. He hasn't lost his vitality as a performer.

"It's interesting to note that in Billy's [Broadway] show [*Movin' Out*], there isn't a brand-new piece of music that he put in the show that could emerge. Sometimes, when you're putting the oldies package together, you add a new song. So he has a hit Broadway show, but when was the last time he had a hit record? Billy made a decision in his war with Columbia Records, it appears. 'I'm not writing, I'm not recording as Billy Joel any more. I'll do a classical record. I'll do a Broadway show, I'll go on tour and make a hundred million dollars. I'm not forced to go into the studio unless you do X, Y, and Z,'—whatever X, Y and Z are—'and it doesn't matter if the contract is a hundred years long. I'm just not going to do it.'"

As for Billy, yet another concept that seems to play tug of war with his head is to retire and live on his royalties, which on an annual basis must be considerable, or to keep on performing and creating in the public eye. While he hasn't recorded any more pop in over a decade, his classical work is showing signs of being well received. He also claims to be working on a new Broadway show that might—dare we even think it?—have new Billy Joel songs in it.

"I get kind of tired of performing,'" he says. "As a matter of fact, sometimes I resent it."

"I've had 'the career'. What I would like for the next year—ten years is to have 'the life,' because I've already had an amazing career. It's been wonderful, it's been fantastic, beyond my wildest expectations. Now I want the life . . . A relationship with someone, a family . . . a home. All those things that are not part and parcel of being a rock star or a celebrity or in show biz or any of that stuff. It's time for me to start living my life. At this late date."

The relationship angle is something that has long been a problem for Billy. He wonders perpetually why he cannot maintain a relationship. Does it stem from the fact that he has nothing to pattern it on, since his father left when he was in grade school? Is it perhaps his own insecurity, not as a performer or a musician but as a human being?

"Billy was insecure about whether the world would like him, like his music, understand him, accept him," Artie Ripp says of the young Billy Joel he discovered and signed all those years ago. "Was he going to have success on a personal level? Was he going to be able to pay his bills? Was he going to be able to be independent? Was he going to be able to run his life the way he wanted—to run his life, whatever that was? I don't think he was insecure as a musician. I don't think he was insecure as a composer. I think he was not secure as a performer. I think that in the beginning, he would kind of hide behind the piano rather than really sit up: 'None of you know who I am.' The insecurity didn't come from him as a talent. The insecurity really came from him saying, You don't know who I am. You never heard my music before. You don't know me, you don't like me. Are you going to like me? Are you going to want to see me again?'

"The other reality is, Billy has written the words and the melodies that millions of people around the world use in conversations with themselves and use as a personal communiqué to someone they care about, whether it's someone they said goodbye to, someone they're having fun with, somebody they want to become attached to.

"He can't have a business insecurity, because certainly he's a rich guy, but he could be insecure, like 'Look what I've done with my personal relationships. I haven't been able to keep Elizabeth, not Christie, not this one, not the other one.' Eventually, everybody winds up going out of his life, with the exception of maybe a few people. If one goes back and tries to find out where and why such a personal insecurity might come from, well, his father left his mother, and left him, when he was like five years old. His father never communicated with him. It was like, 'I reject you. You're a fart that happened to come out of your mother, and I certainly don't want anything to with you. I'm not interested in whether you're alive, whatever you're accomplishing, whether you're good or bad or so on. So having that kind of cold rejection and lack of value to another person—'Okay, you don't like my mother anymore, but you care about me. Happy birthday, you call me up, you want to see me once a year' and so on. I think that helped create some real emotional scars for him.

"The personal tragedy of Billy on an emotional level is something that's terrible and sad, that he's not a happy, joyful guy, but I guess if you piss on people, you wind up drinking a glass of piss yourself. I think that Billy, personally, rather than denigrate me, he could have said, 'Here's a guy who loved me, believed in me, picked me out and recognized that I have talent. He made mistakes that bothered me, that disappointed me, but he never left my side.' I didn't have the money to pay the bills that I said I would pay every month, but I didn't run away from him. I didn't turn around and say, 'You're a piece of shit. You're worthless. Your work is worthless. I don't believe in you.' Even though he would never recognize that thing, and he had to be so venomous in demeaning me—as if I speeded up *Cold Spring Harbor* on purpose. Why didn't he mention I sent him around the world so the world would have its own perspective, that they could know you not from the album from hell but from you in person? At no time did he ever show the graciousness to really appreciate that. It was like your father left you, then I fucked you. Fuck your father. Fuck me. Well, I'm sorry you're the angry young man and you're ugly as you are while in fact you create beautiful, sensitive, memorable musical works and performances. It's too bad that inside, you're Mr. Hyde."

Ironically, his father, who rejected him so in his youth, has grown fond of his oldest son over the years. "It's fantastic what he's done," says Howard Joel. "He works very hard, and he's got a certain measure of luck, but he's a very talented fellow."

"Billy should love himself half as much as others love him," adds his mother, "then he'd be in good shape."

"Billy was offering people his life," adds Howard Bloom. "It was written in his songs. Every fight he ever had with Elizabeth was written in his songs, and people could identify. They could visualize that Italian restaurant."

Billy, on the other hand, has mixed feelings about it all. "I feel what I do is competent," he says. "I know how to write music, I know how to write lyrics and I know how to perform. However, in an age of incompetence, that makes me extraordinary."

Artie Ripp sees it differently: "Billy has a lot of rock and roll in him, but he's a classically trained individual and he's a storyteller and balladeer, without any question. But he is among the unique few. With Dylan, Simon, Springsteen, he stands out as one of those very unique twentieth-century songwriters who wrote words and music and really wrote some immortal pieces of work."

"There are a lot of singers and songwriters who could be around for a long time," Billy counters. "Maybe we won't be doing pubescent pop music aimed at pubescent masculine ritual types who want to bang their heads against the wall—we've gotten more sophisticated."

"I'll always be a musician," he adds. "Since I was four years old, I've been a musician. So I don't want to stop doing that. I like it too much."

I WRITE MY BOOK
AND I HAVE MY SAY AND
I DRAW CONCLUSIONS

Up until now, there has been no really in-depth biography of Billy Joel. I now understand why. Billy is intensely private and has become even more so as time has gone on. If anything, this has fueled the public's fascination with him as a person and a performer. How many other performers who haven't recorded a new song in over a decade could sell out arenas—at $300 a ticket—on a regular basis?

This is not to say that the idea has never been considered, even by Billy himself. Peter Skolnick, now an attorney in New Jersey (he represents David "The Sopranos" Chase, among others), was a literary agent in the early '80s.

"Billy was, at that point, still with Frank Weber," he recalls. "I was approached by Jeff Schock, who had recently joined Frank to take care of promotion and marketing. Jeff and I talked about an authorized biography. I went out to Frank's office to meet with Billy. I must have gotten there early, because I'm standing outside there, having a cigarette, when Billy comes roaring up on a motorcycle. He doesn't know who I am. He goes into the office. Then I came in.

"What I found fascinating and wonderful about the very short meeting we had is he said to me, 'Why would anybody want to read a book about me?' I was amazed. Everyone was fascinated by him. He told me, 'I will do this book if you can find a writer who is so good that he could write a book that is so good, that if the reader had never heard of Billy Joel, he would still say, "Boy, what a terrific book."' That was a very tall order. I actually think that I found such a writer, but at the point when I started putting that all together, Billy famously had his falling out with Frank. That book never happened.

"Billy was genuinely humble. His question about why would anybody really care, I think it was a sincere question, and his whole notion that he wanted a book so good that even if you'd never heard of him, you'd think it was a great book, it was kind of refreshing."

I don't pretend to have written that book, though that was my goal. That's my goal whenever I sit down to write: To make what I know of a subject interesting enough that even someone who doesn't care about the subject will enjoy the book. My test market in such matters is my father, who might have heard the names of many of the people I write about but goes out of his way to avoid the music.

This is not to say that I wanted to do a hatchet job on Billy. Despite his protestations, he is a fascinating enough subject without having to resort to that. During the course of writing this, I came to admire him a bit, and discovered that even people he's vilified in the past—Artie Ripp, in particular—had very little bad to say about him. Billy just tries to live his non-professional life as best he can, out of the public eye, despite being in a profession that is intensely public. I've actually cut material from this book that I felt was derogatory without furthering the story. One of my yardsticks, as a parent, was: Is this something his daughter wouldn't know about him? Others were: Is this something that adds to the book or the story? Is this something anyone else really needs to know?

If anything, Billy became less forthcoming as he became more interesting. Around the time Skolnick and Schock were planning the authorized book, Billy Joel told the *New York Daily News*'s Fred Schruers, "Just don't go around making up stories about why I do what I do, because you don't know. If you want to find out, ask me. I'll tell ya."

In the wake of this came his marriage to a supermodel, his amazing legal woes, more hits, more tours, car crashes, detox—all things that attract public curiosity and scrutiny, and, naturally, they made him withdraw even more. So, sadly, what he told Schruers seems to have ceased being Billy Joel's policy. Despite several polite requests, he didn't see fit to cooperate with this book. Beyond that, his friends are unspeakably loyal, and many have signed non-disclosure agreements.

For example, I've known Phil Ramone for nearly three decades (from my days as an apprentice engineer—not at A&R, but through my work with an organization that honored him and into my membership in the National Academy of Recording Arts and Sciences). However, Phil said at first that he would not talk without Billy's permission and later told me that he just could not do the interview. Richie Cannata, too.

A co-worker of my wife knows another member of the Billy Joel Band and told me to call him. I did, and the band member went off on my wife's unsuspecting co-worker, saying that now he'd have to change his phone and email to keep me from badgering him about this book. I had to email him, assuring him that I would not be badgering him, that I would never contact him about the matter again. And I didn't. This is why the tabloids won't use me.

"He has built a wall around him similar to Michael Jackson or Greta Garbo," is how Artie Ripp describes it. "You can't really find out anything from anybody who has worked with him or been close to him. They have a commitment to respect the confidentiality of that which they know, and this is helping somebody else make something off of somebody they have a relationship with."

"All of us find it a little weird and uncomfortable [talking about Billy]" adds Elaine Schock, who made a large portion of her living talking about Billy during the '80s and '90s as his minister of information.

So some seventeen years after making himself available for the truth, Billy changed his tune to, "I'm not sure I'm comfortable with them knowing as much as they know. I'm not sure if I want people to know much more about me as it is. Not because I'm a misanthrope, but only because I treasure my private life. Frankly, in all truth, I don't think I'm all that interesting. So, it is amazing to me that people want to know so much. I think people would be surprised at how mundane I really am. I don't say that with any false humility. I think it's just my needs and passions aren't that different from anybody else's. Maybe they see themselves in me. Who knows?"

APPENDICES

APPENDIX A: ALBUM CHARTS

Billboard 200 Albums

Top Internet Album Sales

Top Classical Albums

Chart information courtesy of Billboard.com © 2004 VNU eMedia, Inc.
All rights reserved.

APPENDIX B: SINGLES & TRACKS

Pop Singles

The *Billboard* Hot 100

Adult Contemporary

Club Play

Mainstream Rock Tracks

Top 40 Mainstream

APPENDIX C: GRAMMY AWARDS & NOMINATIONS

1978   Record of the Year (Winner): "Just the Way You Are"

1978   Song of the Year (Winner): "Just the Way You Are"

1979   Album of the Year (Winner): *52nd Street*

1979   Best Pop Vocal Performance, Male (Winner): *52nd Street*

1979   Song of the Year: "Honesty"

1980   Album of the Year: *Glass Houses*

1980   Best Rock Vocal Performance, Male (Winner): *Glass Houses*

1982   Album of the Year: *The Nylon Curtain*

1983   Album of the Year: *An Innocent Man*

1983   Best Pop Vocal Performance, Male: "Uptown Girl"

1984   Best Video Album: *Billy Joel Live from Long Island*

1989   Best Pop Vocal Performance, Male: "We Didn't Start the Fire"

1989   Record of the Year: *We Didn't Start the Fire*

1989   Song of the Year: "We Didn't Start the Fire"

1990   Best Pop Vocal Performance, Male: *Storm Front*

1990   Producer of the Year: *Storm Front*

1991   Grammy Legend (Winner)

1991   Best Long-Form Video: *Live at Yankee Stadium*

1991   Best Short-Form Video: *When You Wish Upon a Star*

1993   Album of the Year: *River of Dreams*

1993   Best Pop Vocal Performance, Male: "River of Dreams"

1993   Record of the Year: "River of Dreams"

1993   Song of the Year: "River of Dreams"

2002   Best Pop Collaboration with Vocals: "New York State
        of Mind," Tony Bennett and Billy Joel

APPENDIX D: OTHER AWARDS & HONORS

1975   Cashbox Award for Best New Male Vocalist,
       for *Streetlife Serenade*
1980   American Music Award for Album of the Year, for *Glass Houses*
1981   People's Choice Award, for Favorite Male Pop Performer
1981   Rehabilitation Institute Humanitarian Award
1984   Cable ACE Award for Best Actor in a Comedy or Music
       Program, for "A Television First, Billy Joel"
1987   Cable ACE Award for Best Music Special,
       for "Live from Leningrad"
1987   Cable ACE Best Performance in a Music Special,
       for "Live from Leningrad"
1990   International Rock Award ("The Elvis"), for M.V.P. Keyboard
1990   Cathedral of Saint John the Divine (Humanitarian Award)
1991   Honorary Doctorate of Humane Letters, Fairfield University
1991   Town of Huntington proclaims "Billy Joel Park"
1991   Make-a-Wish Foundation, Honorary Chairman,
       Washington, D.C., Chapter
1992   Inducted into the Songwriters Hall of Fame
1993   Honorary Doctorate, Berklee College of Music
1993   National Association of Recording Merchandisers (NARM)
       President's Award
1994   *Billboard* Century Award
1997   American Society of Composers, Authors and Publishers
       (ASCAP) Founders Award
1997   Honorary Doctorate of Humane Letters, Hofstra University
1999   American Music Awards, Award of Merit
1999   Recording Industry Association of America (RIAA)
       Diamond Award
1999   Inducted into the Rock and Roll Hall of Fame
2000   James Smithson Bicentennial Medal of Honor
2000   Honorary Doctorate of Music, Long Island University,
       Southampton College
2001   Johnny Mercer Award from the Songwriters Hall of Fame
2002   Music Cares Person of the Year

APPENDIX E: GOLD & PLATINUM AWARDS

Platinum Albums
Greatest Hits, Volume I & Volume II . . . . .20 x Platinum
The Stranger . . . . .9x Platinum
52nd Street . . . . .7x Platinum
An Innocent Man . . . . .7x Platinum
Glass Houses . . . . .7x Platinum
River of Dreams . . . . .5x Platinum
Piano Man . . . . .4x Platinum
Storm Front . . . . .4x Platinum
Songs in the Attic . . . . .3x Platinum
The Bridge . . . . .2x Platinum
Complete Hits Collection . . . . .1x Platinum
Greatest Hits, Volume III . . . . .1x Platinum
Kohuept . . . . .1x Platinum
Streetlife Serenade . . . . .1x Platinum
The Essential Billy Joel . . . . .1x Platinum
Turnstiles . . . . .1x Platinum

Platinum Singles
"It's Still Rock and Roll to Me"
"My Life"

Gold Singles
"Just the Way You Are"
"Uptown Girl"
"We Didn't Start the Fire"
"Tell Her About It"

Gold Long-Form Videos
The Video Album Volume I
The Video Album Volume II
Eye of the Storm
Greatest Hits, Volume III: The Video
The Essential Video Collection

Platinum Long-Form Video
Live at Yankee Stadium

BIBLIOGRAPHY

Abel, Olivia. "Passages." *People*, New York, February 2, 2004.

"A Dreamboat Wedding." *People*, New York, April 8, 1985.

Ahrens, Frank. "Billy Joel, Bard of the 'Burbs. The Critics Call Him a Sentimental Hack. But His Legions of Fans Sing Another Tune." *Washington Post*, April 23, 1998.

"Alcohol Behind Joel's Rehab." *Newsday*, New York, June 22, 2002.

Amendola, Billy. "Phil Ramone: Trusting the Drummer." *Modern Drummer*, Pompton Lakes, NJ, March 2002.

American Theatre Wing's Tony Awards. www.tonyawards.com.

Aronowitz, Al. "Retropop Scene: How Do You Bury a Cellar." *The Blacklisted Journalist*, Elizabeth, NJ, February 1, 1996. Bigmagic.com.

Arrington, Carl. "Billy Joel Makes It after 10 Years of Trying." *Us*, New York, April 4, 1978.

"Backstage Notes: Drama Dispatch, Tony Tidbits." www.Backstage.com, New York, June 9, 2003.

"Backstage Pass: Band: Billy Joel Keyboardist: David Rosenthal." *Keyboard*, San Mateo, CA, Fall 1989.

Berry, Walter. "Seeing Red: Billy Joel Is Still Angry, But Now He's Broke." Associated Press, November 29, 1990.

"Billy Joel: A Taxing Divorce?" *Rolling Stone*, New York, March 23, 1989.

"Billy Joel Has a Tantrum." *New York Times*, July 28, 1989.

"Billy Joel Recovering." *New York Times*, April 17, 1982.

"Billy Joel Talks Shop with Music Students." Associated Press, New York, August 2, 1989.

Bloom, Howard. Author's interview, May 8, 2004.

————. "Reinventing Capitalism." Unpublished first draft, 2004.

Bolando, Carolina. "Billy Joel Performs for Students in Mandel." *Chicago Maroon*, November 9, 2001.

Bordowitz, Hank. *Turning Points of Rock and Roll*. Citadel Books, New York, 2004.

Brady, James. "In Step with Billy Joel." *Parade*, New York, March 15, 1998.

Brantley, Ben. "Theater Review: In a Top 40 State of Mind." *New York Times*, October 25, 2002.

Brock, Gary L. "AOL Chat with Billy Joel." AOL, winter 1994.

Brozan, Nadine. "Chronicle: Billy Joel, the Graduate, Offers Some Hints on How to Commence." *New York Times*, June 26, 1992.

————. "Chronicle." *New York Times*, April 15, 1994.

Burton, Alex. "Billy Joel: My Miracle Escape from Japan's Killer Quake." *The Star*, Tarrytown, NY, February 7, 1995.

Cabal, Alan. "Bridge, Tunnel, Beach—Fuck This Town—I'm Heading to Jersey!" *New York Press*, June 17, 2003.

Cannon, Bob. "Just the Way He Is." *Entertainment Weekly*, New York, September 11, 1992.

Carlton, Richard. "The Piano Man." *60 Minutes*, TV One, New Zealand, February 1994.

Charles, Nick, et al. "Pop Quiz with Billy Joel." *People*, New York, June 25, 2001.

Charlie Rose Show via "Names in the News." Associated Press, October 7, 1993.

Childs, Andy. "Billy Joel, Piano Man." *ZigZag*, London, July 1975.

Cocks, Jay. "The Brash Ballad of Billy Joel." *Time*, New York, January 3, 1978.

Cohen, Stephanie, and Hank Bordowitz. "Peter Townshend Q&A." www.MCY.com
in summer 2000.

Columbia biography for *An Innocent Man.*

Columbia biography for *River of Dreams.*

Connor, Tracy. "Depressed Billy Joel Confided Troubles to Friends before Checking into
Rehab Clinic." *New York Daily News,* June 21, 2002.

Couric, Katie. *Dateline NBC,* May 20, 2003.

Cox, Meg. "Billy Joel Suit over Conflict May Spur Some Lawyers to Change Their Tune."
Wall Street Journal, New York, January 13, 1993.

Dannen, Fred. *Hit Men.* Vintage Books, New York, 1990.

Darwent, George. Billy Joel Biography/Interview, 1995, via www.Turnstiles.org.

DeCurtis, Anthony. "Billy Joel—Rolling Stone." *Rolling Stone,* New York, October 2, 1997.

DeMain, Bill. "Billy Joel: Scenes from a Musical Life." *Performing Songwriter,* Nashville, TN,
January/February 1996.

———. "Billy Joel in a New Romantic State of Mind." *Performing Songwriter,*
Nashville, TN, November 2001.

Dobnik, Verena. "Little Kids Rock Is a Real-life 'School of Rock.'" Associated Press,
New York, October 28, 2003.

Doerschuk, Bob. "The Piano Man Rocks On." *Keyboard,* San Francisco, CA, December 1981.

"Domestic News: In-law and Outlaw." United Press International, September 26, 1989.

Dougherty, Steve. "A $90 Million Matter of Distrust Pits Billy Joel against His Ex-Manager."
People, New York, October 9, 1989.

Duffy, Thom. "Billy Joel Rides the Tide of Success into His 40s." *Billboard,* November 4, 1989.

Edwards, Mark. "All Shook Up." *Sunday Times,* London, May 13, 2001.

Elliot, Susan, "Billy Joel." *High Fidelity,* New York, January 1978.

Erlewine, Stephen Thomas. "Attila Review." www.allmusic.com.

Fabrikant, Geraldine. "Billy Joel Takes His Lawyers to Court." *New York Times,*
September 24, 1992.

Family Productions biography for *Cold Spring Harbor.*

Farquhar, Michael, et al. "Names and Faces." *Washington Post,* August 25, 1994.

Gentile, Bruce. Video of Billy Joel Cold Spring Harbor Park dedication, 1991.

———. Unpublished interview with Mark Perry, September 22, 2002.

———. Author's interview and correspondence, October 26, 2004.

George, Nelson. *Top of the Charts.* New Century Books, Piscataway, NJ, 1983.

Gerosa, Melina. "Christie's Happy New Year." *Ladies' Home Journal,* New York, January 1995.

Gibson, Sandy. Author's interview and correspondence, October 9, 2003.

———. Author's correspondence, September 10, 2004.

———. Author's correspondence, September 12, 2004.

———. Author's correspondence, September 30, 2004.

"Giuliani Camp: Song Promotes Drugs, Masturbation." Associated Press, New York,
February 7, 2000.

Gliatto, Tom; "'I Am Alive' (Model Christie Brinkley Survives Helicopter Crash)."
People, New York, April 18, 1994.

Gliatto, Tom, with Craig Tomashoff, Nancy Matsumoto, and Bryan Alexander. "Suddenly It's
All Over but the Lawyering." *People,* New York, April 25, 1994.

Goldman, Michael H. Lecture at Princeton University, March 1994, via www.Turnstiles.com.

Goodman, Fred. "An Innocent Man." *Spy*, New York, March 1991.

———. "It's Music Crusader vs. Ultimate Insider in $90 Million Billy Joel Legal Brawl." *New York Observer*, March 8, 1993.

Gottschalk, Earl C., Jr. "Stars Struck: Celebrities Often Turn Their Finances Over to Others—and Lose Their Shirts." *Wall Street Journal*, New York, October 19, 1990.

Graff, Gary. "Piano Man Offers His Final Notes for the Pop World." Reuters, August 14, 1997.

———. "Pop Quiz: Q&A with Billy Joel." *Oakland Press*, Oakland, MI, August 1997.

Hamilton, Kendall. "Daydream Believers." *Newsweek*, New York, April 18, 1997.

Handelman, David. "The Bond between Christie and Alexa." *Redbook*, New York, January 1998.

Harmon, Brian, Debbie Tuma, and Tracy Connor. "Piano Man Sings the Rehab Blues." *New York Daily News*, June 21, 2002.

Hassles' history via www.LIrock.com.

Hay, Carla. "Bright Lights, Big Productions." *Billboard*, New York, May 24, 2002.

Heckman, Don. "Pop Festival Excitement Grows as Night and the Stars Appear." *New York Times*, April 3, 1972.

Hinkley, David. "Rock On! Forget What You Heard. It's Still Rock 'n' Roll for Billy Joel." *New York Daily News*, August 17, 1997.

Holden, Stephen. "Billy Joel on the Dark Side." *New York Times*, December 29, 1982.

———. "Billy Joel Reaches Out to Embrace Pop." *New York Times*, August 3, 1986.

———. "Billy Joel Plays New York in a Feisty State of Mind." *New York Times*, June 25, 1990.

———. "Adrift from Pop, Billy Joel Takes a Classical Turn." *New York Times*, September 14, 1997.

Holly, Debbie, and Ed Morris. "Joel 'Shamelessly' Endorses Brooks Hit." *Billboard*, New York, November 23, 1991.

Isacoff, Stuart. "Billy Joel: Neo-Romantic." *Piano Today*, Winter 1996.

Jerome, Jim. "I'm Still Just Another Heavy Hitter off the Street." *People*, New York, March 6, 1978.

———. "Cubans Would Never Again Say 'Yanquis, Go Home!' after the 1979 'Bay of Gigs.'" *People*, New York, March 19, 1979

———. "Backstage with Billy Joel." *People*, New York, December 13, 1993.

Joel, Billy. "If I Knew Then What I Know Now." *Musician*, New York, April 1995.

———. "Billy Joel: 2000 Years: The Millennium Concert" live chat. MSN Live. May 1, 2000.

"Joel Leaves Rehab, Says He'll Attend Premiere." *USA Today*, New York, June 27, 2002.

"Joel Lights a Fire in the Classroom." *Newsday*, New York, January 19, 1990.

"Joel's Ex-guitarist Stegmeyer Dies in Apparent Suicide." *Newsday*, New York, August 26, 1995.

Kandlikar, Dipti. "'Piano Man' Comes to Rochester." www.Turnstiles.org, February 24, 1996.

Kaufman, Joanne. "Was Roger Daltrey Your Camp Counselor?" *Wall Street Journal*, New York, June 26, 2003.

Keil, Beth Landman, and Ian Spiegelman. "Intelligencer: Uptown Girl at Discount Price." *New York*, April 10, 2000.

Kendall, Kris. "Nothing Sweeter: The First Annual Bubblegum Achievement Awards." www.6is9/jaguaro.org, January 28, 2003.

Klosterman, Chuck. "The Stranger." *New York Times Magazine*, September 15, 2002.

Knippenberg, Jim. "Billy Joel: One of the Brightest of the New Stars." *Cincinnati Enquirer*, January 20, 1974.

Kolodner, John David. "Billy Joel: From Barroom to Big Time." *Concert*, April 1974.

Konigsberg, Eric. "Piano Man, Part Two." *New Yorker*, December 3, 2001.

Kozak, Roman. "Billy Joel: Superstar with His Own Entertainment Complex." *Billboard*, New York, August 9, 1980.

Lambert, Wade, and Milo Geyelin. "Legal Beat." *Wall Street Journal*, New York, September 26, 1989.

Landis, David. "Lifelines." *USA Today*, August 2, 1990.

Lang, Michael. Author's interview, April 16, 1998.

Lipson, Karin. "Riches to Ruins." *Newsday*, New York, January 7, 2003.

McAleer, Dave. *The Book of Hit Singles Top 20 Charts*. Backbeat Books, San Francisco, CA, 2001.

Malkin, Mark S. "Intelligencer: Billy Joel in Who's the Plaintiff." *New York*, October 10, 1994.

————. "Intelligencer: VH-1 Keeps the Faith with Billy Joel." *New York*, February 10, 1998.

Mazur, Irwin. Author's interview and correspondence, May 25, 2004.

————. Author's correspondence (email), June 30, 2004.

McCollum, Brian. "Billy Joel Is Playing in a Lower Key." *Detroit Free Press*, November 18, 1998.

Nadboy, Arie. "I Am the Edu-Tainer." *Island Ear*, March 1996.

Neuhaus, Cable. "He Sang of Their Troubles, But Grateful Citizens Say Thank You Anyway to Billy Joel." *People*.

Newman, Melinda. "A Matter of Trust: Billy Joel Suing Former Lawyers." *Billboard*, New York, October 3, 1992.

————. "Joel Sees Pop Exit with Greatest Hits 3." *Billboard*, New York, July 26, 1997.

————. "The Piano Man Is Changing His Tune"; Billboard News Service, New York, August 18, 1997.

————. "The Beat." *Billboard*, New York, January 29, 2002.

New York State Department of Motor Vehicles police accident report, by Detective Paul E. Fabiano, January 31, 2003.

"Notes on People: Dakota Blocks Billy Joel's Bid to Buy Apartment." *New York Times*, June 28, 1980.

Orth, Maureen, Janet Huck, and Peter S. Greenberg, "Making of a Rock Star." *Newsweek*, October 27, 1975.

Palmer, Robert. "Pop: 5 Nights of Billy Joel at the Garden." *New York Times*, June 25, 1980.

Patterson, M. C. "What Christie Did for Love." *McCalls*, New York, January 1995.

"Pop Music Icon Billy Joel Signs Book Publishing Deal with Scholastic." Scholastic Books press release, May 18, 2004.

"Radio Bars Song." *New York Times*, December 30, 1978.

Ragogna, Mike. Liner notes for *You've Got Me Humming: The Best of the Hassles*. Razor and Tie Records, New York, 1999.

Rathbun, Keith. "A Conversation with Billy Joel." *Cleveland Scene*, March 16, 1996.

Recording Industry Association of America. www.riaa.com.

Ripp, Artie. Author's interview, May 8, 2004.

Robins, Wayne. "Just the Way He Is." *Newsday*, New York, August 2 1989.

————. "Next Batter, Billy Joel." *Newsday*, New York, June 22, 1990.

————. "Billy Joel Gets the Blues." *Newsday*, New York, August 10, 1993.

———. "Billy Joel." *Newsday*, New York, October 29, 1999.

Rockwell, John. Untitled review. *New York Times*, February 23, 1974.

———. "Billy Joel Sings the Praises of New York." *New York Times*, December 10, 1978.

———. "Pop: Billy Joel Brings Cuban Crowd to Its Feet." *New York Times*, March 6, 1979.

Rogers, Sheila. "Billy Joel Has No Qualms About Rockin' at Age 40." *Rolling Stone*, New York, November 12, 1989.

Rosten, Leo. *The Joys of Yiddish*. McGraw-Hill, New York, 1968.

Rush, George. "People: The Final Chorus of Piano Man Suit." *New York Daily News*, October 26, 1993.

Ryan, Matt, and Jimmy Jam. "Billy Joel Interview." WNCI Morning Zoo, Columbus, OH, July 21, 1997.

Sandow, Greg. "Ode to Billy Joel." *Entertainment Weekly*, New York, October 9, 1992.

———. "A Piano Man Turns from Pop to Classical." *Wall Street Journal*, New York, November 6, 2001.

Sauter, Michael. "Billy Joel: To Russia with Love." *Entertainment Weekly*, New York, August 9, 1996.

Schilling, Jerry. Author's interview, March 16, 2004.

Schock, Elaine. Author's interview, August 4, 2004.

Schruers, Fred. "Cool Hand Billy." *Sunday News Magazine*, New York, January 17, 1982.

Schwartz, Tony. "Billy the Kid." *Newsweek*, New York, December 11, 1978.

Shapiro, Laura. "She's Got a Way." *New York*, October 28, 2002.

Sheff, David and Victoria. "The Playboy Interview." *Playboy*, New York, May 1982.

Simonson, Robert. "Billy Joel Working on New Musical about the Music Business." *Playbill*, New York, June 7, 2004.

Skolnik, Peter. Author's interview, December 9, 2004.

Smith, Joe. *Off the Record*. Warner Books, New York, 1988.

Smith, Liz. "She's Got a Way That Moves Him." *Newsday*, New York, September 20, 2004.

Soocher, Stan. *They Fought the Law: Rock Music Goes to Court*. Schirmer Books, New York, 1998.

Stevens, Amy. "Lawyers and Clients." *Wall Street Journal*, New York, December 10, 1993.

Tallmer, Jerry. "Billy Joel Grapples with the Past." *The Villager*, New York, July 16, 2003.

Tannenbaum, Rob. "It Takes Two." *New York*, October 28, 2002.

Thomas, Bill. Author's interview, September 25, 2003.

Timberg, Scott. "The Twyla Zone Grows." *Los Angeles Times*, October 24, 2004.

Torgoff, Martin. "Special Bridge Tour Edition." Root Beer Rag (Billy Joel Fanzine), winter 1986.

Tour program for *52nd Street*, 1978.

Tuma, Debbie, and Anne E. Kornblut. "Uptown Girl Goes 4 It, Weds Again." *New York Daily News*, September 22, 1996.

"Tying the Knot." *Tampa Tribune*. Tampa, FL, September 24, 1996.

Van Matre, Lynn. "Billy [Shrinking Violet] Joel Fights His 'Obnoxious' Image." *Chicago Tribune*, October 21, 1982.

Verna, Paul. "The Billboard Interview." *Billboard*, New York, May, 11, 1996.

www.lapdonline.org/bldg_safer_comms/gi_gangs/gang_signs.htm.

Waddell, Ray. "Joel and John's Face to Face Dates Still Breaking Box Office Records." *Billboard*, New York, March 9, 2002.

————. "Joel/John Still Jumping." *Billboard*, New York, November 9, 2002.

Wasserzieher, Bill. Author's correspondence (email), July 30, 2004.

Watts, David. "Take the Billy Joel Challenge." *Tower Records' Pulse*, Sacramento, CA, November 1989.

Welsh, Jonathan. "Try: 'We dig it here in Allentown, don't let anybody put it down.'" *Wall Street Journal*, June 11, 1997.

Westerman, Chantal. "Billy Joel's New Direction." *Good Morning America*, New York, August 18, 1997.

————. "Billy Joel's Greatest Hits." *Good Morning America*, New York, August 19, 1997.

Whitburn, Joel. *The Billboard Book of Top 40 Hits*. Seventh edition, Watson Guptill Publications, New York, 2000.

————. *Top Pop Albums 1955–2001*. Record Research Books, Menomonee Falls, WI, 2001.

White, Timothy. "Looking Back in Anger." *Crawdaddy!*, New York, November 1978.

————. "Billy Joel Is Angry." *Rolling Stone*, New York, September 4, 1980.

————. "The Rolling Stone Interview." *Rolling Stone*, October 15, 1992.

————. "Billy Joel: 1994 Recipient of the Century Award." *Billboard*, New York, December 3, 1994.

————. "A Portrait of the Artist." *Billboard*, New York, December 4, 1994.

Williams, Stephen P. "Captain Billy Joel, Designer Man." *New York Times*, August 3, 2000.

Wolf, Jeanne. "Christie's Secret Strength." *Redbook*, New York, September 1999.

"Woman Wants Billy Joel to Pay for Damage to Her House." Associated Press, April 27, 2004.

"Wreck May Get Billy Joel Premium Rate Hike." United Press International. April 27, 2004.

Yacuboski, Philip. "Billy Joel Lecture at the University of Scranton." *King's College Crown*, Wilkes-Barre, PA, March 12, 1996.

Yetnikoff, Walter, with David Ritz. *Howling at the Moon*. Broadway Books, New York, 2004.

Zibart, Eve. "The Hicksville Slugger." *Washington Post*, October 8, 1978.

Zulaica, Don. "LiveDaily Interview: Liberty DeVitto, Drummer for Billy Joel." www.livedaily.com, March 14, 2001.

Zwecker, Bill. "Wedding of Decade Stumps the Snoops." *Chicago Sun Times*, September 24, 1996.

NOTES

Introduction

(p. xi) "Critics have accused Joel of trying to have it all ways . . .": Schwartz, 1978.

(p. xi) "He has mastered the art of making lyrics . . .": Palmer, 1980.

(p. xii) "When he got criticized it really hurt him . . .": Schock, 2004.

(p. xii) "I think of myself . . .": Joe Smith, 1988.

(p. xii) "I don't feel that I have to be very accessible . . .": Robins, 1999.

(p. xii) "Everybody who knows Billy cares a great deal about him . . .": Schock, 2004.

(p. xiv) "I don't know what happened with his father . . .": Bloom interview, 2004.

(p. xiv) "Billy has his own distrust of people . . .": Mazur interview, 2004.

Chapter 1

(p. 1) "Ahh, life is a cesspool.": White, December 4, 1994.

(p. 2) "What is a child supposed to do about that? . . .": Lipson, 2003.

(p. 2) "My father, Carl . . . had to leave . . .": White, December 4, 1994.

(p. 3) Howard and Rosalind performed together in the college's productions . . . : According to Billy, in Tallmer, 2003.

(p. 3) "My family didn't have a pot to pee in . . .": White, December 4, 1994.

(p. 3) "We . . . took pictures of the heaps of . . . dead people . . .": White, December 4, 1994.

(p. 4) "He was never the same when he came back . . .": White, December 4, 1994.

(p. 5) "My father was my idol as a pianist as a kid . . .": White, December 4, 1994.

(p. 6) "After four years of little Billy's storm song . . .": Bolando, 2001.

(p. 6) "I hated every minute of it until I quit . . .": Family Productions biography.

Chapter 2

(p. 7) Rosalind was still a relatively young and attractive woman . . . : According to Billy in Sheff, 1982.

(p. 7) "We weren't like everybody else on the block . . .": Ahrens, 1998.

(p. 7) "We were blue-collar poor people . . .": Columbia biography for *An Innocent Man.*

(p. 8) "We went hungry a lot . . .": White, 1978.

(p. 8) "Roz did the best she could . . .": Gentile interview, 2004.

(p. 8) "My grandfather . . . was the most inspiring presence in my life . . .": Darwent, 1995.

(p. 8) "He would sneak us into operas, ballets . . .": Tallmer, 2003.

(p. 9) "I guess I started writing when I was about seven years old . . .": Family Productions biography.

(p. 9) Billy's early school days: Via Sheff, 1982.

(p. 9) "By the time he was seven . . .": White, December 4, 1994.

(p. 9) "Billy reads books the way other people eat M&Ms": Bloom interview, 2004.

(p. 10) "I . . . remember doing an Elvis Presley impression when I was in the fourth grade . . .": Sheff, 1982.

(p. 10) "I think it was because of his father leaving the family like that . . .": Mazur interview, 2004.

(p. 11) "The way Brubeck messed around with time signatures . . .": Watts, 1989.

(p. 11) "This is the flag of the Jews": Darwent, 1995.

Chapter 3

(p. 12) "You got into junior high, you could go one of three ways . . .": Cocks, 1978.

(p. 12) "We'd just play handball all day . . .": Schwartz, 1978.

(p. 12) "We were hitters. I mean I had a gang . . .": Kozak, 1980.

(p. 13) "We used to sneak off to find Italian-style clothes . . .": Schruers, 1982.

(p. 13) As the Los Angeles Police Department points out . . . :
   www.lapdonline.org/bldg_safer_comms/gi_gangs/gang_signs.htm.

(p. 13) "I never said I was tough . . .": Van Matre, 1982.

(p. 14) "I've got two different sized nostrils . . .": Sheff, 1982.

(p. 14) "I just wanted to break out in general . . .": Darwent, 1995.

(p. 15) Orbison advice to the Beatles: Bordowitz, 2004.

(p. 16) "If you're going to be a concert pianist . . .": Elliot, 1978.

(p. 16) "I had no intention of becoming a concert pianist . . .": Westerman, August 18, 1997.

(p. 17) "I thought, 'these guys don't look like Fabian . . .": Columbia biography for
   An Innocent Man.

(p. 17) Attitude toward Beatles: Via Sheff, 1982.

(p. 17) "When I was a teenager . . .": Sheff, 1982.

(p. 17) "I became a musician partially because of my physical limitations . . .":
   White, December 4, 1994.

(p. 17) "When these guys first asked me to join them . . .": White, 1978.

(p. 18) "Her name was Virginia Callahan . . .": Hinkley, 1997.

(p. 18) "Then, at the end of the night . . .": Bolando, 2001.

(p. 18) "If you were from the more industrial . . .": Sheff, 1982.

(p. 18) "Rock is a religion . . .": Bloom interview, 2004.

(p. 19) "The first time I remember actually being . . .": White, December 3, 1994.

(p. 20) "What are you looking at me for? . . . : Almost verbatim from DeMain, 1996.

(p. 21) "Long Island was the soul counter . . .": Gentile interview, 2004.

(p. 21) "The first song Billy ever recorded . . .": Hassles' history via www.LIrock.com.

(p. 22) "I told them, 'The hell with it . . .": Columbia biography for *An Innocent Man.*

Chapter 4

(p. 24) "Jon Small always used his penis as a brain . . .": Gentile interview, 2004.

(p. 25) "The Hassles had really become one of the hot bands . . .": Mazur interview, 2004.

(p. 25) "Harry Weber suffered from debilitating depression . . .": Gibson, September 30, 2004.

(p. 25) "He was sniffing a lot . . .": Hassles' history via www.LIrock.com.

(p. 26) "Billy had come in . . .": Mazur interview, 2004.

(p. 26) "I'm a better organist than I am a piano player . . .": Doerschuk, 1981.

(p. 26) "I was told . . .": Mazur correspondence, June 30, 2004.

(p. 26) "Harry laid himself on the tracks one night . . .": Gentile interview, 2004.

(p. 26) "I saw the Hassles' first gig . . .": Gentile interview with Mark Perry, 2002.

(p. 27) Hamptons in the '60s: Cabal, 2003.

(p. 27) "Billy sang . . .": Mazur interview, 2004.

(p. 27) "Dizek was really the glamour part . . .": Gentile interview, 2004.

(p. 27) "I arranged for somebody from United Artists records . . .": Mazur interview, 2004.

(p. 27) "We recorded our first single and album . . .": Mazur interview, 2004.

(p. 28) "Our management was bad . . .": Hassle's history via www.LIrock.com.

(p. 28) "I didn't really know the inner workings . . .": Mazur interview, 2004.

(p. 29) "If you wanted to learn the record business . . .": Mazur interview, 2004.

(p. 29) Draft board episode: Sheff, 1982.

(p. 30) "It was a pretty good album . . .": Mazur interview, 2004.

(p. 30) "After three confusing years . . .": Family Productions biography.

(p. 30) "Billy was always alright with me . . .": Hassle's history via www.LIrock.com.

(p. 31) "After gigs, very early in the morning . . .": Gentile interview, 2004.

(p. 31) "Billy and I . . . wanted to continue to play together . . .": Hassle's history via www.LIrock.com.

(p. 32) "Jon and Billy no doubt thought . . .": Gentile interview, 2004.

(p. 32) "It was some ridiculous concept that they had . . .": Mazur interview, 2004.

(p. 32) "*Attila* received rave reviews . . .": Family Productions biography.

(p. 32) "as if a drill has punctured . . .": Erlewine, "Attila Review."

(p. 32) "Billy and Jon were getting gigs . . .": Gentile interview, 2004.

(p. 33) "I went to see Billy play with El Primo . . .": Gentile interview, 2004.

Chapter 5

(p. 34) "Liz was wise to Jon . . .": Gentile interview, 2004.

(p. 35) "I got a call from Billy one night . . .": Mazur interview, 2004.

(p. 35) "There's a lot of frustration living in the suburbs . . .": Childs, 1975.

(p. 35) "As it turns out . . .": Ahrens, 1998.

(p. 35) "blackout drinker . . .": Gentile interview, 2004.

(p. 36) "Billy was very excited . . .": Gentile interview, 2004.

(p. 36) "I did like two-dozen reviews . . .": White, December 3, 1994.

(p. 36) "Landscaping sucked . . .": Kandlikar, 1996.

(p. 36) "It was hard work . . .": Couric, 2003.

(p. 36) "When the guys started telling me . . .": Childs, 1975.

(p. 37) Gaslight information: Aronowitz, 1996.

(p. 37) "I tuned in once . . .": Wasserzieher correspondence, 2004.

(p. 37) "Billy is two years younger than Elizabeth . . .": Gibson interview, 2003.

(p. 38) "I was absolutely devastated . . .": Klosterman, 2002.

(p. 39) "We found Billy in the cedar closet . . .": Gentile interview, 2004.

(p. 39) "I was into a real self-pity trip . . .": White, 1992.

(p. 39) "One day, I get up . . .": Mazur interview, 2004.

(p. 39) Conversation at Meadowbrook: Verbatim from Mazur interview, 2004.

(p. 39) "I somewhat represented myself as a doctor . . .": Mazur interview, 2004.

(p. 39) "Billy had a tendency in those days . . .": Mazur interview, 2004.

Chapter 6

(p. 41) Post-Meadowbrook dialogue: Mazur interview, 2004.

(p. 41) Paramount first-look option: Mazur interview, 2004.

(p. 42) Moishe Levy incident: Mazur interview, 2004.

(p. 43) Michael Lang incident: Mazur interview, 2004.

(p. 43) "I sucked": Joe Smith, 1988.

(p. 44) "sell a hundred records . . .": Joe Smith, 1988.

(p. 44) "Artie produced some great, great records . . .": Gibson interview, 2003.

(p. 46) "Bob Krasnow had a deal with them . . .": Gibson interview, 2003.

(p. 47) Tony Martell account: Bloom, "Reinventing Capitalism," 2004.

(p. 47) Dialogue between Artie Ripp and Michael Lang: Verbatim from Ripp interview, 2004.

(p. 48) "This is somebody who will be an important talent . . .": Ripp interview, 2004.

(p. 48) Dialog between Michael Lang and Artie Ripp: Ripp interview, 2004.

(p. 49) Dialog with Irwin Mazur: Ripp interview, 2004.

(p. 49) "You wanted a record deal in thirty days . . .": Mazur, 2004.

Chapter 7

(p. 50) "I didn't know what I was signing . . .": Sheff, 1982.

(p. 50) "I was only twenty . . .": Childs, 1975.

(p. 50) "The record company gave me a piano . . .": Family Productions biography.

(p. 50) "One day, the ultimate shit goes down . . .": Gentile interview, 2004.

(p. 51) "As you sign a record contract . . .": Childs, 1975.

(p. 52) "The studio itself is a sterile . . .": Ripp interview, 2004.

(p. 52) "It's not easy for me to listen to myself . . .": Joel, 2000.

(p. 52) "Billy needed to play and sing at the same time . . .": Ripp interview, 2004.

(p. 52) "I think of myself as a piano player . . .": Darwent, 1995.

(p. 53) "I'm living in a beautiful little hamlet . . .": Family Productions biography.

(p. 53) Hicksville of the Hamptons: Via Sheff, 1982.

(p. 53) "I remember taking the ride . . .": Gentile interview, 2004.

(p. 54) "Gulf & Western's record holdings . . .": Bloom, "Reinventing Capitalism," 2004.

(p. 54) "It all of a sudden struck me . . .": Ripp interview, 2004.

(p. 55) "Artie started totally flipping out . . .": Gibson interview, 2003.

(p. 55) "The strangest thing occurred . . .": Ripp interview, 2004.

(p. 55) "But at the end of the day . . .": Ripp interview, 2004.

(p. 56) Smashing the album: Klosterman, 2002.

Chapter 8

(p. 57) "How do I establish Billy . . .": Ripp interview, 2004.

(p. 57) "I sent Billy out . . .": Ripp interview, 2004.

(p. 57) "Touring made zero economic sense . . .": Mazur interview, 2004.

(p. 58) "They'd like to present me . . .": Family Productions biography.

(p. 58) "During those early days of being on the road . . .": Mazur interview, 2004.

(p. 58) "Traveling across the country . . .": Kolodner, 1974.

(p. 58) "I literally lived on the road . . .": Childs, 1975.

(p. 59) Mar y Sol incident: Mazur interview, 2004.

(p. 60) "My wife was on the stage with me . . .": Mazur interview, 2004.

(p. 60) "We did really well . . .": Childs, 1975.

(p. 60) "The first real excitement . . .": Heckman, 1972.

(p. 60) "It was one of the first outings . . .": Gentile interview, 2004.

(p. 61) "People at Columbia Records . . .": Ripp interview, 2004.

(p. 61) Reunion with Howard Joel: Via Sheff, 1982.

(p. 62) "'Captain Jack' was a 'look-out-the-window' song . . .": Zibart, 1978.

(p. 62) "It's about coming out of the New York suburbs . . .": Kolodner, 1974.

(p. 63) "Clive [Davis, president of Columbia Records] invited me . . .": Yetnikoff, with Ritz, 2004.

(p. 63) "If you go back in his career . . .": Bloom interview, 2004.

(p. 63) "We all moved . . .": Mazur interview, 2004.

(p. 63) "Billy and Elizabeth were living . . .": Gibson interview, 2003.

(p. 64) "I had to figure out . . .": Ripp interview, 2004.

(p. 64) "I took on something like two million . . .": Ripp interview, 2004.

(p. 64) "Billy says he's not going to record . . .": Gibson interview, 2003.

(p. 65) "I went through the *Godfather* thing . . .": Schwartz, 1978.

(p. 65) "The characters that Bill Murray and Steve Martin do . . .": White, 1980.

(p. 65) "If somebody asked for a Sinatra song . . .": Doerschuk, 1981.

(p. 65) "What you're doing in a piano bar . . .": Doerschuk, 1981.

(p. 66) "It's disgusting . . .": Gibson interview, 2003.

(p. 66) "After a while, the music business in LA . . .": Childs, 1975.

(p. 66) "I've never given myself . . .": DeMain, 1996.

Chapter 9

(p. 67) Conversation with Jerry Moss: From Ripp interview, 2004.

(p. 67) "Eventually . . .": Ripp interview, 2004.

(p. 67) "I was playing songs . . .": Isacoff, 1996.

(p. 67–68) Atlantic records interest: Via Ripp interview, 2004.

(p. 68) "In conjunction with Billy's lawyer . . .": Ripp interview, 2004.

(p. 68) Becky Mancuso-Shargo story: Based on Ripp interview, 2004.

(p. 69) Conversation with Clive Davis: Based on Mazur interview, 2004.

(p. 70) "the sound of universes colliding": Orth et al., 1975.

(p. 70) "I wanted to be on Columbia Records . . .": Newman, July 26, 1997.

(p. 70) "Clive has a secret meeting . . .": Goodman, 1991.

(p. 71) Conversation with Ahmet Ertegun: From Ripp interview, 2004.

(p. 71) "able to sell Billy's records . . .": Gibson, September 12, 2004.

(p. 71) "My deal with Columbia . . .": Ripp interview, 2004.

(p. 72) "Basically, I stepped out . . .": Ripp interview, 2004.

Chapter 10

(p. 74) "Some of the things on *Piano Man* . . .": Knippenberg, 1974.

(p. 75) "I wrote 'You're My Home' . . .": Sheff, 1982.

(p. 75) "I don't make my songs for any audience . . .": Joel, 2000.

(p. 75) "It took time for Billy to find a band . . .": Ripp interview, 2004.

(p. 76) "Michael became a confidant of Billy's . . .": Mazur interview, 2004.

(p. 76) "By the time it came to interest by Columbia . . .": Gibson, September 10, 2004.

(p. 76) "Artie made a nice financial deal . . .": Mazur interview, 2004.

(p. 77) "Elizabeth would sit in the lobby . . .": Gibson interview, 2003.

(p. 77) "Clive Davis was executed out of the company . . .": Ripp interview, 2004.

(p. 78) "When I was drumming for Henry Gross . . .": Gentile interview, 2004.

(p. 79) "'Piano Man' was me . . .": Arrington, 1978.

(p. 79) "I was talking about the cold, hard business . . .": Zibart, 1978.

(p. 79) "I have a real cynicism . . .": Rockwell, 1978.

(p. 79) "I like to be as eclectic as possible . . .": Childs, 1975.

(p. 79) "I never do the same thing twice . . .": Columbia biography for *An Innocent Man*.

(p. 80) "I was with Caribou Management . . .": Zibart, 1978.

(p. 80) "When I was in LA . . .": Rockwell, 1978.

(p. 81) Sleeping under the piano: Schwartz, 1978.

(p. 82) "Billy rejected the first recording . . .": Schilling interview, 2004.

(p. 82) "So we kind of hit it off . . .": Schilling interview, 2004.

(p. 82) "Michael [Stewart] felt comfortable . . .": Childs, 1975.

(p. 83) "Liberty used to work with Mitch Ryder . . .": Tour Program for *52nd Street*, 1978.

(p. 83) "Billy looked at it as a band . . .": Schilling interview, 2004.

(p. 84) "I heard Ronnie in my head . . .": White, 1980.

(p. 84) "I was moving back to New York . . .": DeMain, 2001.

(p. 84) "I thought, 'This is one of the greatest woman singers ever . . .": Doerschuk, 1981.

(p. 84) "'Angry Young Man' was written about his tour manager . . .": Schilling interview, 2004.

(p. 85) "When I got back to New York from LA . . .": DeMain, 2001.

Chapter 11

(p. 86) "The very next day . . .": Sheff, 1982.

(p. 86) "She's the person who hired me . . .": Schilling interview, 2004.

(p. 87) "I was regarded as Billy's girlfriend . . .": Schruers, 1982.

(p. 87) "She was a good manager for him . . .": Gibson interview, 2003.

(p. 87) "a mom-and-pop operation": Arrington, 1978.

(p. 87) "I could never understand how Paul McCartney . . .": Gibson interview, 2003.

(p. 88) "For years . . . we were the opening act . . .": Knippenberg, 1974.

(p. 88) "He came to my room one night . . .": Schilling interview, 2004.

(p. 88) "There was no class distinction . . .": Schilling interview, 2004.

(p. 88) "Probably no manager worked Walter Yetnikoff better . . .": Schilling, 2004.

(p. 89) "Billy Joel . . . was struggling. . . .": Yetnikoff, with Ritz, 2004.

(p. 89) "CBS down in Australia . . .": Schilling interview, 2004.

(p. 90) "Before *Turnstiles* there was that cooling-off period . . .": Schilling interview, 2004.

(p. 90) "By the end of 1976 . . .": Kozak, 1980.

(p. 90) "Hearing Billy Joel at the 1971 Puerto Rican Pop Festival . . .": Rockwell, 1974.

(p. 91) "I got a call from his wife at the time . . .": Joe Smith, 1988.

(p. 91) "Love me, love my band . . .": Tour Program for *52nd Street*, 1978.

(p. 91) "The first time I saw Liberty . . .": Amendola, 2002.

(p. 92) "Phil liked my guys right off the bat . . .": Columbia biography for *An Innocent Man*.

(p. 92) "We did songs in five takes . . .": Columbia biography for *An Innocent Man*.

(p. 92) "Everybody at the label loved him . . .": Verna, 1996.

(p. 93) Conversation with Mazur and Bishop: Mazur interview, 2004.

Chapter 12

(p. 95) "I was in the middle of a meeting . . .": Joe Smith, 1988.

(p. 95) "Everybody was down on it . . .": Darwent, 1995.

(p. 95) Phoebe Snow story: Via DeMain, 1996.

(p. 96)"That edge of anxiety . . .": "Billy Joel Talks Shop with Music Students," 1989.

(p. 96) "People who think it's me . . .": Jerome, 1978.

(p. 96) "'Just the Way You Are' was a big hit . . .": White, 1980.

(p. 97) "'He studied piano' . . .": Klosterman, 2002.

(p. 97) "If you go back in his career . . .": Bloom interview, 2004.

(p. 98) "It wasn't the song . . .": "Radio Bars Song," 1978.

(p. 98) "I didn't have trouble . . .": DeMain, 1996.

(p. 98) "When I wrote . . .": Sheff, 1982.

(p. 98) "They missed the point . . .": Sheff, 1982.

(p. 98) "It was actually three different songs . . .": DeMain, 1996.

(p. 99) "I try to go back to Long Island . . .": Arrington, 1978.

(p. 99) "Basically . . . when *The Stranger* finally came out . . .": Ripp interview, May 8, 2004.

(p. 100) "There are acres of bodies . . .": Isacoff, 1996.

(p. 100) Australia story: Via Schilling interview, 2004.

(p. 101) "While I was working for CBS . . .": Mazur interview, 2004.

Chapter 13

(p. 102) "When I come up with a melody . . .": Sheff, 1982.

(p. 102) "*52nd Street* was a much different album . . .": White, 1980.

(p. 102) "I am not a virtuoso pianist . . .": Doerschuk, 1981.

(p. 103) "I wrote that one thinking about a young person . . .": DeMain, 2001.

(p. 103) "It's about anybody who's ever had a hangover . . .": Sheff, 1982.

(p. 103) "My music and lyrics . . .": Sheff, 1982.

(p. 104) "Though the two have to fit together . . .": Holden, 1986.

(p. 104) "Zanzibar" story: Via DeMain, 1996.

(p. 106) "The reader should be put on notice . . .": Soocher, 1998.

(p. 106) "'My Life' [is] a song that turned sour for me . . .": "Billy Joel Talks Shop with Music Students," 1989.

(p. 106) "Some of them grew up to be doctors . . .": Holden, 1997.

(p. 106) "I give birth to these songs . . .": Sheff, 1982.

(p. 106) "Everything I've done is different . . .": Sheff, 1982.

(p. 106) "Now I see somebody coming at me . . .": Soocher, 1998.

(p. 107) "My father had lived in Cuba . . .": Jerome, 1979.

(p. 107) "I'm not down here on some capitalist venture . . .": Jerome, 1979.

(p. 107) "Hey, is it horny in here . . .": Jerome, 1979.

(p. 108) "Mr. Joel's presence at this three-day festival . . .": Rockwell, 1979.

(p. 108) "We listen to him on radio . . .": Jerome, 1979.

(p. 108) "Big halls are rip-offs . . .": Knippenberg, 1974.

(p. 108) "Because we're doing bigger rooms . . .": Doerschuk, 1981.

(p. 109) "I sat down at the piano one show . . .": Darwent, 1995.

Chapter 14

(p. 127) "The song is an out and out attack . . .": Sheff, 1982.

(p. 127) "'It's Still Rock and Roll to Me' wasn't against . . .": Schruers, 1982.

(p. 128) "I thought about doing an album . . .": Zibart, 1978.

(p. 128) "What else could the song be about?": Kandlikar, 1996.

(p. 128) "In the midsection of the song . . .": Doerschuk, 1981.

(p. 128) "I don't think we'll ever play . . .": Joel, 2000.

(p. 129) "At this point, Elizabeth and I . . .": Kozak, 1980.

(p. 129) "She said Billy's business . . .": Soocher, 1998.

(p. 129) "I had questions about somebody's brother . . .": Deposition, via Soocher, 1998.

(p. 130) "When you are working with managing . . .": Kozak, 1980.

(p. 130) "People think I've got this multimillion-dollar mansion . . .": White, 1980.

(p. 130) "He has won a huge following . . .": Palmer, 1980.

(p. 131) "I was turned down for an apartment . . .": Sheff, 1982.

(p. 131) "a growing feeling that there are already enough celebrities . . .":
"Notes on People: Dakota Blocks Billy Joel's Bid to Buy Apartment," 1980.

(p. 131) "I was an expert at taking people . . .": Bloom interview, 2004.

(p. 132) "Ten years after I had worked at Gulf & Western . . .": Bloom interview, 2004.

(p. 132) "I thought I was so cool . . .": Schock, 2004

(p. 133) "As writers, one of the first things . . .": Bloom interview, 2004.

(p. 133) "I met my first husband . . .": Schock, 2004.

(p. 133) "Timothy White . . . had already written this story . . .": Schock, 2004.

(p. 134) "I liked controlling Alan Grubman . . .": Yetnikoff, with Ritz, 2004.

(p. 134) "The only way Billy signed again . . .": Gibson interview, 2003.

(p. 135) Signing with Columbia: Via Soocher, 1998.

(p. 135) "For years, I didn't think . . .": Schruers, 1982.

Chapter 15

(p. 136) "The more he kept doing drugs . . .": Gibson interview, 2003.

(p. 136) "Around late spring of 1980, we were talking . . .": Darwent, 1995.

(p. 136) "When you're on a motorcycle . . .": Schruers, 1982.

(p. 136) "a motorcycle fetishist . . .": Bloom interview, 2004.

(p. 136) "A motorcycle . . . is an amusement . . .": Sheff, 1982.

(p. 137) "You know those roads out on Long Island . . .": Bloom interview, 2004.

(p. 137) "I felt absolutely helpless . . .": Columbia biography for *An Innocent Man*.

(p. 137) "There's a scar on every single knuckle . . .": Darwent, 1995.

(p. 137) "We were afraid for Billy's life . . .": Bloom interview, 2004.

(p. 137) "Dexterity is not a problem . . .": Darwent, 1995.

(p. 138) "The biggest thing I learned from the accident . . .": Holden, 1982.

(p. 138) "Not only did she hit him . . .": Bloom interview, 2004.

(p. 139) "There was cocaine . . .": Bloom interview, 2004.

(p. 139) "It really shook me up . . .": Van Matre, 1982.

(p. 139) "She's a good friend . . .": Darwent, 1995.

(p. 140) "If it were up to her . . .": Gibson interview, 2003.

(p. 140) "I think what had happened . . .": Goodman, 1991.

(p. 140) "I shouldn't have gotten married . . .": Klosterman, 2002.

(p. 140) "[Elizabeth] was bored . . .": Soocher, 1998.

(p. 140) "Elizabeth suggested several other managers . . .": Gibson interview, 2003.

(p. 141) "Elizabeth's brother is a dog . . .": Gibson interview, 2003.

Chapter 16

(p. 142) "We have a trio called the Mean Brothers . . .": Darwent, 1995.

(p. 142) "The album . . . opens with four songs . . .": Darwent, 1995.

(p. 143) "When I was through with the album . . .": Van Matre, 1982.

(p. 143) "He loved the Beatles so much . . .": White, December 4, 1994.

(p. 143) "I feel like I almost died . . .": Columbia biography for *An Innocent Man*.

(p. 143) "I tried to remember . . .": Holden, 1982.

(p. 144) "We used a lot of the panning . . .": Darwent, 1995.

(p. 144) "Allentown is a metaphor for America . . .": Neuhaus, "He Sang of Their Troubles . . ."

(p. 144) "I just wrote a song . . .": Neuhaus, "He Sang of Their Troubles . . ."

(p. 144) "It was literally the fifth time . . .": Darwent, 1995.

(p. 145) "I like the straight-force piano resonance . . .": Darwent, 1995.

(p. 145) "I wasn't trying to make a comment . . .": Holden, 1982.

(p. 146) "I wanted the album jacket to look . . .": Darwent, 1995.

(p. 146) Nylon *shmata* conversation: Via Yetnikoff, 2004.

Chapter 17

(p. 148) "I just have to get used . . .": Darwent, 1995.

(p. 148) "One of the first relationships . . .": Newman, July 26, 1997.

(p. 149) "I saw her getting on a plane . . .": *Charlie Rose Show*, 1993.

(p. 149) "I started playing piano . . .": Yacuboski, 1996.

(p. 149) "We were friends first . . .": *Charlie Rose Show*, 1993.

(p. 149) "[Billy was] a strong support for me . . .": Patterson, 1995.

(p. 149) "I met him at the apartment . . .": Bloom interview, 2004.

(p. 151) "I decided I wanted to have as much fun . . .": Columbia biography
        for *An Innocent Man*.

(p. 151) "You should communicate . . .": Columbia biography for *An Innocent Man*.

(p. 152) "You say something really tender . . .": Columbia biography for *An Innocent Man*.

(p. 152) "Uptown Girl' is a joke song . . .": DeMain, 1996.

(p. 152) "'An Innocent Man' was written . . .": Newman, July 26, 1997.

(p. 153) "The song says I'm not living in the past . . .": Columbia biography
        for *An Innocent Man*.

(p. 153) "Billy never thought of himself . . .": Bloom interview, 2004.

(p. 154) "When Billy did his week at the Garden . . .": Gentile interview, 2004.

(p. 154) "The reason we're going on the boat . . .": "A Dreamboat Wedding," 1985.

(p. 155) "A lot of people have told me . . .": "A Dreamboat Wedding," 1985.

(p. 155) "When I married Christie . . .": Klosterman, 2002.

(p. 155) "Her name is a feminine version of Alexander . . .": Brock, 1994.

Chapter 18

(p. 156) "It got to a point . . .": Robins, 1999.

(p. 156) "Liberty DeVitto was sharing with me . . .": Gentile interview, 2004.

(p. 156) "The only premise for *The Bridge* . . .": Holden, 1986.

(p. 157) "I realized there's been a lot of connections . . .": Torgoff, 1986.

(p. 157) "I named my daughter . . .": Holden, 1986.

(p. 157) "I found out I could hold my own . . .": Torgoff, 1986.

(p. 157) "I hated that thing": Newman, July 26, 1997.

(p. 157) "I had gotten to the last song . . .": Torgoff, 1986.

(p. 158) "I had a writing studio . . .": Torgoff, 1986.

(p. 158) "remember this good time . . .": Newman, July 26, 1997.

(p. 158) "a guitar oriented song that had some grit in it": Newman, July 26, 1997.

(p. 159) "The band had a bunch of stickers printed . . .": Gentile interview, 2004.

(p. 159) "had all the cocaine in the world . . .": Gentile interview, 2004.

(p. 160) "I went on tour with him a lot . . .": Schock interview, 2004.

(p. 160) "I think they were just thrilled . . .": Sauter, 1996.

(p. 160) "I went to Billy's big concert . . .": Yetnikoff, with Ritz, 2004.

(p. 161) "It's my show!": "Billy Joel Has a Tantrum," 1989.

(p. 161) "It was a real prima donna act . . .": "Billy Joel Has a Tantrum," 1989.

(p. 161) "It separated the wheat from the chaff . . .": Watts, 1989.

(p. 161) "Ever since we played Russia . . .": Sauter, 1996.

(p. 162) "I remember the evening . . .": Yetnikoff, with Ritz, 2004.

(p. 162) "would fire him as Joel's attorney . . .": Fabrikant, 1992.

(p. 163) "took more monies from the revenues . . .": Via Soocher, 1998.

(p. 163) "I would never let anyone dictate . . .": Joel, 1995.

(p. 164) "To have to translate . . .": Gottschalk, 1990.

(p. 164) "When Frank . . .": Goodman, 1991.

(p. 164) "even know how much he has to send . . .": Gentile interview, 2004.

(p. 164) "You were right . . .": Yetnikoff, with Ritz, 2004.

(p. 164) "I'm really hurt by the whole thing . . .": Robins, 1999.

Chapter 19

(p. 165) "That was a difficult thing for me to do. . .": Duffy, 1989.

(p. 165) "At one time, I wasn't sure . . .": Rogers, 1989.

(p. 165) "After thirteen years . . .": Robins, 1990 .

(p. 166) "Doug Stegmeyer went through a lot of money . . .": Gentile interview, 2004.

(p. 167) "He was asked to do one at NYU . . .": Schock interview, 2004.

(p. 167) "Mick Jones is a songwriter . . .": Robins, 1999.

(p. 167) "He has an inside track . . .": Duffy, 1989.

(p. 167) "I don't have as much faith . . .": Robins, 1999.

(p. 168) "He wanted me to come with songs . . .": Watts, 1989.

(p. 168) "I turned forty this year . . .": Rogers, 1989.

(p. 168) "I wanted to list all the different icons . . .": Kandlikar, 1996.

(p. 168) "I'm a history nut . . .": Watts, 1989.

(p. 168) "Part of the point of that song . . .": Duffy, 1989.

(p. 169) "the greatest teaching tool . . .": "Joel Lights a Fire in the Classroom," 1990.

(p. 169) "[It] surprised me . . .": Robins, 1990.

(p. 169) "It's a nightmare . . .": Newman, July 26, 1997.

(p. 169) "'Uptown Girl' or . . . some silly novelty song . . .": Nadboy, 1996.

(p. 169) "There's no backlog . . .": Holden, 1986.

(p. 169) "was written back in 1983 . . .": Newman, July 26, 1997.

(p. 169) "It's kind of an ode to manic depression . . .": Newman, July 26, 1997.

(p. 170) "The baymen are being put out of business . . .": Robins, 1999.

(p. 170) "The Baymen love this song . . .": Robins, 1999.

(p. 170) "If these guys disappear . . .": Robins, 1999.

(p. 171) "It's a man's ultimate expression . . .": Holly and Morris, 1991.

(p. 171) "I actually wrote that [musically] thinking . . .": Newman, July 26, 1997.

(p. 171) "There's some malevolence in the album . . .": Duffy, 1989.

(p. 172) "I've got a pretty good slice . . .": Rogers, 1989.

(p. 172) "I trusted him totally . . .": Soocher, 1998.

(p. 172) "It's really quite a shocking story . . .": Lambert and Milo, 1989.

(p. 172) "an audit and investigation revealed major incidents . . .": Dougherty, 1989.

(p. 172) "All this came to light when . . .": "Domestic News: In-law and Outlaw," 1989.

(p. 172) "the worst I've ever seen": Dougherty, 1989.

(p. 172) "He was de facto manager . . .": Schock interview, 2004.

(p. 173) "I'm finding I can get a lot of things done . . .": Duffy, 1989.

(p. 173) "The assumption that artists need . . .": Joel, 1995.

(p. 173) "Musicians can manage themselves . . .": Goldman, 1994.

(p. 173) "The reason for the length of this tour . . .": Berry, 1990.

(p. 174) "I went to Shea to see the Stones . . .": Robins, 1990.

(p. 174) "The concert reinforced the image of Mr. Joel . . .": Holden, 1990.

(p. 174) "How does a little pup like me . . .": Berry, 1990.

(p. 175) "Roz was so drunk . . .": Gentile interview, 2004.

(p. 175) "a famous brothel . . .": Gentile video, 1991.

(p. 176) "Now, thirty-six years later . . .": Holly and Morris, 1991.

Chapter 20

(p. 177) "He submitted some of his actual works . . .": Brozan, 1992.

(p. 177) "Well, here I am, mom . . .": Brozan, 1992.

(p. 177) "They're deliberately trying to make this litigation . . .": Soocher, 1998.

(p. 178) "He sued everyone who's ever had a drink . . .": Soocher, 1998.

(p. 178) "None of this came to light . . .": Newman, 1992.

(p. 179) "from the outset of their attorney-client relationship . . .": Newman, 1992.

(p. 179) "duties of care and undivided loyalty . . .": Fabrikant, 1992.

(p. 180) "I thought having a manager . . .": Newman, 1992.

(p. 180) "The record companies want to deal with a house lawyer . . .": Cox, 1993.

(p. 180) "Allen [Grubman] is tough . . .": Goodman, 1993.

(p. 180) "If you're a lawyer getting paid by a label . . .": Cox, 1993.

(p. 180) "I had no axe to grind . . .": Goodman, 1993.

(p. 181) "This isn't a crusade . . .": Cox, 1993.

(p. 181) "They don't know the difference . . .": Gottschalk, 1990.

(p. 181) "I'm a piano man . . .": Gottschalk, 1990.

(p. 182) "The essence of the album . . .": Robins, 1993.

(p. 182) "It's really a play on the phrase . . .": Newman, July 26, 1997.

(p. 182) "I realized . . . I just can't write . . .": McCollum, 1998.

(p. 182) "I used to be afraid of being in my forties . . .": Jerome, 1993.

(p. 183) "He's hardly the writer of empty pop hits . . .": Sandow, 1992.

(p. 183) "It's sort of like . . . intercourse . . .": Carlton, 1994.

(p. 183) "Rock is a cannibalizing business . . .": Jerome, 1993.

(p. 183) "That song started out very fast . . .": Newman, July 26, 1997.

(p. 184) "The basic inner something . . .": Robins, 1993.

(p. 184) "I had a classical piano piece . . .": Newman, July 26, 1997.

(p. 184) "I love hearing Alexa's voice . . .": Jerome, 1993.

(p. 184) "She likes a lot of this 'high life.' . . .": Carlton, 1994.

(p. 185) "He actually asked us to put a song on it": Cannon, 1992.

(p. 185) "I like to play and make music . . .": Newman, July 26, 1997.

(p. 185) "I love it when he's on the road . . .": Carlton, 1994.

(p. 185) "Sure there are still groupies . . .": Jerome, 1993.

Chapter 21

(p. 186) "I'm married to Christie Brinkley . . .": Robins, 1989.

(p. 186) "Outside of Rocky's Sports Arena . . .": Gentile interview, 2004.

(p. 187) "We just dropped . . .": Gliatto, April 18, 1994.

(p. 187) "I would look out the window . . .": Gliatto, April 18, 1994.

(p. 187) "We have been there to support each other . . .": Gliatto et al., April 25, 1994.

(p. 188) "'Shameless' had already become a big hit . . .": Schock interview, 2004.

(p. 188) "Some believe Joel's roving eye . . .": Quoted in Patterson, 1995.

(p. 188) "My divorce was a long time coming": Patterson, 1995.

(p. 188) "We had so many laughs and adventures . . .": Wolf, 1999.

(p. 188) "I was on tour with Billy . . .": White, December 4, 1994.

(p. 189) "When you have scheduled time . . .": Handelman, 1998.

(p. 189) "I enjoy my daughter's company . . .": Ryan and Jam, 1997.

(p. 189) "I owed it to her . . .": Wolf, 1999.

(p. 189) "Now that she's gone . . .": Patterson, 1995.

(p. 189) "the Colorado disaster": Handelman, 1998.

(p. 190) "We first met in a hotel . . .": Brady, 1998.

(p. 190) "just prior to the *Storm Front* tour . . .": Brock, 1994.

(p. 190) "The funny thing is . . .": Zulaica, 2001.

(p. 190) "When I get together with Elton . . .": Couric, 2003.

(p. 190) "He had a nine-foot piano . . .": Nadboy, 1996.

(p. 190) "He's a very caring man . . .": DeCurtis, 1997.

(p. 191) "When we're on stage together . . .": Ryan and Jam, 1997.

(p. 191) "It definitely lights a fire under you . . .": Newman, July 26, 1997.

(p. 191) "He's a better piano player . . .": Brock, 1994.

(p. 191) "I still don't know how that room held together . . .": Burton, 1995.

(p. 191) "Caroline hadn't done a lot of things . . .": Schock interview, 2004.

(p. 192) "We understood the news reports . . .": Burton, 1995.

(p. 192) "It was a tough tour . . .": Schock interview, 2004.

(p. 192) "I can make a lot of money . . .": McCollum, 1998.

Chapter 22

(p. 193) "It's done . . .": Rush, 1993.

(p. 193) "Everybody's being a lot more cautious . . .": Stevens, 1993.

(p. 194) "She's very lovely . . .": Schock interview, 2004.

(p. 194) "If the press had gotten wind . . .": Zwecker, 1996.

(p. 194) "I'm happy for her . . .": Tuma and Kornblut, 1996.

(p. 194) "I wanted to concentrate on students . . .": Rathbun, 1996.

(p. 194) "What I have on this mission . . .": Nadboy, 1996.

(p. 195) "I think it's such a good thing for people . . .": Rathbun, 1996.

(p. 195) Mr. Joel goes to D.C.: Via Thomas interview, 2003.

(p. 196) "This was actually suggested by Columbia Records . . .": Westerman, August 19, 1997.

(p. 197) "I've been writing classical music . . .": Graff, August 14, 1997.

(p. 197) "We do Traffic and Hendrix . . .": Doerschuk, 1981.

(p. 197) "He has a stable of songs . . .": "Backstage Pass: Band: Billy Joel Keyboardist: David Rosenthal," 1989.

(p. 197) "I just thought that song was so great . . .": Newman, July 26, 1997.

(p. 198) "I recorded that song a few years ago . . .": Newman, July 26, 1997.

(p. 198) "[Dylan] sent a guy to my house . . .": Graff, August 1997.

(p. 198) "A Bob Dylan song is not supposed to be . . .": Newman, July 26, 1997.

(p. 198) "People still have certain beliefs about Allentown . . .": Welsh, 1997.

(p. 199) "We came up with an idea . . .": Ryan and Jam, 1997.

(p. 199) "Even sailboaters who look down their noses . . .": Williams, 2000.

(p. 199) "I'm not going to become wealthy . . .": Brady, 1998.

(p. 200) "I threw out a number . . .": Williams, 2000.

Chapter 23

(p. 201) "Oh, you know, what Sting does . . .": Cohen and Bordowitz, 2000.

(p. 201) "Writing orchestral work . . .": Duffy, 1989.

(p. 202) "I love other kinds of music . . .": Holden, 1986.

(p. 202) "I've been listening almost exclusively . . .": Nadboy, 1996.

(p. 202) "This is magnificent music . . .": Isacoff, 1996.

(p. 202) "I let these symphonies pound . . .": Sandow, 2001.

(p. 202) "It was a real sense . . .": DeMain, 2001.

(p. 203) "'The Longest Time' could be a Haydn piece . . .": Hinkley, 1997.

(p. 203) "I was always writing classical music . . .": DeMain, 1996.

(p. 203) "I was listening to a classical station . . .": Graff, August 1997.

(p. 203) "I have a drive to create another kind . . .": Newman, July 26, 1997.

(p. 203) "Classical music was like the girl next door . . .": Bolando, 2001.

(p. 203) "I was kind of seduced by this . . .": McCollum, 1998.

(p. 203) "After thirty-five years of the affair . . .": Bolando, 2001.

(p. 204) "My greatest fear . . .": Isacoff, 1996.

(p. 204) "In the classical world . . .": Graff, August 14, 1997.

(p. 204) "I wanted to write music about where I came from": Holden, 1997.

(p. 204) "I've got to get this stuff orchestrated . . .": Graff, August 1997.

(p. 205) "The classical world is pretty much running out . . .": DeMain, 2001.

(p. 205) "When I got into rock . . .": Knippenberg, 1974.

(p. 205) "The stuff that I'm writing . . .": Nadboy, 1996.

(p. 205) "My left hand was always a piece of ham . . .": Isacoff, 1996.

(p. 205) "My brother is a classical conductor . . .": DeMain, 2001.

(p. 206) "Even with my pop albums . . .": Konigsberg, 2004.

(p. 206) "One of the things you like . . .": Isacoff, 1996.

(p. 206) "It's not all that different . . .": DeMain, 2001.

(p. 206) "The last song I wrote . . .": Couric, 2003.

(p. 207) "A lot of times I feel like I've written a complete piece . . .": Graff, August 14, 1997.

(p. 207) "If . . . there's some sort of emotional code . . .": DeMain, 1996.

(p. 207) "I suspect I wouldn't be very good . . .": Newman, July 26, 1997.

(p. 207) "I write my best stuff . . .": Tannenbaum, 2002.

(p. 207) "Don't think they haven't tried": Tannenbaum, 2002.

(p. 207) "The recording artist who has been doing my songs . . .": Newman, July 26, 1997.

(p. 207) "I've had it . . .": DeCurtis, 1997.

(p. 208) "I don't feel like a rock star today . . .": Sheff, 1982.

(p. 208) "The New Year's Eve concert . . .": Joel, 2000.

(p. 208) "Remarkably enough . . .": Joel, 2000.

(p. 208) "the song glorified drug use . . .": "Giuliani Camp: Song Promotes Drugs, Masturbation," 2000.

(p. 209) "This is a hell of a show . . .": Waddell, March 9, 2002.

(p. 209) Most successful touring package: Waddell, November 9, 2002.

(p. 209) "I couldn't have been born . . .": Newman, July 26, 1997.

(p. 211) "My first reaction . . .": Lipson, 2003.

(p. 211) "I might owe Neckermann . . .": Lipson, 2003.

(p. 211) "I talked with my brother . . .": Tallmer, 2003.

(p. 211) "I came away . . .": Lipson, 2003.

Chapter 24

(p. 212) "drifted off the side of the roadway . . .": New York State Department of Motor Vehicles, 2003.

(p. 212) "an operation on his nose and face . . .": New York State Department of Motor Vehicles, 2003.

(p. 212) "gone by him at a high rate of speed . . .": New York State Department of Motor Vehicles, 2003.

(p. 213) "The seat Alexa was sitting in . . .": Couric, 2003.

(p. 213) "In my whole life, I've only had two car accidents . . .": Couric, 2003.

(p. 213) "He hit my bushes . . .": "Woman Wants Billy Joel to Pay . . . ," 2004.

(p. 214) "It looks like his insurance premiums . . .": "Wreck May Get Billy Joel Premium Rate Hike," 2004.

(p. 214) "I think that he can be irresponsible . . .": Ripp interview, 2004.

(p. 214) "use phony draft cards . . .": Schwartz, 1978.

(p. 214) "blackout drinker . . .": Gentile interview, 2004.

(p. 214) "cajoled me into helping him . . .": White, 1980.

(p. 214) "I've become more of a baritone . . .": McCollum, 1998.

(p. 215) "seemed to have ingested . . .": Harmon et al., 2002.

(p. 215) "You know, sometimes I'm in a bar . . .": Nadboy, 1996.

(p. 215) "I mean, he fell down the stairs?": Gibson interview, 2003.

(p. 215) "[She was why I] started drinking all that wine . . .": Klosterman, 2002.

(p. 215) "His ex-girlfriend just got married . . .": Harmon et al., 2002.

(p. 215) "I can abuse alcohol . . .": Couric, 2003.

(p. 215) "I was the guy who got the phone call . . .": Gentile interview, 2004.

(p. 216) "He may have felt that he was drinking too much . . .": Harmon et al., 2002.

(p. 216) "I told my daughter . . .": "Joel Leaves Rehab, Say's He'll Attend Premiere," 2002.

(p. 216) "He would do anything for his daughter": Schock interview, 2004.

(p. 216) "Billy has felt his drinking . . .": "Alcohol Behind Joel's Rehab," 2002.

(p. 216) "I was on a binge . . .": Couric, 2003.

(p. 217) "I'm an alcohol abuser . . .": Couric, 2003.

Chapter 25

(p. 218) "There is an overt theatricality . . .": Rockwell, 1974.

(p. 218) "Writing a Broadway musical? Certainly": Duffy, 1989.

(p. 218) "Billy could turn Broadway upside down . . .": Robins, 1999.

(p. 219) "He was insisting that I do this . . .": Robins, 1993.

(p. 219) "A project of that nature . . .": Brock, 1994.

(p. 220) "In all of history . . .": Timberg, 2004.

(p. 220) "I want to do a narrative . . .": Couric, 2003.

(p. 220) "Just the fact . . .": Newman, 2002.

(p. 220) "This was really Twyla Tharp's vision . . .": Couric, 2003.

(p. 221) "It's a full-length ballet . . .": Shapiro, 2002.

(p. 221) "[This] is not about exploiting Billy Joel . . .": Hay, 2002.

(p. 221) "Billy Joel is an amazing storyteller . . .": Hay, 2002.

(p. 221) "I've always referred to my songs . . .": Couric, 2003.

(p. 221) "I went, not knowing what I was going to see . . .": Newman, 2002.

(p. 221) "I always thought his music could be on Broadway . . .": Ripp interview, 2004.

(p. 222) "shimmering portrait . . .": Brantley, 2002.

(p. 222) "All these people in buses are going by . . .": Tallmer, 2003.

(p. 223) "I'm working on a book . . .": Simonson, 2004.

(p. 223) "Having somebody with such an amazing body of work . . .": Newman, 2002.

(p. 223) "It will be a lot of fun . . .": Newman, 2002.

(p. 223) "Whatever subject we touch on . . .": Klosterman, 2002.

(p. 224) "In my whole life . . .": Klosterman, 2002.

(p. 224) "He talks like a guy . . .": Klosterman, 2002.

(p. 224) "I'd like to have a successful long-term relationship . . .": Connor, 2002.

(p. 224) "I was recently on a date with a woman . . .": Klosterman, 2002.

(p. 224) "He's looking for a real relationship": Connor, 2002.

(p. 225) "Reassuring a child . . .": "Pop Music Icon Billy Joel Signs Book Publishing Deal with Scholastic," 2004.

(p. 225) "There's nothing wrong with leaving . . .": Liz Smith, 2004.

Chapter 26

(p. 226) "Billy can be an intense guy . . .": Schilling interview, 2004.

(p. 226) "Billy was probably the most significant . . .": Ripp interview, 2004.

(p. 226) "When Billy played LA a few years ago . . .": Gibson interview, 2003.

(p. 227) "What's the difference between a pop artist . . .": Bloom interview, 2004.

(p. 228) "It's easier to manage money . . .": Mazur interview, 2004.

(p. 228) "You get up on stage . . .": Joel, 2000.

(p. 228) "I'm glad that people like my music . . .": "Joel, 2000.

(p. 228) "We carry two acoustic pianos . . .": Doerschuk, 1981.

(p. 228) "A star . . . is a big ball of gas . . .": Carlton, 1994.

(p. 228) "I look in the mirror every morning . . .": DeMain, 1996.

(p. 229) "That's what makes it fun . . .": Nadboy, 1996.

(p. 229) "I think success is . . .": McCollum, 1998.

(p. 229) "You don't necessarily have to be on the cutting edge . . .": Robins, 1999.

(p. 229) "I'm not cutting edge and I haven't been . . .": McCollum, 1998.

(p. 229) "I don't want to be an oldies act . . .": Charles et al., 2001.

(p. 229) "I don't like writing . . .": Schwartz, 1978.

(p. 230) "You have to have the desire . . .": Newman, August 18, 1997.

(p. 230) "Is that merely a cover for him . . .": Ripp interview, 2004.

(p. 231) "I get kind of tired of performing . . .": Nadboy, 1996.

(p. 231) "I've had 'the career' . . .": Couric, 2003.

(p. 231) "Billy was insecure . . .": Ripp interview, 2004.

(p. 233) "It's fantastic what he's done . . .": White, December 4, 1994.

(p. 233) "Billy should love himself half as much . . .": Via White, December 4, 1994.

(p. 233) "Billy was offering people his life . . .": Bloom interview, 2004.

(p. 233) "I feel what I do is competent . . .": White, December 4, 1994.

(p. 233) "Billy has a lot of rock and roll in him . . .": Ripp interview, 2004.

(p. 233) "There are a lot of singers and songwriters . . .": Van Matre, 1982.

(p. 233) "I'll always be a musician . . .": Tour Program for *52nd Street*, 1978.

Afterword

(p. 234) "Billy was, at that point, still with . . .": Skolnik interview, 2004.

(p. 235) "Just don't go around making up stories . . .": Schruers, 1982.

(p. 236) "He has built a wall around him . . .": Ripp interview, 2004.

(p. 236) "All of us find it a little weird . . .": Schock interview, 2004.

(p. 236) "I'm not sure I'm comfortable . . .": Joel, 2000.

INDEX

Joel, Billy, *110–125*
awards and honors of, viii, ix, x,
    xi, 77–78, 97, 106, 110, *114*,
    121, 122–123, 124, 125, 126,
    128, 135, 144, 146, 154, 171,
    174–175, 195–196, 208,
    222–223, 225
birth of, 4
car accidents of, 212–214
charitable work of, viii, ix,
    109, 120, 155, 158, 161, 170
and draft, 29, 145
health of, vii–viii, xiii, 38–39,
    136–138, 171–172, 212–217
and Holocaust, 210–211
and Kobe earthquake, 191–192
motorcycle accident of, 136–138
relationships of, vii, viii, ix,
    xiii–iv, 34–35, 36, 37–38, 41,
    50–51, 53, 136, 139–141,
    148–152, 154–155, 186–189,
    191–192, 215, 223–225
and religion, 11, 97–98
and September 11, 2001, 210
suicide attempt of, 38–39
as "William Martin," viii, 65
Joel, Carl, 2–3, 4, 210–211
Joel, Elizabeth, vii, viii, xiii, 24,
    25, 31, 34–35, 36, 37–38, 41,
    50–51, 53, 63–64, 66, 67, 71,
    75, 76, 77, 80, 81, 82, 83,
    86–90, 91, 98, 105, 107, 111,
    120, 128–131, 134, 136,
    139–141, 151, 155, 159, 177,
    178, 199, 226, 227, 232
Joel, Howard, 1–4, 5, 6, 7, 11,
    61–62, 97, 233
Joel, Judy, 1, 4, 10, 11
Joel, Rosalind, 1, 3, 4, 5, 6, 7, 8,
    11, *110*, 154, 158, 175,
    215–216, 233
Joey Dee and the Starliters, 20
John, Elton, xi, xii, 41–42,
    54–55, 80, 187, 189–191,
    202, 207, 209, 210, 216–217,
    219, 229
John (Executive Lounge), 66
Johnny Thunders and the
    Heartbreakers, 60
John Paul II, Pope, 174
Johnson, Lyndon, 29
Jones, Mick, *120*, 167–168
Jones, Quincy, 91, 157, 174
Jones Beach, 170
Joo, Richard, 205–206, 223
Joplin, Janis, 69
"Journey's End," 21
"Jumpin' Jack Flash," 88

Just Sunshine, 43
"Just the Way You Are," xi,
    94–97, 103, 106

Kamali, Norma, 154
Kama Sutra, 44–45, 46, 64, 72
Kaufman, Howard, 82
Kaylan, Howard "Flo," 45
"Keeping the Faith," 153, 155,
    209, 222
Kendricks, Eddie, 73
Kennedy, John F., 15
Kennedy, John F., Jr., 194
Kennedy, Robert, 24
Kenny, Gerard, 33
Khan, Steve, 102, 104, 127
Kiel Opera House, 78
King, Ben E., 152
King, Carole, 197–198
Kinks, 17
Kirwin, Danny, 81
Kiss, 129
Kleinow, Sneaky Pete, 52
Klores, Dan, 180–181
Klosterman, Chuck, 223
Knapp, Mike, 188
Knechtel, Larry, 52, 78
Kohuept, 161, 197
Kooper, Al, 36
Koppelman, Charles, 77
Kortchmar, Danny "Kootch,"
    182, 183–184
Krall, Diana, 223
Krasnow, Bob, 46–47
Kristofferson, Kris, 107
Kyle, 47, 52, 54

LaBelle, Patti, 228
Ladysmith Black Mambazo, 182
Lang, Michael, 43, 47, 47–49,
    71, 72, 76, 134, 227
The Late Show, 183
Lauper, Cyndi, 118, *119*, 157–158
"Leader of the Pack," 19
League of American Theatres
    and Producers, 222
"Leave a Tender Moment
    Alone," 152
Ledbelly, 33
Led Zeppelin, 31, 142, 202
Lee, Katie, *125*, 224, 225
Lehigh University, 144
Lehigh Valley Economic
    Development Corp., 198
Lemon Pipers, 33
Lenin, Nikolai, 143
Lennon, John, xiv, 15, 16, 17,
    131, 143, 175

Leo, Arnold, 170
Leone's, vii
"The Letter," 59–60
Letterman, David, 183
Levitt, 5
Levy, Morris, 28–29, 30, 42, 44,
    163
Lewis, Jerry Lee, 190
Lewis, Terry, 171
Liebowitz, Annie, 153–154
"Light as the Breeze," 187–188,
    197
Lincoln Center, 78
Lipps Inc., 127
"Little Kids Rock," 200
Little Richard, 15, 151, 190
Lola (pug), 214
London, Rick, 130, 133, 164,
    172, 177–178, 193
London Symphony, 204
"The Longest Time," 203
Long Island Symphony, 204
Long Island University, 166–167
Lopez, Vinnie, 60–61
"Los Angelenos," 80, 135
Los Angeles Times, 132
Lost Souls, 20, 21, 23, 25–26,
    102, 110, 198
Lott, Trent, 195, 196
Lovin' Spoonful, 44–45, 46, 226
Ludlum, 146
"Lullabye (Goodnight, My
    Angel)," 184, 186, 196,
    206–207, 225
Lutz, Helen, ix
Lyman, Frankie, 28

Ma, Yo-Yo, 206
MacDonald, Ralph, 104
MacPherson, Elle, 148, 149
Madison Square Garden, 106,
    130, 131, 148, 154, 161, 208,
    210, 214–215
Madonna, 163, 228
Magid, Larry, 209
Mahavishnu Orchestra, 59
Mainieri, Mike, 104
Malo, Ron, 78
Mamas and the Papas, 44
Mancuso-Shargo, Becky, 68
Mann, Herbie, 59
Manson Family, 31
Marden, Phil, *112*
Maritime Music, 172, 215
Marks, Leonard, 164, 172, 177,
    178, 179, 180–181, 184, 193
Marley, Bob, 60, 73
Martell, T.J., 135